"Local color, endearing ruminations, and Harris's obsessive love for the City of Light shine through in these pages. *C'est formidable!*"

—DAVID DOWNIE,
author of *A Taste of Paris*

"*In Portrait in Red*, L. John Harris takes on the role of a Paris *flâneur* who comments on all he sees, hears, feels, and tastes. Harris's expert eye and palette tease out the nuances of life on the streets of the French capital."

—ZACK ROGOW,
coauthor of *Colette Uncensored*

PORTRAIT IN RED

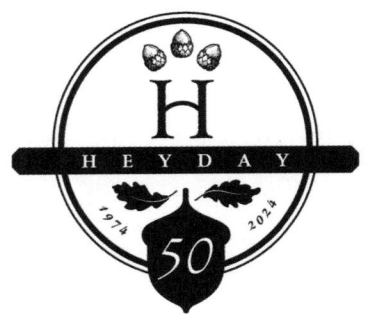

Also by L. John Harris

The Book of Garlic

The Official Garlic Lovers Handbook

Foodoodles

Café French

My Little Plague Journal

PORTRAIT IN RED

A Paris Obsession

L. JOHN HARRIS

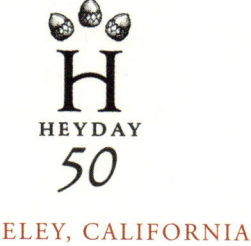

BERKELEY, CALIFORNIA

Library of Congress Cataloging-in-Publication Data
Names: Harris, Lloyd J., 1947- author.
Title: Portrait in red : a Paris obsession / L. John Harris.
Description: Berkeley, California : Heyday, [2024] | Includes
bibliographical references.
Identifiers: LCCN 2024011100 (print) | LCCN 2024011101 (ebook) |
ISBN: 9781597146494 (hardcover) | ISBN 9781597146500 (epub)
Subjects: LCSH: Girl in red. | Girls—Europe—Portraits. | Harris, Lloyd
J., 1947—Art collections. | Portrait painting, European—Expertising.
Classification: LCC N7649.G57 H37 2024 (print) | LCC N7649.G57 (ebook) |
DDC 704.9/426—dc23/eng/20240423
LC record available at https://lccn.loc.gov/2024011100
LC ebook record available at https://lccn.loc.gov/2024011101

Cover Art: *The Girl in Red*, artist unknown
Cover Design: Archie Ferguson
Interior Design/Typesetting: Archie Ferguson

Published by Heyday
P.O. Box 9145, Berkeley, California 94709
(510) 549-3564
heydaybooks.com

Printed in East Peoria, Illinois, by Versa Press, Inc.
10 9 8 7 6 5 4 3 2 1

Dedicated to my mother and father

CONTENTS

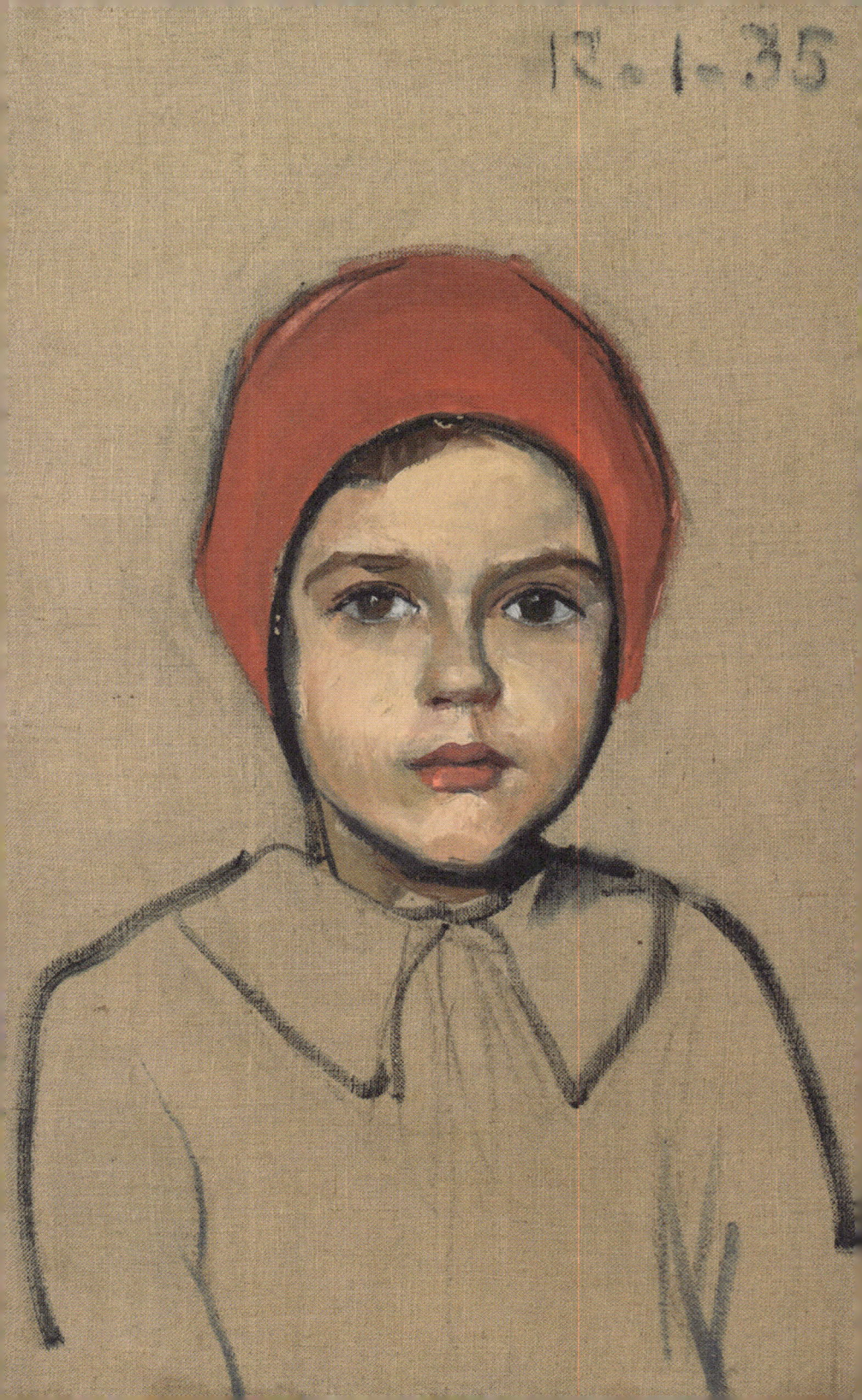

PROLOGUE

○

She looks at me with dark, sad eyes, a young girl, about ten years old, perhaps a bit older. The sadness I sense is deeper than her years would suggest, something you might see in the eyes of a refugee, a runaway, or a victim of abuse. She seems so alone. But she is not alone. There is someone in the room with her, the artist who has painted this portrait of a girl wearing a vivid red head covering. Who is this mysterious girl? Who is the artist—male or female? French or foreign? From where I'm standing, on the corner of rue Guénégaud and rue Mazarine in Paris's Saint-Germain-des-Prés, I don't see a signature on the canvas, though a date is prominent in the upper right-hand corner—12-1-35 (January 12, 1935).

Is the girl wearing a hat or bonnet or headscarf? I can't tell as I approach closer. The unframed canvas, along with other random discards, leans against the wall of a residential building, next to its entry door, between two art galleries. This is up the block from La Palette, a café where I have just had lunch. It's July 26, 2015, around one in the afternoon. I arrived in Paris yesterday to begin a three-week writing assignment for a food magazine, and this is my first full day in the City of Light.

My guess is that the canvas has come from one of the many art galleries in the area of Saint-Germain-des-Prés and the Latin Quarter, logically one of the two on either side of the apartment building where it sits. The painting—I assume an oil painting—seems unfinished. The face is nicely painted, but the girl's upper body is just a series of long, black brushstrokes that outline a broad-collared blouse or jacket. The face, too, is outlined in black. The red head covering, whatever type of headwear it is, lacks detail. The canvas that surrounds the girl is blank except for the date scrawled in black.

Behind the canvas, in the stack of odds and ends, is a fragment of a cloth-covered wooden panel that might be part of a dismantled gallery display, left for passersby. Such giveaways are not an uncommon sight in Paris. What's uncommon is that a good painting is among them.

I pick up the canvas to take a closer look. Definitely no signature or any other identifying information, front or back. The small nails holding the canvas to the sides of the stretcher bars are rusty, and there is a darkened area running along the bottom front of the canvas, as if the painting had sat outside in wet weather. It seems to me that there is a lot of history in this little painting. I feel oddly drawn to the girl who stares out at me with a story she does not tell.

When I gently run my index finger over the surface, the painted areas feel raised, indicating paint, not a printed surface, as with a giclée print, those awful copies of famous paintings made with inkjet printers. The canvas, *la toile*, feels rough and dry and looks old. This is a real painting, and though hard to believe, it appears to be abandoned, not forgotten, accidently dropped or parked temporarily. Still, I wait to see whether there might be someone coming to reclaim it from one of the adjacent galleries. Rather unlikely, given that most galleries are closed now for the summer holidays, *les grandes vacances*.

I wonder whether an art dealer has forgotten the painting in the rush to leave town? More likely, a dealer has cleaned up a gallery and thrown out unwanted items before leaving. An anonymous, seemingly unfinished portrait bought for a song at an estate sale or flea market would be better off in the hands of someone who loved it than sitting unsold in a gallery or stashed in a closet. Or so I rationalize. It's just too good, too powerful to leave to an uncertain fate or outright destruction. Maybe I'm its fate. But why it is "good" and "powerful" is not something I carefully think through. It just *is*. Like a bite of a dish that puts a smile on your face before you identify the ingredients.

Several minutes pass as I stand on the sidewalk with the canvas, lost in my musings, waiting for the painting's embarrassed owner to arrive and reclaim it. Hoping they don't.

No one does.

So, with canvas in hand and a vague sense of guilt, I continue my stroll toward the Seine, where I'll turn left at Quai de Conti and head along Quai Malaquais and Quai Voltaire to rue du Bac. Then left on Bac, past the modern art icon Galerie Maeght, to blvd. Saint-Germain. My apartment is just a few hundred yards up blvd. Saint-Germain from the corner.

I hold the canvas with the painted side facing toward me as I walk, the stretcher bars facing out. Am I hiding the canvas to avoid detection by someone who might recognize and claim the painting? Perhaps. But I also feel uncomfortable walking along the street with an uncovered canvas. It may be common in Paris where art is so much a part of everyday life, but I can't recall ever seeing someone back home doing so. In any case, one would certainly want to protect the painted side of a canvas while moving along crowded, narrow and often wet Parisian streets.

Back at the apartment, I assess my mysterious find, a captivating image of a young girl, presumably living in Paris just five dark years before the onset of World War II and the German Occupation. Edgar Degas once said, "We were created to look at one another, weren't we?" I can't stop looking at her. It feels like an important moment at the outset of my stay in Paris, but I can't say exactly why. That it will launch me on a journey that will change my life I cannot begin to know.

PORTRAIT IN RED

I

THE JOURNEY BEGINS

2015–2016

Berkeley · New York · Paris ·
London · Berkeley · Los Angeles ·
Berkeley · New York · Berkeley

A CORNER TABLE

○

I've come to Paris on a journalistic mission following a short visit to New York. I view professional travel in terms of missions, to distinguish it from sightseeing, my travel motive when I was young. The way I look at it now, once you've seen the sights, there is little reason to return unless there is a clear objective, a mission. Or, in certain cases, because an internal necessity pulls you back, an inexhaustible passion for a place that Lucian Freud, the great British portrait painter, described as "traveling down." With Paris I have both motives for returning—mission and passion.

My first task whenever I arrive in Paris, after dropping off my bags in my apartment, is to secure a corner table on the terrace of café Les Deux Magots, an eight-minute walk from my apartment along blvd. Saint-Germain, past all the fancy clothing and furniture shops and their gorgeous window displays. This is ritual—not sacred ritual but Paris ritual, though they often feel the same. Before unpacking, before shopping for food or contacting friends, I reconnect with this dream café and the dream of Paris.

It's late afternoon and the cafés and streets of the Rive Gauche (Left Bank) are packed with locals and tourists. Across from the Deux Magots, on rue Bonaparte, joyous bells chime on the hour at the Église Saint-Germain-des-Prés, the remains of an abbey complex built in the sixth century. The bells tell me I am in Paris, really in Paris!

I have my journal and a newspaper purchased at a kiosk en route to the café, but won't engage with either of these until I get a good look at Paris from my electric terrace perch. Yes, the Deux Magots is one of Paris's most touristy haunts, almost on a par with the Eiffel Tower, Notre Dame Cathedral and the Louvre. Why, then, am I so eager to merge with the crowds of Americans, Chinese, Germans, British, Russians, Scandinavians, Indians, Japanese, Saudis and all the rest—both inside and outside the café, on the terrace and sidewalk?

A café doesn't ascend to this pinnacle of prominence without good reason, and I don't resist it, an engaging nexus of dramatic urban geography, classical architecture, cultural history, exotic faces and soul-stirring bells. It's not a café in Rome, Vienna, New York, London, or San Francisco, all fine in their own right. And definitely not a Berkeley café where the coffee seems more important than the café culture. This is the notorious Rive Gauche, Saint-Germain-des-Prés, one of the world's most glamorous urban focal points. I think of it as the *Rêve* Gauche (the Dream Bank). Even my most tourist-averse expat friends in Paris frequent the Deux Magots terrace, and there are plans to meet here tomorrow evening for a reunion.

As I sip slowly on a glass of champagne, a *coupe*, the bells tell me it's 5 p.m. I imagine I'm on the prow of a giant passenger ship with the vast ocean of Parisian culture floating in front of me. I position myself as far away as possible from the cigar- and cigarette-smoking *tout-Paris* crowd that inhabits the café at tables along the sidewalk, the way ravenous pigeons inhabit the charming little square—le square Laurent Prache—across from the café on rue Bonaparte, at the foot of the Saint-Germain church.

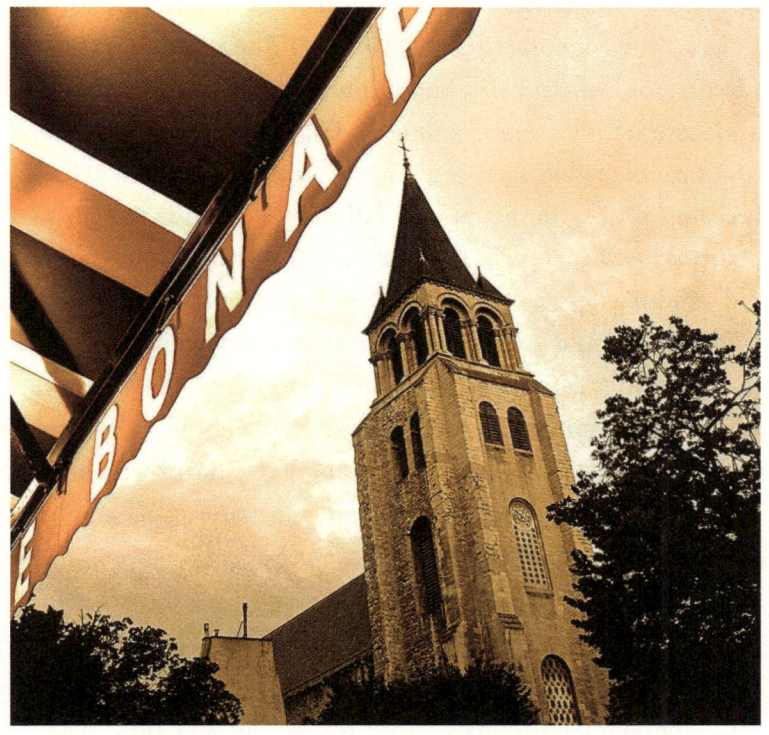

The bell tower of the Église Saint-Germain-des-Prés across from Le Bonaparte's terrace, just up the block from Les Deux Magots

The very heart and heat of the tourist season is upon us, but I don't mind. July and August are the months that the Parisian folks with whom I swap living quarters want to be in Berkeley, away from the crowds and the heat. Their elegant apartment on blvd. Saint-Germain is worth the hot and muggy sacrifice. As if being in Paris anytime, anywhere, can be considered a sacrifice.

My mission this summer for the online food journal *Zester Daily* is to report on the status of a Parisian café staple, the croque monsieur. The editor at *Zester* has agreed to include one of my cartoonish illustrations with the article, a perk that augments the meager fee. There are all kinds of reasons to come to Paris, and if it must be to *flâne* (stroll) cafés and critique a Parisian sandwich, I'm your *gastro-flâneur*. The ubiquitous grilled ham-and-cheese croque, with its glaze of *béchamel* sauce, on the cusp of culinary icon and cliché, has a colorful history in Paris, though it's only about a hundred years old. And it's not as easy to make—or, more precisely, to make well—as it would appear. My mission is to taste and evaluate as many croques as I can stomach in search of the best. My stomach is braced for the onslaught.

As I savor my coupe, enthralled by the spectacle that shimmers before me, I have no intimation of anything being different from recent missions to Paris, save for the lingering effects of having just seen Gustav Klimt's *Portrait of Adele Bloch-Bauer I* (1907), known as the *Woman in Gold*, at the Neue Galerie in New York. I'd been inspired to change my usual itinerary—Berkeley-London-Paris—after seeing the film *Woman in Gold*, about the restitution of this astonishing portrait stolen by the Nazis from a wealthy Jewish family in Vienna. I had to see her face to face—in the flesh, as it were.

So it is a more art-centric than food-centric beginning to my mission in Paris. Still, that I would soon encounter a discarded portrait on a sidewalk and fall under its spell is not something I could ever have imagined, though the area of my brain that engages with art was on high alert after seeing the Klimt. Magic, like its romantic partner Love, is always a surprise.

Just across from the Deux Magots, on the south side of blvd. Saint-Germain, is the old-school Brasserie Lipp, a bit long in the tooth perhaps, but still, another Paris landmark, at least for foreign foodies like me. I look forward to their *blanquette de veau*, the classic veal stew from Normandy made with a rich and creamy *velouté* sauce. The dish is really good at Lipp—I've been enjoying it since the 1990s—though the brasserie is best known for Alsatian *choucroute garnie* and for its snooty garçons and maître d's. Noted artists, writers, politicians and intellectuals have been frequenting Lipp for over a century, and one wonders what part its heavy German-inspired Alsatian food played in the formulation of the equally heavy midcentury philosophy, existentialism, dished up by Lipp regulars Jean-Paul Sartre and Simon de Beauvoir.

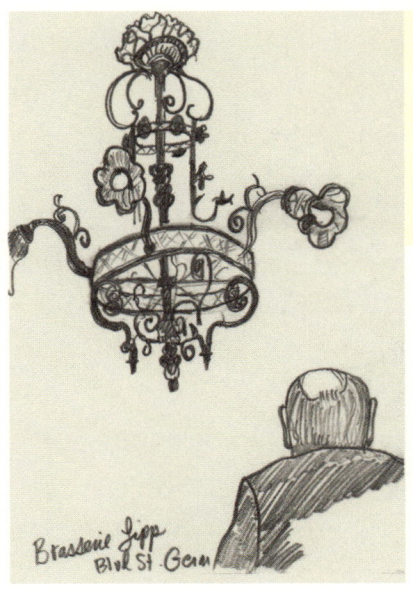

This sketch is from an old journal. A Lipp customer is seated in front of me and under an iron chandelier.

Brasserie Lipp, the Deux Magots and its neighboring competitor, Café de Flore, form a cultural power triangle on blvd. Saint-Germain. They've been the daily hangouts of some of the most celebrated creatives of the last hundred years. I feel the weight of that history as I scribble notes and doodle in my journal on this delightful first night back in Paris, as all my first nights back in Paris are.

After my drink at the Deux Magots, I jump ship and float down rue Bonaparte a short block to rue de l'Abbaye. There I steer left to rue St. Benoît, where a modest little bistro, Au Pied de Fouet, serves real French food to real French people. It's cheap, fast, traditional and good. I'm sure most tourists walking by are put off by the limited menu posted on the door of this cramped hole in the wall. Not I.

Finishing a delicious plate of lamb braised with cumin and served with buttery *pommes purée*, I pay *l'addition*—just under 20 euros, including a glass of wine—and make my dreamy way back to my apartment. *J'ai bien mangé* (I am full). *Je suis content* (I am happy).

FIRST CROQUE

o

My Paris apartment takes up the entire fourth floor of a Haussmann-era building. It's elegantly furnished and filled with art. The owners—he, *Parisien*, she, *Américaine*—have installed a well-equipped guest space for friends and their adult children. I use it as my office and for coffee breaks, perfect for a live/work Paris *séjour* (stay).

I consider it "my" apartment because, after several stays, it feels, indeed, like mine. The location is in the 7th arrondissement, nicely situated near the border of the 5th and 6th arrondissements, which include the neighborhoods of Saint-Germain-des-Prés and the Latin Quarter. It's just a few blocks from the Musée d'Orsay, the Bon Marché fancy food market and countless art galleries, antique shops, bistros and cafés, like my regulars, the Deux Magots, Café de Flore and La Palette. On the Right Bank, just across the Seine's Pont Royal and only minutes by foot from the apartment, are the Louvre and the Tuileries. My Paris hood. I fall asleep this first night *chez moi* to the vague rumblings of the Metro trains that pass deep beneath me.

My jet lag symptoms are minimal in the morning, thanks to the brief stopover in New York, so I'm ready to go to work. After a *café crème* at a small café near the apartment, I head to La Palette on rue de Seine for my first croque monsieur. It's a delightful, leisurely, twenty-minute stroll to the café through the 6th. The café has strong ties to the Left Bank art scene, but these days it's mostly a hangout for Parisian millennials, well-to-do older residents and the global tourist bobos who frequent the area's high-end art galleries, shops, cafés and restaurants.

La Palette is just one long block from the École des Beaux-Arts, the famed art and architecture school associated with France's centuries-old chain of conservative art institutions (The Academy) that artists of the late nineteenth and early twentieth centuries rebelled against to create a "modern" art. Passing by the school en route to La Palette, I notice that the gates are open to its large entry courtyard on rue Bonaparte. This, after several years of closure for renovations funded by Ralph Lauren. I make a mental note to come back and explore the campus.

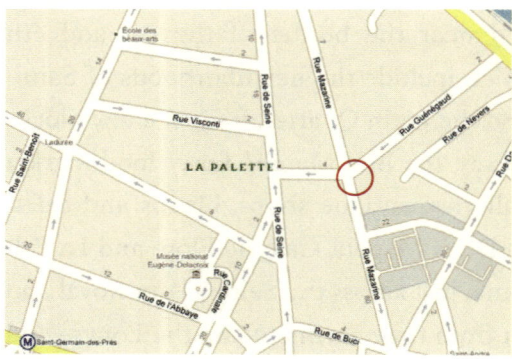

La Palette in the 6th arrondissement and the location (red circle) of the first sighting of The Girl in Red, *ground zero*

Arriving at the café, I note that the table I'd like to sit at is empty and sports a Reserved sign. This is always the case with this sidewalk power table next to the entrance to La Palette, reserved for regulars. I settle for a small table on the terrace and peruse a menu. My assumption is that the croque will be first class (I've been to the café many times but have never had its croque monsieur), but there are no guarantees, given the now well-documented decline in the quality and quantity of traditional Parisian cafés. Paris's shrinking reputation today among the world's culinary capitals (Hong Kong, Copenhagen, New York, San Francisco and the Costa Brava in Spain) has been noted by food critics for decades, and they may be right, though I have my reservations. Paris will always be Paris, and for the most part, Paris couldn't care less what the rest of the world thinks about its food or anything else for that matter.

There is also a croque madame on La Palette's menu, the same sandwich as the monsieur, but served with a fried egg on top. Legend has it that the egg represents a woman's broad-brimmed hat, and hence the madame. *Croquer* is a French verb meaning "to crunch" or "to munch" and nothing says "café" more than the "crunchy mister." Marcel Proust, a café society fixture before he withdrew to his sickbed to write his master-piece, *In Search of Lost Time*, mentions the croque in the novel. The working title of my *Zester* article is a somewhat snarky homage to Proust—"In Search of Lost Croques"—based on an assumption that my croque critique will reveal a decline in this signature café treat.

I place my croque order and prepare to take pictures dis-creetly and document in my journal what I find. The lunch crowd is buzzing around me, and as at the Deux Magots yesterday, I'm happy as a clam in chowder.

The croque arrives in due course accompanied by a rather sparsely dressed green salad. The leaves look dry, no vinegary sheen. I request from the garçon some lemon wedges to add sparkle (acid/moisture) to the greens (one returns a dish in Paris at one's peril) and then dig into the croque. It's served on

Paris's ubiquitous high-end rustic loaf from the legendary Poilâne bakery, and the construction of the sandwich is unusual—open faced. Sufficiently cheesy and crusty, it lacks the creamy béchamel sauce one expects. I also prefer a less heavy, less sour *pain de mie* (French white bread) for croques. Nonetheless, a well-prepared and tasty *déjeuner* confection.

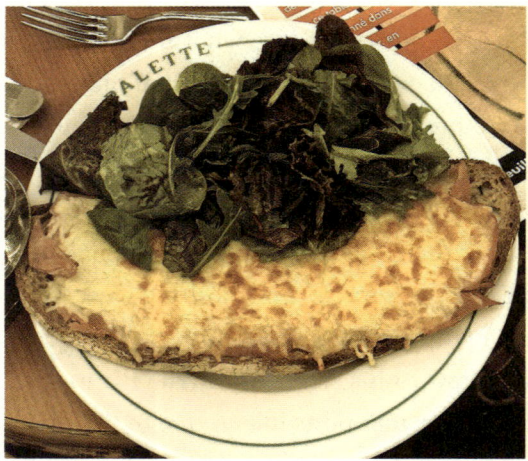

The croque monsieur at La Palette is a nontraditional open-faced version on rustic Poilâne bread.

Having noted in my journal the ingredients, cooking method, flavor and appearance of the croque, I pay the bill and head toward the Seine for a leisurely stroll home. So far, so good. Day one, croque one. I am delighted to be back in my food journalist groove, totally unprepared for what will stop me short just a few steps from the café in a junk pile on rue Guénégaud—a portrait of a young girl. I pick it up, examine it carefully, and after a long ruminative pause, take it home.

NOT THE *MONA LISA*

o

Arriving back at the apartment with my found object, my guilty treasure, I measure the canvas—15" × 22"—and name it, rather literally and after careful consideration, *The Girl in Red*. Red because it's the only dominant color in the portrait besides black—the so-called absence of color. There is a bit of brown in her eyes and eyebrows and in the few strands of hair that peek out from her head cover, and hints of a pale gray-blue in areas of the image's bold black outline.

Placing the painting on the mantel over the fireplace in the apartment's grand salon, I can't take my eyes away from it. The girl seems to be looking through me to something off in the distance. I see her, but she doesn't see me. I turn the canvas to face the mirror at an angle so that I can see the front, back and side of the canvas simultaneously—as an object, not just a painting. The date—12-1-35—seems oversized, given the relatively small scale of the canvas. The rather slapdash quality of the numerals suggests to me a male artist, but one can't be sure. The dried-out, grayish wood of the stretcher bars supports the date, too—old, but not ancient. Even without knowing a lot of details about the year 1935—in Paris, in France, in Europe, in the world—it colors my impression of the portrait, as if the artist is telling me something important about that time, that day, Paris.

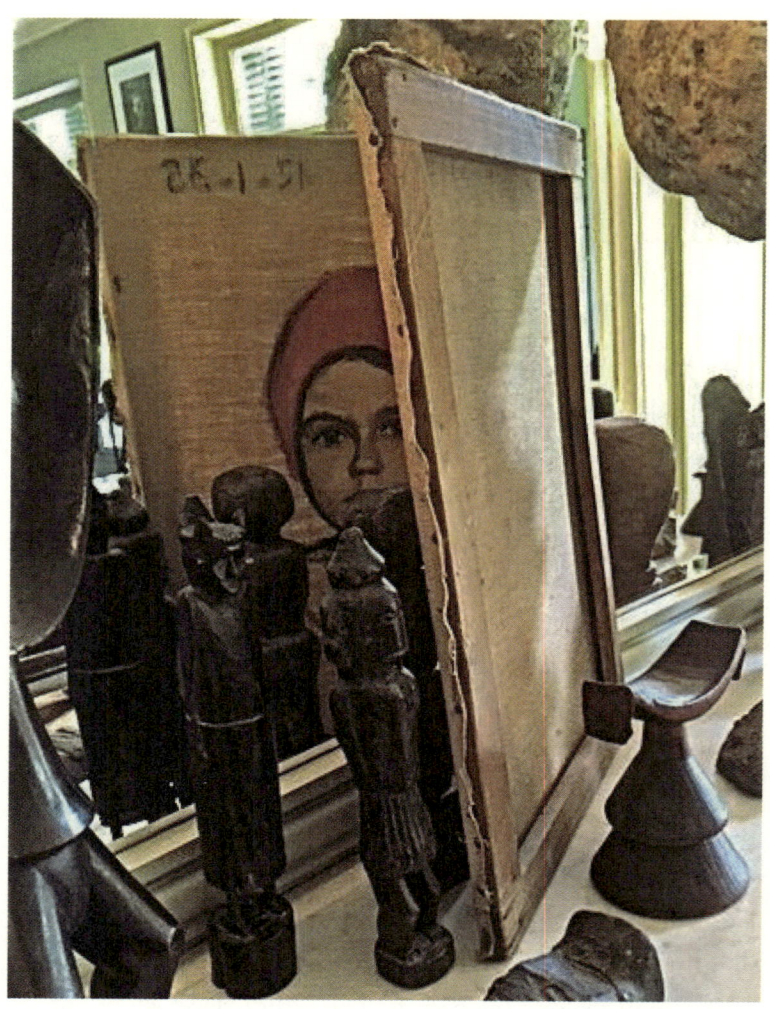

On the salon mantel facing the mirror, The Girl in Red
surrounded by African and Indonesian figurines

What *was* happening in 1935? The basics are well
known: The Nazis were already in power in Germany, and
the Spanish Civil War was just around the corner. World
War II was brewing, and by 1940 Paris would be occupied by

the Germans. But despite the portentous date and the artist's obvious skill, the work has, it seems to me, minimal commercial value. "Unfinished, unsigned and anonymous" goes through my mind. It's hard to put a high price on that. I would like to be wrong, but after discovering the low values of the pieces in my mother's small art collection at her passing in 1990, most of it the work of known (at least in Los Angeles) and more or less successful working artists, I have no illusions.

The highest appraised and insured values for Mildred Rose Harris's collection were for her African art pieces and for several museum-quality paintings by noted Romanian artists of the 1920s and '30s sold to her by their expat owners in LA. They had escaped with their art from Nicolae Ceauşescu's authoritarian regime in the 1980s. None of these works exceeded values beyond the low few thousands of dollars.

My mother's own portrait, painted when she was forty-five years old, is by Eckard Heidrich, a German artist who was teaching at UCLA in the 1960s. It has today a modest value by the standards of contemporary art—$8,000–$13,000 according to the prices of his work I find online on the Saatchi Art website. No biographical information on the artist is given, except for the year of his birth, 1930.

Though stunning, and in some ways radical (a textured white stripe runs down the left edge of the canvas to balance my mother's face set off to the right), the portrait is not the *Mona Lisa*. Nor is it a grand John Singer Sargent commissioned by some industrialist to immortalize his wife's social status and to showcase her beauty. It's just the work of a talented young artist commissioned by an adoring husband to depict the stark beauty of his beloved.

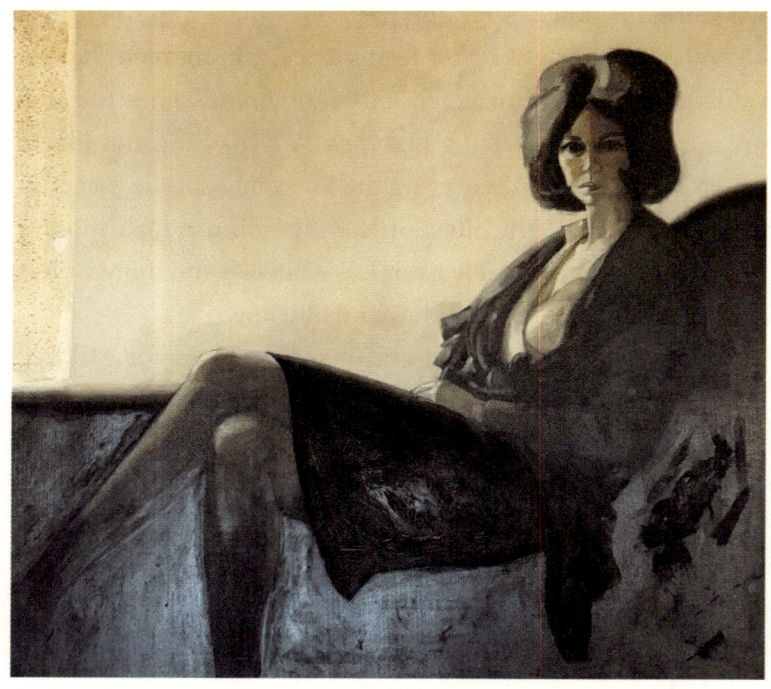

Portrait of Mildred Rose Harris *by Eckard Heidrich, 1963*

The Girl in Red is not the *Mona Lisa* either. Far from it. Nor does it match the drama of Heidrich's portrait of my mother. On the other hand, as a competent and expressive painting from the mid-1930s, it's compelling and, indeed, valuable. But if not commercially valuable, then in what sense? Aesthetically? Historically? Personally? Perhaps all three.

Who was the artist? The sitter? Why was it left unfinished? Is it, in fact, unfinished? Who discarded it, and why? And, my more immediate question, what should I do with it? One obvious impulse is to show *The Girl* to galleries around the 5th and 6th arrondissements to see whether anyone recognizes it. The problem is, most of them are now closed for the summer. Another impulse is to post the portrait on Facebook and see how my "friends" react. This I will do.

Still another impulse is to finish the painting myself, channeling the unknown artist and their technique to fill in the background and torso (pastiche). Or treat the canvas parodically with a dash of Dada. This would involve going against the artist's style to create irony and humor (kitsch). Since my art school days at UC Berkeley in the late 1960s, I have had a fetish for the mediocre and often unfinished or poorly finished paintings one buys for a song at flea markets and which I've collected over the years, intending to alter, finish or re-finish them. Picasso did something like this in the 1950s, transforming *The Young Italian*, a painting by the mostly forgotten nineteenth-century academic and religious painter Victor Orsel, into his own playful lithographic image, *The Italian Woman* (*L'Italienne*, 1953). I own one of these lithographs.

The story goes that a zinc photolithographic plate of Orsel's painting, created for an *affiche* (poster) in the studio of Picasso's printer, Fernand Mourlot, was lying around, waiting to be ground down for reuse. Picasso saw it and got permission from Mourlot to take the zinc home and play with it. He added, graffiti-style, antic characters—Pan, Bacchus, a female nude—in the empty areas framing the woman's head and torso, and added bold black lines around her features and shawl. The next day, he brought his modified—some would say disrespectful—version of Orsel's work back to Mourlot's studio to be printed—in two stages, as it turned out. My proof from the second stage is signed in pencil by both Picasso and Mourlot. Also, in Picasso's hand beneath the signatures, the words *bon à tirer*, literally "good to pull," meaning also "ready to print."

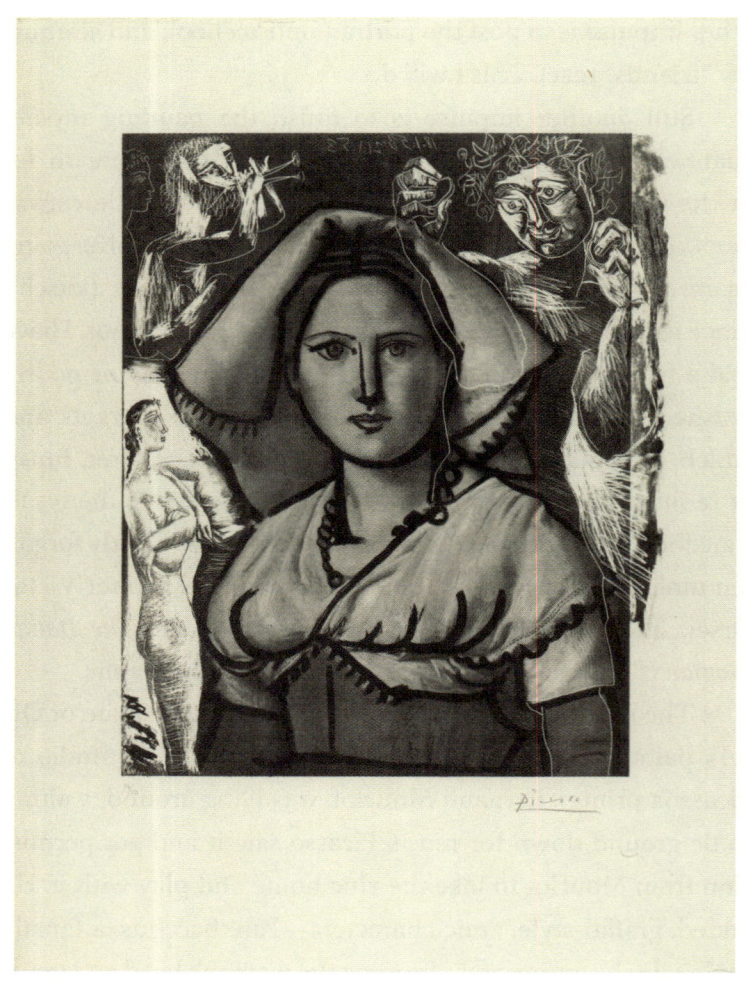

The Italian Woman *by Pablo Picasso, 1953,*
based on the painting
The Young Italian *by Victor Orsel*
circa 1820

o

I note an echo in my *Girl* of the broad black outlines of Picasso's piece. I could modify *The Girl* in the same way, thickening the lines around the nose and lips and adding doodles and caricatures in the background *à ma façon* (in my own style), bringing my found *Girl* back to life just as Picasso had done with his *Italienne*. But I'm exhausted now from the excitement of my first full day in Paris, and hungry again, my first croque monsieur a distant memory. So there is, finally, the impulse to ignore my impulses and just bring the painting back to Berkeley to be enjoyed for what it is—one of an infinite number of anonymous portraits of a human face.

THE GIRL'S AURA

○

After taking the first photo of *The Girl in Red*, I crop the image, leaving as a border some of the black leather of the chair on which I had propped the canvas. I am already thinking about how to frame the piece when I return to Berkeley. To frame a painting underscores its presence and value as art, *n'est-ce pas*?

I have now posted my photo on Facebook. The "socially mediated" image of *The Girl*, to use the parlance of postmodern criticism, is a digital reproduction—filtered, low resolution, pixilated, a copy. She is now simultaneously a public and private image. And evocative, as the first online comments attest: "I love the painting and the intrigue." And, "Love this and love her. So touching. I smell book—and film!" The comments keep coming, and keep me going.

Although I wasn't conscious of it at first, the title I have chosen—*The Girl in Red*—is an homage to Klimt's *Woman in Gold*, which I had just seen in New York. I considered other titles: *Girl in a Red Cap* and *Portrait of a Young Parisienne* among them. The pantheon of Western art history is full of paintings of girls or women in red hats, notably Johannes Vermeer's *Girl with a Red Hat* (1669) and Pierre-Auguste Renoir's *Girl in a Red Hat* (1913). But is my *Girl* wearing a hat? It's not clear what kind of head covering it is. My title seems just right.

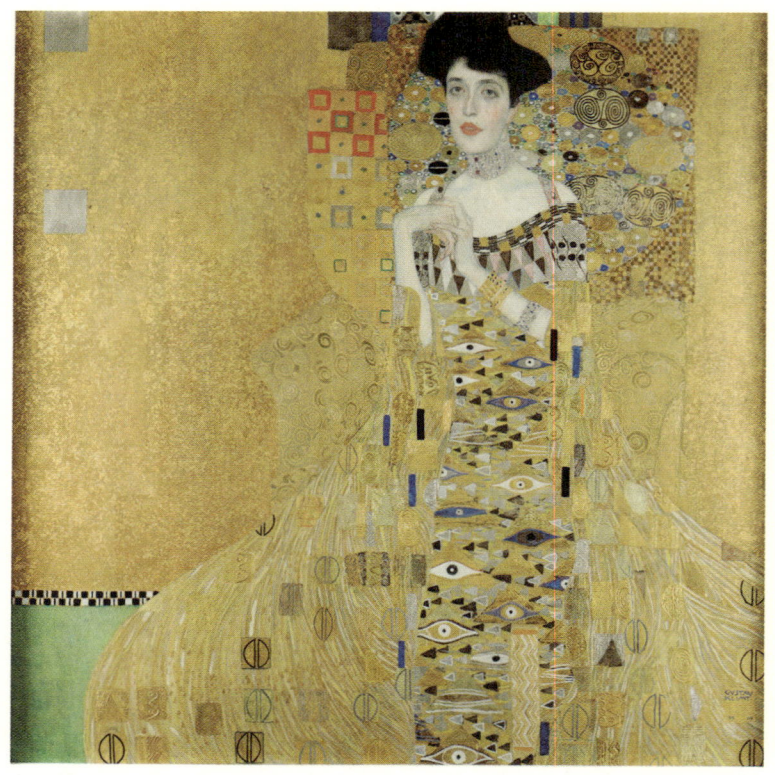

Portrait of Adele Bloch-Bauer I (Woman in Gold)
by Gustav Klimt, 1907

One online commenter, a childhood friend, has challenged the title, Klimt homage notwithstanding, suggesting that "girl in red" has inappropriate connotations, something out of Nabokov's *Lolita*, the novel Nabokov had to publish in France in 1955 with Olympia Press because US publishers wouldn't touch a book about an older man "involved" with a twelve-year-old girl. I confess to feeling grandfather pangs when I am around my sons' friends who are starting to make babies, and I would love nothing more than to dote on a granddaughter in my looming dotage. But my two-dimensional *Girl* touches something in me much deeper than all that. The painting's emergence in my life soon after seeing the Klimt is a truer rationale for my title and my strong reactions to this portrait of a young girl and its dark date.

If you have seen the movie *Woman in Gold*, or read the book the film is based on, you know the incredible story of the painting as it has lived through time and space. All of the painting's experiences, from the time it was created in Vienna, to its theft by the Nazis, to its later restitution to the family that commissioned it, to its sale by its rightful owner to the Neue Galerie in New York in 2006—all constitute key elements not only of its provenance (the historical record of ownership) but its aura, its one-of-a-kind authenticity as a work of art. Even this text contributes, however nominally, perhaps fancifully, to the aura of the Klimt, and now to the aura of *The Girl in Red*.

Aura, an aesthetic concept developed in the 1930s by the German Jewish philosopher and Marxist critic Walter Benjamin as Western art was passing through the upheavals of modernism against the backdrop of wars and revolutions, is still a concept of interest in contemporary art criticism. Benjamin's aura and its political and aesthetic implications are presented in his famous essay, "The Work of Art in the Age of Mechanical Reproduction," a challenging text I have struggled to read through, let alone fully understand.

In the essay, Benjamin writes: "In even the most perfect reproduction, one thing is lacking: the here and now of the work of art—its unique existence in a particular place. It is this unique existence—and nothing else—that bears the mark of the history to which the work has been subject." This sounds like a positive attribute of an artwork, and it indeed is from

most perspectives; but it's loaded with negative social and political connotations in Benjamin's critique.

First published in German in 1935 (in English in 1936) the
essay must rank high on the list of that year's most significant
literary achievements. Tragically, Benjamin committed suicide
in 1940 while fleeing France to Spain as the Germans advanced
on Paris. He was hoping to reach the United States, where
many of his colleagues associated with the Frankfurt School
at Goethe University in Frankfurt had emigrated, when he was
stopped at the Spanish border. Fearing a forced return to Paris
and the Gestapo, he took an overdose of morphine.

Before finding *The Girl*, I had already encountered Benjamin's expansive body of work while researching Paris café
history for my *Zester* food articles. Benjamin's examination
of the poet Charles Baudelaire, the quintessential bohemian
artiste-flâneur who worked and virtually lived in cafés, is full
of insight into nineteenth-century Paris and the function
of the café as the showcase for an emerging avant-garde in
poetry, theater, music and the visual arts. Hence the Baude-
lairean rigor of my gastro-flâneuring—well, café hopping—to
deconstruct the croque monsieur in postmodern Paris.

As I understand the central point of Benjamin's aura concept—taking the word far beyond its more common meaning as
some sort of mystical or spiritual energy field emanating from
a human body—is that mechanical ("technological" in some
translations) reproductions (photographs, book and magazine illustrations, movies and, now, the digital images of social media) lack the full impact and meaning of the authentic,
original object—its unique existence in a particular place. The
power of the auratic presence is not *in* the image per se but

in the relationship between the work and the viewer who is affected (manipulated, in political terms) by the work's unique existence—in churches, museums, public buildings and the grand homes of the elite.

I am admittedly a Johnny-come-lately to Benjamin's Marxist critique of art and social/economic power and that of his Frankfurt School cronies in the 1930s and beyond. Their German Critical Theory, followed by French post-structuralism, invaded academic circles in the US in the 1960s and 1970s, the years when my focus shifted from the visual and literary arts at UC Berkeley to the culinary arts. I missed out on the dense deconstructions of Jacques Derrida and Michel Foucault's assault on colonial power structures. In other words, I got swallowed up by French gastronomy, not French postmodernism—and by Berkeley's French-inspired "new gastronomy," the so-called California cuisine revolution.

But if I have it right, mechanically reproduced and thus inexpensive copies available to a mass audience break an artwork's power as a cult or fetish object controlled by powerful and privileged elites—the rich, the royal, the religious. Reproducibility democratizes art, causing a "withering" of its aura, and creates a liberating role for art that counters its historically repressive function in society (theoretically speaking) from ancient times through the medieval period, the Renaissance and the Enlightenment, to the modern era. All news to me—the idea that art can be "repressive"—but I'm learning.

Benjamin, with his focus on cinema as the ultimate aura-free tool for revolutionary change and resistance to fascism, has been diagnosed by some contemporary critics with a utopian naïveté. Art's aura did not wither, as demonstrated by the global Hollywood star system that emerged in the 1930s, becoming just another iteration of the power of the aura over the masses. Even Benjamin loved Charlie Chaplin and Mickey Mouse, comic stars of the twentieth century's cinematic zeitgeist.

Although Benjamin was challenged and no doubt disappointed by the political machinations of his time and the use of cinema and print media as propaganda tools by both radical-right fascists and radical-left communists, his novel analysis of art and mass culture (modernity) has stood the test of time and has been incorporated into the work of many cultural theorists who followed him. One of them, the brilliant English art critic, novelist and painter John Berger, applied Benjamin's Marxist ideas in a popular TV series and follow-up book in the 1970s, *Ways of Seeing*. These works had a huge influence in England and Europe on how art, especially visual art, was seen as a political medium at the turn from the modern to the postmodern.

But by 2001, in a collection of essays titled *The Shape of a Pocket*, Berger, still a Marxist at heart, seems to ignore Benjamin and the social sins of the auratic image when he rhapsodizes in an essay about the Spanish painter Miquel Barceló: "What any true painting touches is an absence, an absence of which without the painting, we might be unaware. And that would be our loss." An evocative but enigmatic observation typical of Berger who, as much as he positively abhors capitalism's profit motive—and still shouts this at every opportunity—seems, as he ages, to love painting even more, as if his passions for painting and against greed are playing leapfrog in his brain.

So *The Girl* has old-fashioned capitalist/elitist aura. *Tant pis!* as the French might say (Oh well, too bad). I can dare to ask, now, with passionate tongue in cheek, "Will *The Girl in Red*'s commodity value increase as awareness of her auratic presence grows?" I have just posted online that I will accept a preemptive offer of $1 million before taking the painting to the auction block.

So far, no takers.

Here, then, in Paris in 2015, on blvd. Saint-Germain, *The Girl in Red* is entering a new phase of its existence after decades lost in the shadows—being analyzed, talked about, joked about and, I hope, appreciated. But, most important, being seen. Walter Pater wrote of the *Mona Lisa* in his *Studies in the History of the Renaissance*, "She is older than the rocks among which she sits; like the vampire, she has been dead many times and learned the secrets of the grave." *The Girl* is not the *Mona Lisa*, but like the *Mona Lisa*, she and her aura are back from the dead.

THE RED AND THE BLACK

○

The dominant reds and blacks in my found portrait bring to mind, here in Paris, Stendhal's *The Red and the Black*, a novel I have never read, or attempted to read, until now. Many of my Francophile friends are familiar with the nineteenth-century classic from their French language and literature classes in college, but few have read it more recently. I've decided to give it a shot after seeing online here in Paris the BBC miniseries first broadcast in the 1990s.

I confess that after several hours with the novel (a 1938 translation titled *Scarlet and Black* just purchased at Shakespeare and Company), I've been unable to get past the first few hundred pages of the rather tedious literary realism. The love affair that develops at the outset of the story between the protagonist, the ambitious young lower-class Julien Sorel, and Madame Rénal, the unhappy upper-class wife of the small town's mayor, is such a slow and erotically repressed slog (Mme. Rénal's hands seem to be the sole focus of Sorel's emerging lust) that when their affair is finally consummated, I completely miss it.

At one point a bit further on in the narrative, when Julien speaks of the adulterous act more directly, I spiral back to locate it. I find the moment embedded in a paragraph so opaque that one wonders if Julien himself missed it. I feel like a kid again looking for the dirty parts of my parents' novels—*Lady Chatterley's Lover*, *Peyton Place*, and the like.

I am not alone in having a "Stendhal problem." The amusing British essayist and lecturer Alain de Botton, in a talk on Stendhal and "French passions" at the Institute Français in 2011 (I've listened to it on YouTube), confesses his inability to "get on with" *The Red and the Black*, preferring Stendhal's nonfiction books (especially *On Love*) and his essays on art, music, and travel.

For de Botton, it's the "artificial and cold" prose of Stendhal's novels that puts him off. He considers his Stendhal problem a personal defect, but refers to others in this camp, somewhat defensively, as "the happy few." Add me to the list.

But I digress. It's the title of Stendhal's novel and the book's red and black color symbolism that are relevant to *The Girl in Red*. One critique of the novel proposes that the colors red and black represent the tension in the narrative between the sacred (the black robes of the clergy) and the profane (the red uniforms of the army). Julien is torn between his passion to become a priest (black) and his obsession with Napoleon (red), a man of action on the battlefield and in the boudoir.

In the realm of the visual arts, there is no color as alive as red, the color of blood. According to Henri Matisse, "A thimble full of red is redder than a bucket full." As for black, it has an intensity and mystery that both subdues and highlights vivid colors such as red, yellow and blue. Odilon Redon once commented that "black is the most essential color." Against black, red really pops. The Nazis knew this well when they placed their black swastika against a blood-red field. Their red, black, and white design was formally adopted as the National Socialist flag in September of 1935.

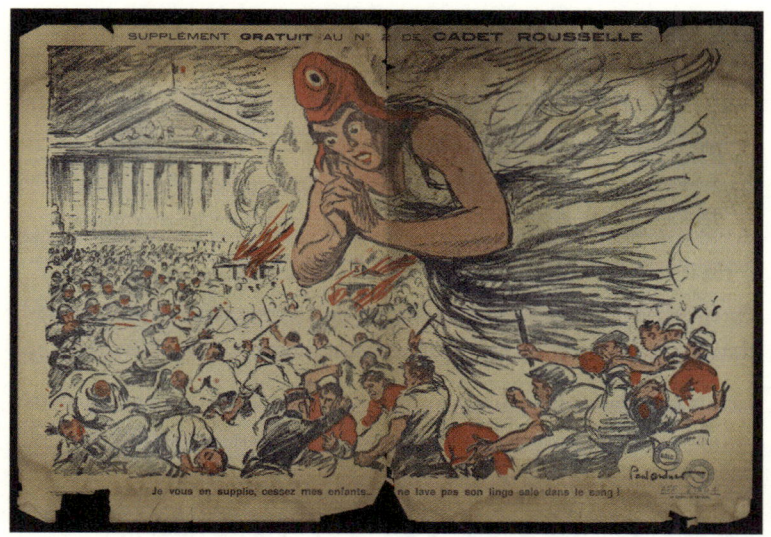

Marianne, in her bonnet rouge, *exhorts the French to resist the right-wing protestors*

It's not surprising that France's blood-red liberty cap, the *bonnet rouge*, has been worn during political uprisings and protests from the French Revolution to the present day. It evolved from the red Phrygian caps and helmets worn since Roman times as symbols of freedom. The bonnet rouge played a role on February 6, 1934, when many far-right protestors were killed in an antiparliamentary riot against the police. In an illustrated broadside published in the magazine *Cadet Rousselle*, Marianne, the personification of France, wearing the red liberty cap, exhorts the left to resist the protestors. The unrest led to the collapse of the Daladier government, giving rise to the antifascist resistance in France

The fascist right also claimed the red-capped Marianne. On the April 1935 cover of *Le Témoin* (*The Witness*), a nationalist humor magazine published and illustrated by the celebrated designer Paul Iribe, Coco Chanel is the model for Marianne, colored by Iribe in red, black and blue. Chanel and Iribe were lovers from 1931 until his death in 1935, and they embraced the same right-wing politics (and antisemitism).

Given this omnipresent image of the red-bonneted Marianne in the prewar period, on both sides of the political spectrum, could viewers of *The Girl in Red* in 1935, and thereafter, no matter who and how few, fail to see a symbolic connection with this budding Marianne? Could the painter of the portrait? I can't.

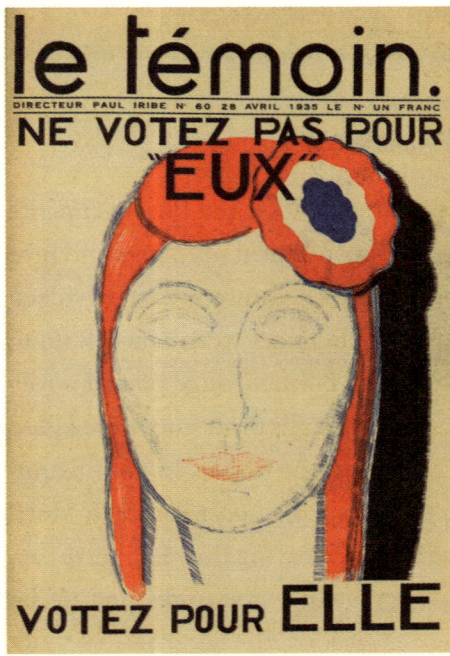

On the cover of Le Témoin *magazine* (The Witness), *Paul Iribe turns Coco Chanel into Marianne.*

In the realm of modernist painting, red and black appear as powerful pictorial elements in their own right, as in Edgar Degas's *La Coiffure*. In this work, red colors the background behind figures outlined in black. Note that from the Renaissance to the birth of modernism outlines around faces and bodies were *verboten*. With the technique of *sfumato*, Renaissance artists applied thin layers of translucent paint to make the transition between background and foreground objects invisible. Leonardo was the master of sfumato, and the *Mona Lisa* has no hard lines.

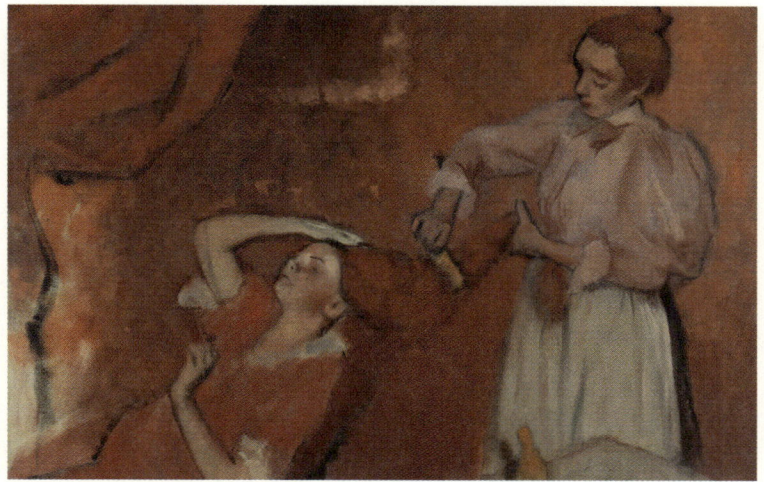

La Coiffure by Edgar Degas, 1896

Granted, the black outlines in *The Girl in Red* are quite heavy, perhaps awkwardly so; and the unfinished background needs no separation from the central image, as is the case with the red-on-red Degas. Nevertheless, with *The Girl*'s face and upper body placed in the center of a more or less raw canvas, the black lines anchor her in the emptiness of negative space, giving the face and head covering an enhanced presence. A modern presence.

On the interpretive level, I'd venture to say that our unknown artist's bold black lines and date provide a dark foil for the innocence of *The Girl*'s young red lips and simple red head covering, and for her undeveloped torso. I'll go even further: The portrait's black elements foreshadow the tragedy that will soon engulf France and the entire world.

MEET AURA'S COUSIN, PATINA

o

My social media postings continue to elicit interesting re-actions, the latest from David Downie, the prolific author of books about Paris. A longtime American expat in Paris, Downie and I have not met face to face, though we are "friends" on Facebook. I have read his fine books, such as *Paris, Paris*, and he has read my Paris food articles, and now my posts about *The Girl in Red*. You could say our relationship is inauthentic—in the Benjaminian sense. It's digital, *Facebook à Facebook*, not real, not *mano a mano*. It lacks aura, the authenticity of actuality. Nevertheless, his comment is very real and appreciated, an educated guess about the story told by *The Girl*: "Serendipity! Very intriguing. I'd guess the painting was done by an art school student. Who knows? The Beaux-Arts is right nearby, and a zillion artists have lived in the neighborhood for the last two centuries . . . Paris is still wonderful for this kind of experience. Living is an experiment in found art."

Yes, plausible, and I love Downie's last line about living as an experiment in found art. But sadly, and all too often tragically, living can be an experiment in lost art. Having recently read *The Hare with Amber Eyes*, Edmund de Waal's heartbreaking story of his family's art treasures—indeed their very lives—stolen by the Nazis, I feel a connection between de Waal's discovery of his family's collection of antique *netsuke* (miniature carved sculptures from Japan) and my discovery of *The Girl in Red*. Both discoveries have opened doors: his to his family's lost narrative via objects with stories, and mine to the meaning of art in my life via a painting with aura and, I would add, patina. De Waal knows all about patina from his work as a ceramicist engaged with the effects of heat and time on the color and texture of his materials. He also understands patina as a literary device, its ability to illuminate stories over time: "It is not just things that carry stories with them. Stories are a kind of thing, too. Stories and objects share something, a patina."

I'd describe patina as both the physical expression of an object's presence in time and its experience translated into stories told over time. But what is the scientific description of the chemical process that patinizes the surface of objects? One online source describes it this way: "A thin layer that variously forms on the surface of stone; on copper, bronze and similar metals (tarnish produced by oxidation or other chemical processes); on wooden furniture (sheen produced by age, wear, and polishing): or any such acquired change of a surface through age and exposure."

The Girl in Red has a goodly amount of patina: the rust on the nails that hold the canvas to the aging, grayish stretcher bars; the dry paint, chipped off in spots; and the darkened lower edge of the perhaps soiled, perhaps water-stained, and slightly fraying canvas. All of this patination, actual and literary, adds, I believe, to the painting's aura, revealing exposure not only to the physical elements but to the wear and tear of time, enhanced by the painting's date and the unknown stories one senses and imagines.

Admittedly, I'm an obsessive lover and collector of old things—furniture, textiles, guitars, art, books, garden artifacts, even houses. Since childhood I have been drawn to objects with patina, though I wouldn't have known that word as a boy. I remember my paternal grandfather Sol's garden in Los Angeles in the 1950s. Papa Sol had imported a cement replica of the seventeenth-century fountain in Brussels known as the *Manneken Pis* ("Little Pissing Man") showing a small naked boy peeing into a basin. Quite a scandal in the extended family, but not for my parents, my older brother and me. We thought it was funny, somewhat naughty, and certainly characteristic of Sol Harris (né Hrekowitch)—a self-styled Polish/Jewish dandy, a veteran of the French Foreign Legion serving in the Sahara and Tonkin in the late 1890s, and a lover of all things French, even the French themselves. He was especially grateful to the French community in San Francisco for loaning him the money to start a textile business in the early 1900s (S. Harris & Co.).

Sol's fountain had been installed at the back of his garden with the boy's "plumbing" hooked up to a running hose. There was a mature fig tree nearby, which seemed quite foreign to me, and along with the fountain created a magical space I loved. The fig tree stood near the entrance to a repurposed garage that contained a huge pool table and an aquarium filled with exotic fish. All the grandchildren would gravitate to this room.

Although the pissing fountain was not officially an antique (being less than one hundred years old), the mossy green sheen that grew on the worn basin made it all look ancient and mysterious. This was not the gorgeous verdigris (greenish gray; in French, *vert-de-gris*) patina that forms on oxidized copper and bronze, used as a pigment in medieval and Renaissance painting until modern and more stable green pigments were developed. It was more slime than sublime.

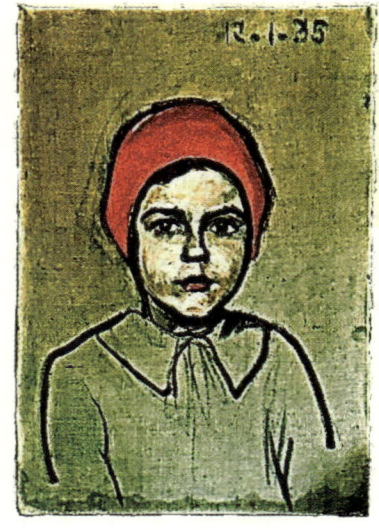

A digital simulation of a heavily patinated (slimy, grimy) Girl in Red "left out" in the elements

But what about on the surface of a painting? Does patination affect a work's aesthetic and monetary value? A painting, of course, is not an object/tool like a piece of wooden furniture or a musical instrument. If a violin's or guitar's sound changes over time and becomes, thanks to the aging of the wood and its effect on vibration (tone), increasingly beautiful (Stradivarius violins and Torres guitars, for example), does a painting's ability to induce what philosophers and psychologists call aesthetic emotion likewise increase as its surface changes with age? Does the human eye and brain translate the effects of age in an artwork as beauty? Or are the changes extrinsic to the work of art as such?

I love the aging surfaces of old oil paintings, the crackling texture caused by the differential drying out of paint and varnish (*craquelure*), and the slight darkening or yellowing or fading of the painting's pigments and varnishes over time. This added value that I perceive in the age and physical decline of a painting, a merger of patina and aura, was noted in an article about the great postminimalist German-born American artist

Eva Hesse and her mixed-media piece *Expanded Expansion* (1969). In an article, "All about Eva," in *The Nation*, following the opening of Hesse's show at the Jewish Museum of New York in May of 2006, the late art critic and philosopher Arthur Danto wrote: "But one cannot erase from consciousness everything that has happened between then and now. . . . So the discolorations, the slackness in the membrane-like latex, the palpable aging of the material, inflect the whole experience."

I suspect that many traditional art restorers and conservators would not agree with Danto (and me) about the virtues of the "post-studio life" of an artwork—as some enlightened curators refer to these "negative" changes in a work over time—and would attempt to reverse the changes as far as possible. Thankfully, the restorers who brought Hesse's darkened and brittle rubberized cheesecloth panels "back to life" simply cleaned and repaired them only where the cloth was severely torn.

For me, these elements of patina, literal and literary, are the visual and emotional cues of time passing, and combined with aura, offer clues to my deep attraction to the eighty-year-old *Girl in Red*.

THE RED AND THE GOLD

○

When I stopped in New York en route to Paris to visit the Neue Galerie and the *Woman in Gold*, I had a foodie agenda alongside my art agenda—to eat at the boutique museum's Viennese-style Café Sabarsky with a dear friend from Berkeley, the young cellist Tessa Seymour. She is now living in New York after her graduation from the Curtis Institute of Music in Philadelphia. Her holiday visits to Berkeley while at Curtis have led to a close friendship and opportunities to hear the progress with her instrument.

I had heard good reports about the café's "authentic" apple strudel, and seeing *Woman in Gold* was going to be, I imagined, mere icing on the Sabarsky's strudel. The Neue's café—the décor and the feel—did not disappoint. Tessa and I were transported to Klimt's Vienna, circa 1900. But the strudel didn't justify the hype. Authentic, perhaps, but it was not as sweet as I would have wanted, and both the pastry and the filling were much too dry for my taste. (One has to be suspicious of any dish advertised as authentic.)

To be fair, compared to the butter-rich, caramelized and succulent Normandy tarte, *tarte Tatin*, which may have already been on my mind's palate as my Paris flight loomed, few apple-based desserts from around the world would *not* seem dry. The best examples of our beloved American apple pie are notable exceptions.

"Dry" does not apply to Klimt's golden, bejeweled Bloch-Bauer portrait. It is a juicy visual confection. Compared to the comparatively bland *Girl in Red*, the Klimt explodes with dramatic and erotic effects. The more I looked at the painting, before and after the strudel, the more I felt its rich brilliance, its tragic irony and its deep aura. You cannot look at it as merely a stunning portrait of a young, glamorous woman. It's a portrait of a place and a time, with all the gaudy sensuality of Vienna's avant-garde Secessionist version of Art Nouveau.

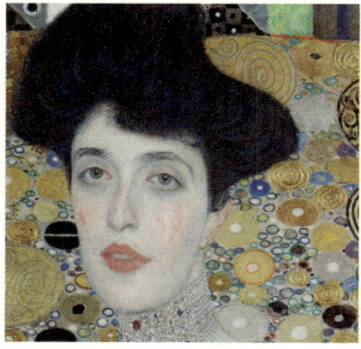 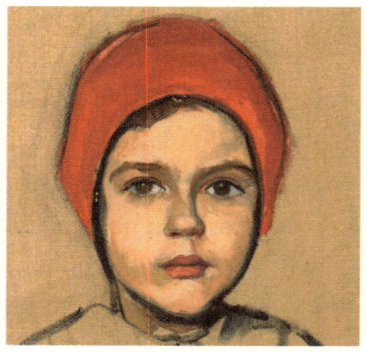

Woman in Gold (*detail*)   The Girl in Red (*detail*)

Although I have not yet fully digested all the connections between *Woman in Gold* and *The Girl in Red* with just a few days in Paris under my belt, they are coming into focus: two portraits, two young females, both with full red lips and soulful eyes, painted in two great cities, Vienna and Paris, where the Nazis would soon destroy vibrant Jewish communities and devour fabulous art collections. It is impossible not to acknowledge the sad serendipity that has brought these two very distinct yet uncannily connected images into my life.

HEUREUX HASARD

○

Artists, and I am referring to creative makers of every stripe, have a special relationship to chance. They don't really believe in it, especially when locked into their creative zone. When I'm in Paris I feel locked in 24/7. The French painter Jean Dubuffet once wrote, "Very often a long-sought secret is revealed to me through a chance encounter without any relation to the subject." You don't have to be a great artist like Dubuffet to experience this magical zone of revelatory chance. A French expression I like to use to represent Dubuffet's "secrets revealed to me" is *heureux hasard*, loosely translated as "happy chance." The appearance of *The Girl in Red* feels like just such a secret, revealed to me here in a magical Paris.

According to my French teacher back in Berkeley (she *is* French) who has now seen *The Girl* via email, *sérendipité* would be the more accurate French word. Yes, but the origin of the term is, in fact, English—serendipity—coined by a British man of letters in the eighteenth century, Horace Walpole. Walpole's neologism came to him after his reading of a Persian fairy tale (my paraphrase): While traveling in the land of Serendip (Ceylon), three young Persian princes help describe and locate a lost camel using chance encounters with revealing clues. This fairy tale also influenced Edgar Allan Poe and led to his introduction of detective fiction into English.

Add also Carl Jung's synchronicity (acausal connections) to the family of heureux hasard, a concept he developed in the 1920s and '30s in conjunction with his theories about dreams and archetypes and the collective unconscious. Jung, who countered Sigmund Freud's materialist view of the unconscious and its contents with a more expansive philosophical and spiritual one, was a huge hero for the artists in my 1960s art commune in Oakland—"Colby Street"—a magical realm of heureux hasard brought back into Proustian memory here in Paris by my encounter with the lost and found *Girl*.

Equally heroic for us was the mythologist Joseph Campbell who showed the way forward with his book *The Hero with a Thousand Faces*. Both Jung and Campbell seem somewhat old school today, but in the 1960s and '70s they were "in." New Age (now known as "human potential") self-help gurus such as Ken Wilber and Deepak Chopra had not yet emerged within the countercultural zeitgeist with what seems more like packaged New Age salesmanship than the more scholarly teachings of Jung and Campbell. The former sell their wisdom; the latter profess theirs. Frankly, I'd rather be a benighted *naïf* on Jung and Campbell's team than a gullible groupie on Wilber and Chopra's.

The fact that my mother was reading Jung, Campbell and the diaries of Anaïs Nin (also Alan Watts, J. Krishnamurti and many other east-west gurus) and discussing them all with her Los Angeles circle of artists, writers and analysts during my teens prepared me for all the fuzzy dimensions of human consciousness and aesthetic imagination I would encounter in the art scene I entered soon after I arrived in Berkeley in 1966. I mean, when at thirteen years of age you are invited to take your aging dog (Pal, a collie) to have his doggie aura (yet another meaning of the word aura) read by an "animal psychic" holding forth in a Beverly Hills living room under the auspices of a research psychologist at UCLA studying paranormal phenomena, you are not going to be surprised by the avant-garde antics in your art commune at college. (According to the psychic, Pal's aura was no longer very active. All he could see was a red ball. Yes, Pal had a red ball, but what dog doesn't?)

Avant-garde antics were routine in our commune. We were led by a charismatic and shaman-like teacher (and landlord), Michael Haimovitz, also from LA like me, also the son of a Jewish textile merchant. (Our fathers knew each other.) Michael had just received his MFA at UC Berkeley for his elaborate theatrical "events," not unlike Allan Kaprow's Happenings in New York earlier in the decade, except that Kaprow's productions (unknown to Michael at the time) were group oriented while Michael's events were offered as "gifts," as he described them, to individuals.

Less interested in the psychological than the sensorial, Michael inspired and managed our group's carefully choreographed events to deliver maximum sensory surprises, even shocks, to our gift receivers. He was inspired, he has said, by the "elaborate decorated dances" he organized for his fraternity at Cal and by an event created for him by the Berkeley composer, philosopher and architect Charles MacDermed, who collaborated with Michael in the mid-1960s, before I had arrived on the scene.

One event I worked on in 1968 involved the "kidnapping" of a Comp Lit professor at Cal who lectured on Dada and Surrealism. The event began with a staged bicycle race we took straight out of an episode in Alfred Jarry's novel *The Supermale*, a Dadaist source that influenced many of us at Colby Street. The professor thought he was going to a party at our house, but was invited at the front door to get on a bizarre-looking tandem bike welded together from old bike parts by the sculptor Joe Slusky. The professor's bike mate took him on a race against other riders on Slusky tandems around a small park nearby, viewed by cheering fans dressed in formal white attire.

After several turns around the park, the professor was ushered into a car that drove him to a dinner party at a Victorian home in San Francisco attended by complete strangers (my art scene cronies) who had studied his life and work with the secret help of his wife. We "knew him" intimately; he was clueless about us. The dinner's miniature-scaled food was served *à la Alice in Wonderland* on tiny child-sized plates with children's cutlery and glassware and napkins cut to size. I remember tiny bowls of soup, followed by baby chicken drumettes served with baby peas, and then tiny wedges from a small frosted cake. The juxtaposition of our dinner party banter ("What's your take on Alfred Jarry's College of Pataphysics, Professor?") with the impression that our bodies had grown enormous, our hands gigantic and our mouths cavernous, was "surreal."

The professor seemed to be in a state of disorientation after this expression of Arthur Rimbaud's "systematic derangement of the senses." The event went on from there into the night, ending with a meeting of the College of Pataphysics ("an imaginary science related to metaphysics as metaphysics is related to physics") aboard a beat-up old ferryboat docked near Fisherman's Wharf. It was a chaotic scene as I remember it; not all of the action (speeches, debates, readings from Jarry) came together as I had hoped. Word trickled back from the professor's friends that he was not particularly happy with the event, especially the initial "abduction." Perhaps lecturing on Surrealism is not the same as living it.

Back home at Colby Street after such extravaganzas, we would record our impressions in our journals, share a communal meal, take recreational drugs, go to bed with our partner (or someone else's partner) and, if still conscious, "throw" the *I Ching* (translated as *Book of Changes*), the ancient Chinese divination "game" that Jung believed was an expression of the collective unconscious and what he later termed "the sympathy of all things." The morning after would center us back in our everyday routines: attending art classes, writing in our journals (à la Anaïs Nin), collage making, live modeling, letter writing (by hand), yoga practice, reading *everything*, shopping and house cleaning, attending performances and art exhibits, demonstrating against the Vietnam War, and planning future events with Michael . . . the usual.

One of our communards, the poet Kaaren Kitchell, my first muse in art and love (and the sister of Michael's artist wife, Jane), had been keeping a journal since childhood and relished reading Nin's diaries. Kaaren still identifies, she told me recently, with what Nin wrote in volume 2 of the *Diary* (covering the years 1934–1939): "Reality doesn't impress me. I only believe in intoxication, in ecstasy, and when ordinary life shackles me, I escape, one way or another. No more walls." That's the life Kaaren aspired to at Colby Street, as did we all—no more walls, figuratively and communally speaking. And that's how Kaaren lives today, moving between Paris, Los Angeles, Phoenix and Berkeley.

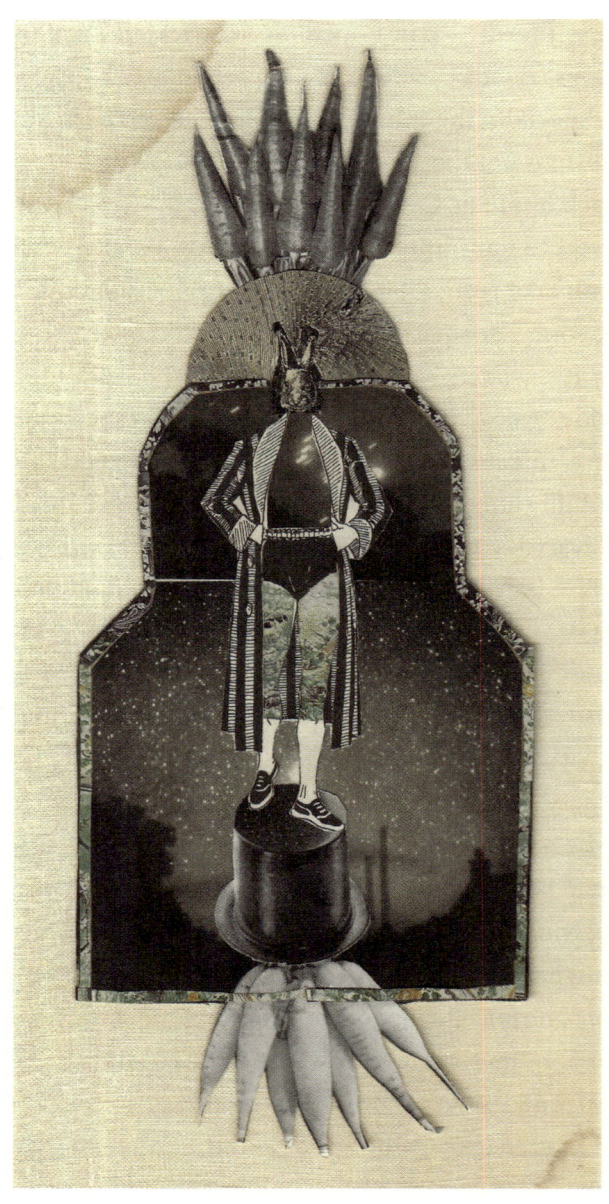

My collage The Rabbit Majesto *from 1969 is the kind of work
I was doing when not involved in Colby Street events.*

o

Intoxication, ecstasy, sympathy, serendipity, heureux hasard, call it what you will—we were countercultural artist/ seekers, a New Agey avant-garde in Berkeley, and our collective unconscious was an open book. Our Cal art professors, especially Peter Voulkas and his former studio assistant, Jim Melchert, both acclaimed pioneers in the transformation of ceramics from craft to fine art, recognized the talent in our group and championed the work Michael and the commune produced, like parents who witness the wild antics of their precocious children.

Although Colby Street operated below the radar of the larger art world, we did have contact with other young artists who had or would have (and a few who still have) larger audiences beyond our Berkeley art scene. Among them was Nancy Spanier, who brilliantly, and innovatively, integrated sculpture and video into her choreography. Nancy performed with José Limón in the 1960s, then launched the modern dance department at the University of Colorado at Boulder. The Nancy Spanier Dance Theatre was formed in 1974 and toured the world, winning many international commissions and awards. Now residing in southern France, Nancy conducts her dance workshops all over Europe with her dancer husband, Paul Oertel, and they document their "performance inventions" on videotape.

When I first met Nancy, the circumstances were, well, surreal—dancing together (total strangers) *tout nu* (stark naked) for an event in 1968 created in honor of Jim Melchert's birthday in December of that year. Events were "in the air," and although this one did not engage the entire Colby Street gang, it took place at the commune. I don't remember all the details of that brief improv with Nancy (she says that we were moving "rather abstractly with touches of subtle seduction"), but it was a thrill to work with her (in more ways than one), and the experience led to my taking dance classes with her and movement classes with Berkeley's Paris-trained mime, Leonard Pitt. All art forms were on the table for me at a time when Berkeley was, according to Larisa Orance, author of *Nancy Spanier: The Arc of a Dancer's Life*, "an incubator of social, political and cultural movements that inspired artists to seek alternative ways of art making." Looking back at that time, I find it hard to distinguish the facts from the fantasies, the real from the surreal, the politics from the art, but this was Berzerkeley circa 1968.

The eruption of these sometimes vague, sometimes vivid memories of my personal art history in Berkeley, triggered in Paris this summer by *The Girl in Red*, tells me that heureux hasard works in multiple time and space dimensions—past, present and future. Returning now to Paris's marvelous present at the legendary English-language bookshop, Shakespeare and Company, I show the shop's book buyer a photo of *The Girl* and share the story. I know the fellow from previous transactions, both purchasing books and selling my own. He seems startled and delighted by the image and the story and suggests that I look at a portrait by the Dutch Fauve artist Kees van Dongen, titled *The Corn Poppy*. There are similarities, he says.

Back at the apartment that afternoon, I look at the van Dongen online and note the red hat and lips, the vacant background and the black outlines, all justifying comparison with *The Girl*. But there is much more modernist caricature than realistic character in the van Dongen. My *Girl* is a real girl.

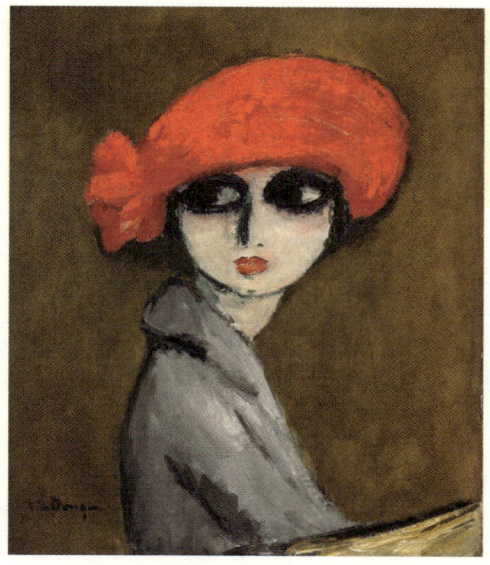

The Corn Poppy
by Kees van Dongen,
1919

There is also online from Berkeley a new Facebook comment from Leonard Pitt, my mime teacher back in the day and the author of a guidebook about Baron von Haussmann's transformation of Paris, *Walks Through Lost Paris*. Also trained as a graphic artist, Lenny extols the virtues of *The Girl*: "No doubt about it, that head is by an accomplished artist and is worth something. . . . There is enormous observation behind each line with years of moving a pencil on paper."

I'm excited by the responses to *The Girl*, though a bit embarrassed that I need outside support for my strong attraction to it. Don't I know what a good painting looks like? I've been away from the art world too long, but I'm back. And I'm curious about what a working painter would say about *The Girl in Red*. As luck would have it, voilà, he appears. Heureux hasard!

FROM RUSSIA WITH
ART AND SOUL

○

After spotting a soulful-looking gentleman in various cafés around Saint-Germain during this first week in Paris, I've wondered who he is. He oozes a bohemian gravitas with his curly white hair, horn-rimmed spectacles and snappy attire (blazer, slacks, silk scarf and loafers without socks—very Left Bank). Can people have aura? This gentleman certainly does.

I next see him at Brasserie Lipp where, after a week of Paris meals in and out, I've come to binge on blanquette de veau. He is several tables away in a window booth near the front door, seated with another fellow who is talking insistently, as if imparting very important information.

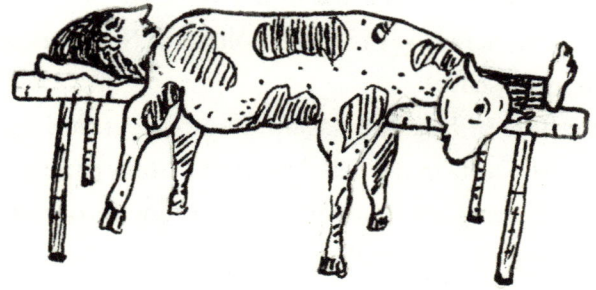

My journal doodle, Blanquette de Veau, *2009,*
inspired by Brasserie Lipp's dish

I focus on my blanquette and plan my strategy. The dish is as delicious as ever, the creamy sauce rich as silk, and when it's *terminé*, I ask the garçon as he's picking up the empty plate whether he knows the gentleman in the corner with the gray scarf. He replies, *"Oui, monsieur,"* but has to ask his manager whether he can give out the name. He returns with it: "Yuri Kuper." I had suspected an artist or writer, and it turns out he's both, an important Russian painter, novelist and playwright.

I recognize neither the name nor the work that I see online. Waiting for the bill, I get the details: born in Moscow in 1940, Kuper has lived all over the world, including Israel, London, Normandy and New York. His paintings, which according to Wikipedia are influenced by Anselm Kiefer, Jean Dubuffet and Giorgio Morandi, feel powerful to me, based on the digital thumbnails I view on my cell phone. I'm particularly attracted to his painting *Garlics* from 1998, for an obvious reason— my obsession with garlic that led to *The Book of Garlic* in 1974. Considered one of the most important Russian painters of the second half of the twentieth century, Kuper is today, I read, the best-known Russian artist in the West. His work is in major museums including the Metropolitan in New York and the Pushkin in Moscow.

In a haze of heureux hasard, induced perhaps by Lipp's blanquette floating in my belly's Sea of Chablis, I approach Kuper and his dinner companion, whom I now recognize as the fellow I've seen talking to Kuper at various cafés around Saint-Germain-des-Prés—talking, never listening. Like some giddy fan in search of an autograph, I introduce myself as a writer and artist from Berkeley, suspecting that Kuper might find the combination of interest. Surprisingly, I am invited to join them for a drink.

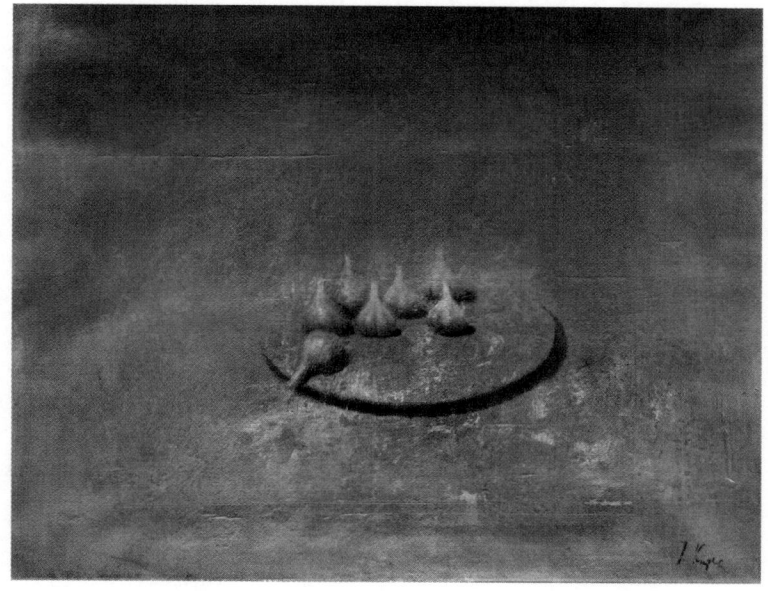

Garlics *by Yuri Kuper, 1998*

Wanting to connect with Kuper since I first saw him, I now have my chance. But his companion, a local art collector and dealer who, I learn, has shown Kuper's work, won't allow it. I will call him Gilbert. He doesn't stop speaking to me, which keeps Yuri out of reach. A handsome middle-aged Frenchman with a prominent Gallic nose and heavily French-accented English, Gilbert insists after a few minutes of small talk that I tell him more about myself. He focuses on me as if Kuper is not even at the table. I feel put on the spot. I don't want to talk about my own art in front of Kuper, at least not at a first meeting. And my mission in Paris and my *Book of Garlic* (published in French translation in the 1980s) are subjects I want to avoid. The French are, generally speaking, not interested in an American's views on food, especially French food, underscored by the minimal sales of the French edition of my book. In fact, I don't want to talk about myself at all, and I'm not ready to mention *The Girl in Red*. I want to talk *to* Yuri, *about* Yuri. But the only way to Yuri is, apparently, through Gilbert, and my efforts are not working.

On an impulse, feeling a little desperate, I mention my guitar collection. Gilbert and I are fellow collector types—he with art, and I mostly with guitars. Surely the guitar collection would provide a common bond between two serious collectors, right? Wrong. Gilbert stops me in midsentence: "*John*, I know *no-sing* about *gee-tars*, so why would I be interested in hearing about your *gee-tar* collection, *John*?"

Yuri sits silently as I process the mounting tension. Gilbert has a way of saying my name with such emphasis that it feels like an insult. He continues in his singsong Frenchie English, "I want to know *some-sing* interesting about you, *John*, like what kind of *woo-man* you like."

Ah, a real Frenchman! I should have counterpunched with something clever like, "Young girls painted on old canvases," but this would have led, no doubt, to my story about finding *The Girl*. I'm still digesting her arrival in my life and don't feel ready to make the painting the focus of a connection with Kuper. I will get his response to it privately in due course. I sense that Gilbert's response to *The Girl* would be dismissive and demoralizing.

All of these considerations are more feeling than thought as I chuckle at Gilbert's question, stalling for time to respond. The soft-spoken, hardly spoken Yuri Kuper just sits there, perhaps embarrassed by his friend's aggressive repartee. Wanting to avoid any awkwardness with Kuper by inadvertently aggravating Gilbert, I politely say my *au revoirs*. I thank them both for inviting me to join them, and for the drink, and rise to leave, never responding to Gilbert's query about *woo-man*.

Gilbert gets up, too. I can't recall whether we shake hands or not, but he offers me his business card and, reaching down to his red leather banquette seat, produces a book, the catalog, he tells me, from a Yuri Kuper show at the Pushkin Museum in Moscow. Handing it to me, Gilbert adds cheerfully, "Great to meet you, *John*. I think you will find this interesting." Kuper, still seated, mumbles something softly as I shake his hand on my way to Lipp's door.

Confused, as if I had simultaneously dodged a bullet and forfeited an opportunity, I slowly walk up blvd. Saint-Germain toward home. The thrill of meeting Yuri Kuper feels diminished by the awkward encounter with Gilbert. I'm determined to follow up with Kuper, but having left the restaurant abruptly, I have failed to get his contact info.

NOT SO HEUREUX HASARD

∘

Settled back in at the apartment, I start browsing through Yuri Kuper's Pushkin exhibit catalog and notice the date: 1995. Why did Gilbert have this ancient catalog at Lipp? And why did he give it to me? Perhaps with the idea of selling me a Kuper? A shiver of heureux hasard runs through me as I note the names attached to the catalog's two introductions, translated from the Russian into English and French. I am acquainted with both men: art historian Peter Selz, who launched and served as director of the UC Berkeley Art Museum in the 1960s and '70s; and Robert Flynn Johnson, an author, art collector and the retired curator emeritus of the Achenbach Foundation's print and drawing collection at the Fine Arts Museums of San Francisco.

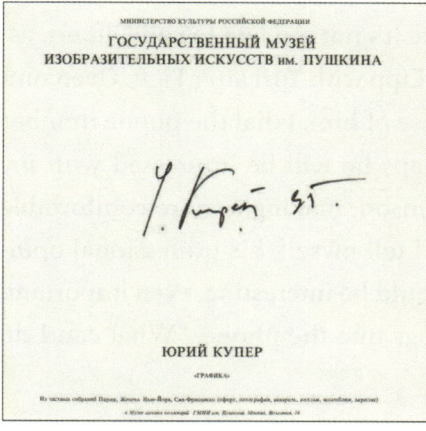

The title page from Yuri Kuper's Pushkin Museum 1995 exhibit catalog with signature and date

Johnson's book advocating for the virtues of anonymous images—*Anonymous: Enigmatic Images from Unknown Photographers* (2005)—is a pioneering work in its field. I became aware of it after meeting Johnson a few years back at a house concert chez moi. He was the guest of a mutual friend who had come to hear Tessa Seymour (my strudel-tasting companion) perform for a group of her local admirers. But I hadn't yet thought of Johnson's book in relationship to *The Girl in Red*. Am I surprised that an advocate for the power of anonymous art and photography should pop up in my life so soon after finding my own anonymous treasure? Not really. Not in the land of heureux hasard.

It is now about 9 p.m., a good time to contact Johnson in San Francisco, midmorning California time. In my email, I tell him all about my encounter with Yuri Kuper and Gilbert. His response is quick and excited, explaining that he hasn't been in touch with Yuri in several years and would love to have his email address. I reply that I will try to get it. I do not mention *The Girl*, keeping the focus for the time being on Yuri. But I very much want to tell him about the portrait and will do so when next we connect.

Now it's 10 p.m. I figure it's not too late to call Gilbert, assuming he stayed longer at Lipp with Yuri after I left. Overcoming my dread of another dose of him, I dial the phone number on his business card. Perhaps he will be impressed with my connection to Selz and Johnson, making a more comfortable rapport possible. After all, I tell myself, his professional opinion about *The Girl in Red* would be interesting, even important.

"Yes, *John*," Gilbert sings into the phone. "What can I do for you, *John*?"

I thank him again for the drink and the catalog and briefly explain, excitedly, my acquaintance with both Peter Selz and Robert Johnson. And I tell him of the request from Johnson for Yuri's email address.

"No, *John*," Gilbert blurts, "I will not give it. Everyone wants to connect with Yuri. I don't care who these people are, and I'm sure Yuri doesn't even remember them. That Moscow show was over twenty-five years ago."

Before I can respond, Gilbert hangs up after a final flourish: "I like you, *John*, but I will not give you Yuri's information. I'm sorry. Good night, *John*."

I am again shaken and confused. Or, as my grandmother would put it in Yiddish, *farmisht*. The repetitive emphasis on my name at the end of his sentences feels like a negation of its value. My value. I will have to find another way to make contact with Yuri. If I must, I will stalk him in Saint-Germain and the Latin Quarter.

From my lips to god's ears: as I approach La Palette the next morning, Yuri is seated alone at the power table on the corner. The needle on my heureux hasard meter is jumping off the scale. I had decided to have my first crème and a croissant at La Palette, outside my regular morning orbit, because it's just a few blocks from Gilbert's art gallery, where I plan to pass by after breakfast. Assuming the gallery is closed for the summer, I'm curious to see whether there are any Kupers visible through the windows without having to engage with Gilbert. Gilbert, my galling Gallic gallerist!

Walking up to Yuri's table I say, "*Bonjour*, Yuri" and reach out to shake hands. We shake, and I'm invited to join him. This time, and without Gilbert's interference, we talk with ease and substance, sipping on crèmes and nibbling on croissants. His soft-spoken Russian-accented English is very good. After a bit of gossip about Peter Selz and Robert Johnson (he does remember them both, of course) and an update on his current work, I express my admiration for his work and explain my connection to his superb *Garlics*. When I show him some of my own foodie drawings from a collection published in 2010, *Foodoodles*, he nods politely, makes approving sounds, but says nothing.

But it's time to get down to business: *The Girl in Red*. I show Yuri the portrait on my cell phone with, it turns out, unnecessary caveats.

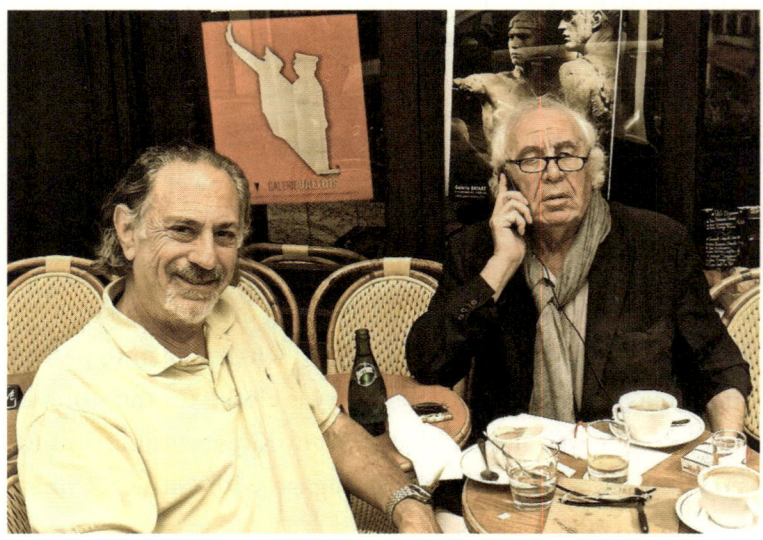

At La Palette with Yuri Kuper,
our garçon takes a photo just as Yuri takes a phone call.

"But this is not mediocre," he says, "and not by a student." "It's well drawn."

Which means, I assume, that the features are anatomically correct, that the eyes are aligned and that the highlights on the forehead, bridge and tip of the nose, cheeks and chin bring those features forward, giving them prominence and balance in relation to the rest of the face. This is the skill, the craft of traditional portraiture. Approval from Yuri is what I had hoped for, and it makes my day.

As I'm talking with Yuri, this major artist sitting with me at one of Paris's iconic artists' cafés, I'm reminded of Woody Allen's hack scriptwriter in *Midnight in Paris* who hangs out with F. Scott Fitzgerald and Pablo Picasso in a magical Paris. "Where am I?" I ask myself. Somewhere between Lewis Carroll's rabbit hole and George Lucas's galaxy far, far away.

Breaking my reverie, I suddenly spy Gilbert walking slowly toward us from several hundred feet up rue de Seine. Had he and Yuri planned to meet this morning? Yuri has said nothing about it. Perhaps it's just their parallel morning routine at La Palette. A grim expression spreads across Gilbert's face as he nears the table and sees me. I brace myself. *Alice in Wonderland* becomes *Night of the Living Dead*. My heureux hasard meter flashes "hazard ahead."

Reaching the table, standing over me, Gilbert unleashes a verbal assault unlike anything I have ever experienced, public or private, including a few nasty lovers' quarrels in Paris cafés with my ex on our last trip together in 2009. Gilbert spits out the word *asshole*, which replaces *John*, and repeats it several times with the same emphasis. He doesn't explain *why* I'm an asshole. He then turns to Yuri and warns him not to give me any personal information, that he would soon regret it if he does.

I sit speechless during all this, shaking my head, laughing nervously and glancing over at Yuri who, again, as at Lipp, has remained remarkably silent while his friend does all the talking, if you can call it that.

After a minute that feels like an hour, Gilbert storms off.

I look at Yuri, asking with my eyes for an explanation. He shrugs, then says, "Don't worry; it's not about you." What it *is* about, he doesn't say and I don't ask. Heureux hasard has morphed this morning into *malheureux hasard* (unhappy chance). I'm once again shaken by Gilbert, this time by what only can be described as limbic rage, not the inquisitorial aggression at Lipp or the imperious telephone call that followed. This explosive dimension of café culture is one I've never experienced on this level, though I've read about even worse episodes in the annals of Parisian café society, including murders, suicides, political riots and acts of terrorism, many splendidly described in *The Other Paris* by Lucy Sante.

Our garçon delivers the bill, and Yuri explains that he is set to leave in the afternoon for Moscow and has to get back to his hotel to pack. We trade contact info, Yuri offers to pay for my café crème and croissant, and we say our goodbyes, agreeing to stay in touch. It's a hard-fought victory, getting Yuri's email address for Robert Johnson and for me. Yuri's favorable comments about *The Girl* help to soothe the venomous sting of Gilbert's angry tongue.

My breakfast at La Palette has been, as they say in the Michelin Guide, and despite the grief, worth a detour. Heading now up rue de Seine toward blvd. Saint-Germain, I decide not to risk a visit to Gilbert's gallery. He might be lurking in the shadows, waiting for me with a sharpened palette knife. I go straight back to the apartment to send Yuri's email address to Robert, and to lie down.

ON A ROLL

○

With Yuri back in Moscow, and Gilbert more or less, and happily, out of my thoughts (and, so far, my cafés), my focus returns to the business at hand: tasting croques. I've already visited some venerable cafés on both sides of the Seine and have encountered mixed results at the mid-to-upper end of the price range.

If a fashionable café in the heart of Paris, whether Right Bank or Left, must average, say, 20 euros per eater to make money, how can it achieve that and have a 7–10-euro toasted ham-and-cheese sandwich on the menu? Even a glass of wine or a café crème hardly gets you there. But add fries and green salad and put the croque on pricey bread (Poilâne) and you have arrived. At Café de la Paix on Place de l'Opéra: 20 euros. At Le Fouquet on the Champs-Élysées, even higher. Both among the best croques I've had, but they are certainly not the same humble croque that emerged at the turn of the century as a bar and café snack food.

My thoughts also turn to getting *The Girl in Red* back to Berkeley, which presents logistical challenges. One doesn't just stuff a painting into a cardboard box and post it *par avion*; it would be smarter to find a specialized shipping company—difficult in the summertime with only a week left in Paris, one packed with social and professional obligations. In any case, I just don't want to risk loss or damage by putting my precious *objet trouvé* in the mail.

Taking the canvas on the plane involves other risks. Boxing it up and putting it through baggage is unacceptable to me, and putting it in an overhead bin, even if it could fit, seems almost as risky. This is no ordinary mass-produced item, like a set of teacups that can be replaced if lost or damaged. It is a one-of-a-kind work of art, an auratic original.

When we talked at La Palette about *The Girl*, Yuri had some advice: "Why don't you just take the canvas off the stretcher bars and roll it up?" He would know, but it seems like a daunting challenge. Some research on the internet brings mixed opinions about the pros and cons. One American artist, the late William Foster Martin, advised against it: "Personally, I have never quite understood the attraction to 'rolling' a canvas with a painting on it. Doing such a thing puts an extraordinary amount of stress upon the painting. . . . I would be terrified to perform this 'rolling' technique, myself."

With my departure looming, I make a decision. Duly terrified, I launch the first phase, removing the canvas from the stretcher bars. I set the canvas on the round dining table in my kitchen/studio and add up all the rusted nails—about twenty-five—that attach the canvas to the wooden bars. Can I remove them without tearing the toile?

I recall a scene in the film *Lust for Life* where Vincent van Gogh receives a bunch of rolled-up canvases that Paul Gauguin has sent to Arles ahead of his arrival. When Gauguin shows up, Vincent can't wait to unroll the canvases and see the work. It's hard to imagine great paintings rolled up for storage or transport. I think of them in massive gilded frames on museum walls, not as pigment on linen stuffed into shipping tubes.

Proceeding with a test extraction, my hands trembling, I remove the first nail with a screwdriver. Digging down between the wood and the nail head, I gently pry upward. I have to be careful not to slip and rip the canvas—or gouge my flesh.

OK, victory! Number one done. "Not so bad," I say out loud. Then the second and third and voilà! No damage to the canvas or the stretcher bars or me. I do it all very slowly and very gently, like bathing a baby in a kitchen sink.

Once I have the painting off the stretcher bars, I take a closer look to see how the frame is assembled. The four corners are mitered and lap-jointed. The joints appear so solid that I'm fairly sure they were glued before tiny, small-headed nails were hammered in at the frame's corners. The weathered wood is no doubt original to the canvas. But one can't be certain.

I now note faint pencil marks on the back of the frame, which indicate, I'm guessing, a price in francs: 15 F. Other than the painting's date, this is the only data point I have as to the provenance or, as it were, the backstory of *The Girl*. Of course, the price may be related to just the frame, not to the painting, as a friend suggests. In either case, my sense is that the canvas and frame are one, united in time, like a long-married couple.

If I'm correct, that the 15 F indicates the price once paid for the painting at a gallery or, more likely, a flea market or estate sale, it's impossible to know the date of that purchase. Obviously, it pre-dates the arrival of the euro—1999. If the transaction dates to circa 1935, the equivalent dollar value of 15 F at that time would have been about $1 and change. Was that the going rate then for a painting of this kind—anonymous and, as many claim, unfinished? Maybe. Picassos then were selling for several hundreds of dollars, not thousands, let alone millions. Today, with inflation, 15 F for *The Girl* in 1935 dollars translates to something like $18, which is, of course, unrelated to any appreciated value as an auratic original.

Vague though all this is, it's the best I can do given the absence of any details of provenance. But now, step two: rolling up *The Girl in Red*. Is the paint on the canvas brittle? Will it crack after eighty years stretched over wood? My hands tremble again.

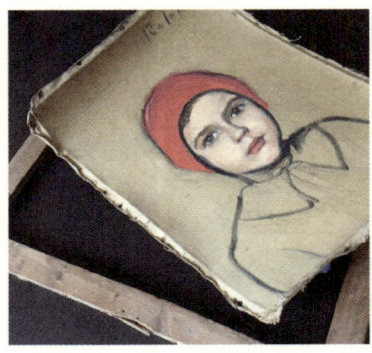

The Girl *off the stretcher bars*

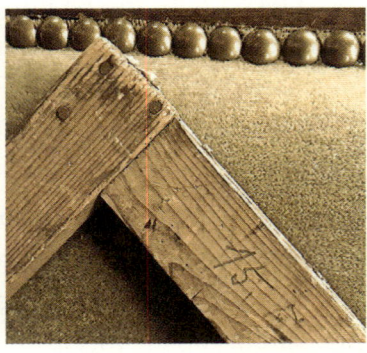

15 F penciled on the stretcher bars

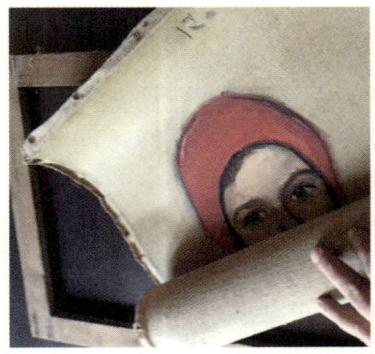

Rolling the canvas

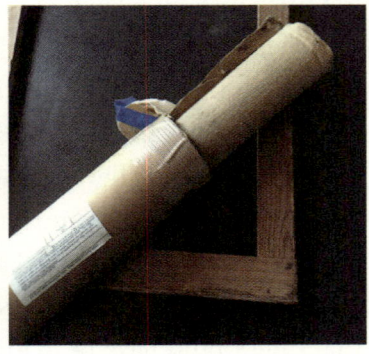

Canvas inserted into cardboard tube

Slowly, gently, I flex the material, and it seems supple. Holding my breath, I begin rolling, not too tightly. When I have it completely rolled up, I take a piece of blue masking tape and wrap it around the roll, which I insert into a heavy cardboard shipping tube I've cut to size with a serrated bread knife. I then tape round disks of cardboard to the tube ends.

I can breathe again. *The Girl* is ready for the trip home, her new home, by my side, where she belongs.

RETURN TO THE SCENE
OF THE CRIME

°

A few days before my return to Berkeley, I'm set to revisit ground zero, "the scene of the crime." I feel a bit off balance. Do criminals always return to the scene of their crimes? It's more or less a myth, I've read, except, oddly enough, for arsonists. Well, that does make sense. When you steal a car, say, you have the car. When you burn down a building, you have to go back to observe the fruits of your labor.

What about metaphorical criminals like me, who commit symbolic crimes, flâneurian crimes? Like walking away with a painting left out on the sidewalk. Isn't the former owner of the painting the guilty one, discarding a very nice portrait to an uncertain fate, perhaps to end up in the *poubelle* (trash)? Yes. But, then, why am I still feeling guilty, as I did on the day I brought my lost *Girl* home?

I don't really believe I stole the canvas, but one friend back home commented on one of my first media posts, saying that I should have waited longer before walking off. But wait for whom—the idiot who threw it out, or the fool who forgot the canvas when she sped off on summer holiday? Or the fellow who left it while returning to his gallery or apartment to relieve himself before hitting the road for Provence or the Dordogne?

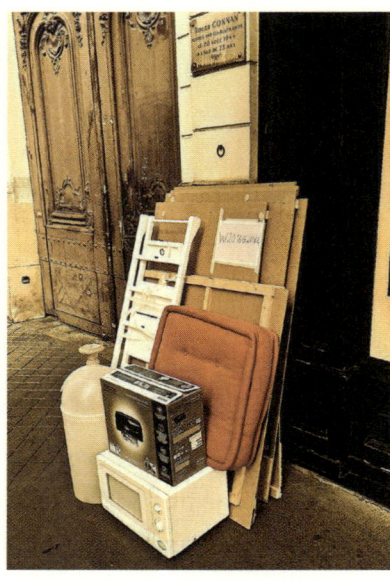

En route to ground zero, I come across a neat stack of abandoned items, not unlike the one in which I found The Girl in Red. *Note the plaque next to the door identifying a young man shot by the Germans on August 20, 1944, just a few days before the official liberation of Paris.*

Guilt enters the picture like a spider, casting its web over my innocence. It's curious to me that guilt feelings are often reserved for the innocent, not the truly guilty, who are usually disassociated from such feelings. But if not literal guilt, perhaps the symbolic guilt of the flâneur, the nineteenth-century observer of the urban landscape who discovers the dark underbelly of the city with, often, brilliant results in the form of visual and literary works that he sells to the highest bidder? This is another aspect of Walter Benjamin's cultural critique, the ironic complicity of the nineteenth-century artist or poet or journalist who sells out to the bourgeois marketplace. Perhaps my guilt can be attributed, albeit anachronistically, to two of these practices.

In his book *Charles Baudelaire: A Lyric Poet in the Era of High Capitalism*, Benjamin writes, "No matter what trail the *flâneur* may follow, every one of them will lead him to a crime."

What Benjamin seems to be getting at is that in Paris, the center of European culture in the nineteenth century, the growing, consuming middle class gives rise to the phenomenon of "the crowd," which paradoxically enables the individual to observe without being observed, to "hide" within the crowd. This new hiddenness links the flâneur (especially the emerging mid-nineteenth-century journalist type) to the criminal elements also lurking within this new urban arena. "The harder a man is to find, the more suspicious he becomes," says Benjamin about Edgar Allen Poe's "The Man of the Crowd." Baudelaire loved Poe and was influenced by his stories.

I should also consider the amorphous, free-floating Jewish version of guilt that emerged, I'm guessing, out of the medieval mythology of the Wandering Jew, the cursed outsider. This mythology dates back ten centuries at least, to the portrayal of the Jew who taunts Jesus while he carries his cross to Calvary. Jesus cursed the Jew to wander the earth as an exile for all time, or at least until the Second Coming. The theme of the Wandering or Eternal Jew becomes, by twentieth century, "The Jewish Question" and leads to Hitler's "final solution."

In this sense, I think, Jews may not fully qualify as flâneurs, because they are, from birth, identified with the outsider in the Christian West. The authentic flâneur, Walter Benjamin's flâneur (other, more flamboyant versions date back to the beginning of the nineteenth century and even earlier), makes a conscious decision to distance himself from bourgeois urban culture, shedding his middle-class skin, as it were—though hiding parodically and perhaps perversely behind the bourgeois attire of the black frock coat and top hat—to become an incognito observer. He willingly abandons the participation to which he is entitled (the female *flâneuse* doesn't fully emerge until the twenty-first century), yet returns to the bourgeois fold at will to sell his creative wares—poems, journalism, novels, art.

The Wandering Jew has no such choices. He is guilty by birth. Perhaps this is a truer source of my unease as I stroll down blvd. Saint-Germain past Deux Magots. I will turn left on rue de Seine and then right at café La Palette onto rue Jacques Callot and up one more block to where rue Guénégaud meets rue Mazarine—the scene of my flâneurian crime, the crime of a "born criminal."

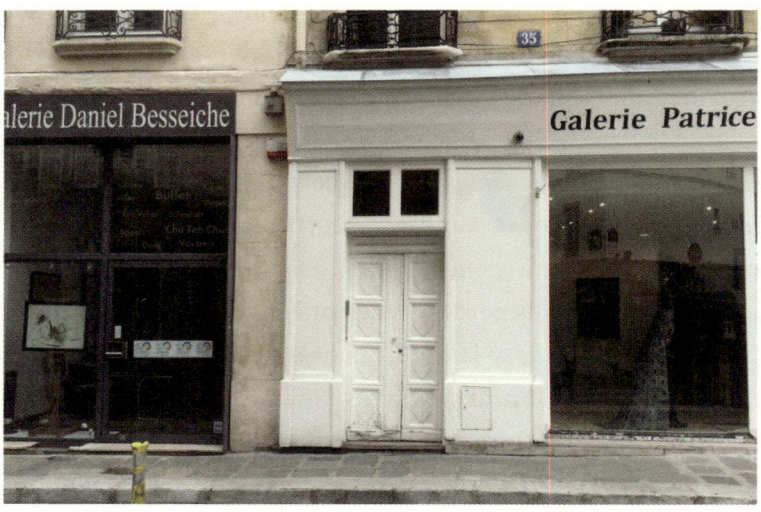

At the corner of rue Guénégaud and rue Mazarine,
ground zero: just to the right of the white apartment
building door marked no. 35 above

To my surprise, and breaking my grim mood, one of the two galleries straddling no. 35 is open, perhaps to take advantage of the busy summer tourist trade. I wander in and engage a young man sitting at a desk. I show him *The Girl* on my cell and recount the story. He doesn't recognize the image and suggests I inquire at an auction house. I thank him for his time and, after a short prayerful pause in front of no. 35, I head toward the river and home.

It was up rue Guénégaud that I ventured just a few weeks ago, carrying my lost and found treasure. I remember being filled with a joy that would only be dampened days later by second thoughts and second guesses and someone's negative Facebook comment about taking the painting too quickly. And now a lingering sense of guilt. Again I ask myself whether this is the residue of Benjamin's "guilty" flâneur? Or is it the cultural inheritance of the Wandering Jew who, despite having established a "homeland," remains unaccepted among the nations that surround him, denied the "natural right to exist," as Saul Bellow put it in his book *To Jerusalem and Back*? A bit of both, perhaps. Guilt by association, both associations.

A RED LETTER DAY

○

The term *red letter day* pops into my head this morning as I start packing for my trip home via London after three short (too short) weeks in Paris. Time flies when you're having croques. At breakfast I read about this term for a special day that dates back to classical antiquity when red ink was used to highlight key words in the Bible and other texts. My morning mood is awash in red, and I'm determined to see, even if only dimly through the windows, whether there are paintings by Yuri on display in Gilbert's gallery. I am ready now. And while in the area, I'll visit yet again ground zero, this time just to say goodbye.

Toward noon, walking down blvd. Saint-Germain, past the upscale shops between rue du Bac and the Deux Magots, including a phenomenal umbrella shop that is more museum than retail store, I come across a tiny pink-and-white-striped umbrella in the middle of the sidewalk. It had rained all night and the streets are now littered with debris, manmade and natural. Anticipating rain in London, I pick up the folded umbrella, open it to confirm its condition, close it, and stuff it into my satchel. In Paris, where it often rains in the summer, I rely on the large collection of umbrellas at my apartment. In London I'll need a small one to carry around.

At the Deux Magots, I take a seat at a table next to two young women speaking English—travel partners, it turns out, from Australia. After ordering a farewell croque, I strike up a conversation with my attractive neighbors. For some reason I have the urge to offer them my newly found pink umbrella, which I produce from my bag. Was I flirting?

"It's a little too feminine for me," I explain. They laugh, and one of the two, a pretty blonde, says, "Well, I'd be willing to swap mine for yours," at which point she produces hers. A solid-red umbrella.

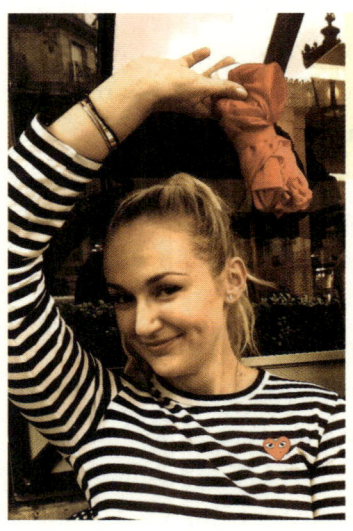

An Australian girl in red at the Deux Magots modeling her umbrella

My turn to laugh. I explain, showing them a picture of *The Girl* on my cell. Both express admiration for the portrait. The blonde and I make the umbrella exchange, and I ask whether I can take a picture of her with the red one. She can't really open it inside the crowded café, so she places it above her head and I shoot the photo—another girl in red. We are chuckling as we share contact information. She asks me to stay in touch and send news about the painting's story.

Leaving the Deux Magots after our air-kisses, and nicely

stuffed with my traditionally made croque's Gruyère cheese, ham and rich béchamel sauce (one of the best croques of the trip), I head toward rue Guénégaud.

Scoring the red umbrella has me thinking about a friend in California, the food writer Michele Anna Jordan, whose cookbooks I published at Aris Books in the 1980s. Michele responded to one of my earliest posts after finding *The Girl*, commenting that my discovery reminds her of Agnès Varda's film *Les Glaneurs et la Glaneuse* (*The Gleaners and I*), released in 2000. It's about people, gleaners, Michele explained, who live off of found objects, sometimes literally—today's dumpster divers.

I vaguely recalled Varda's film, or at least its title, but until Michele's Facebook comment I had not thought of the term *gleaning* in the context of my lost and found painting. How could I not have? I watched a trailer for the film that night on YouTube and determined to rent the DVD once back home in Berkeley. Yes, I had gleaned *The Girl in Red*. I have also gleaned Yuri Kuper and Gilbert. And today I have gleaned a pink-and-white umbrella and turned it red. A red letter day to be sure.

Just as I arrive at rue Guénégaud, an elderly gentleman with snowy-white hair and carrying a cane steps out from the door at no. 35. Again, throwing caution to the wind as I had at Lipp with Yuri, I approach him and ask in French whether he speaks English. "*Oui*," he replies, with questioning eyes. I proceed to explain how I found a painting leaning against the wall next to the door of his building and show him *The Girl* on my cell phone. I ask whether he knows anything about it. He doesn't, but is intrigued and asks me to send him the image to show his friends in the neighborhood. I of course agree. We exchange names (his, Lucien Godin) and email addresses.

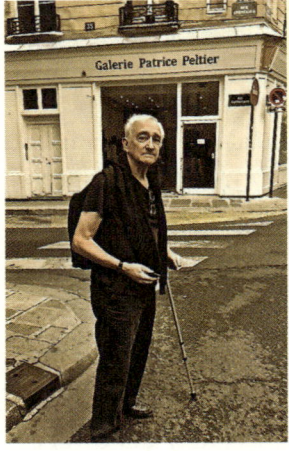

Lucien Godin, outside his apartment at 35, rue Guénégaud

Before parting, Godin speculates that with so much art activity in the area associated with the École des Beaux-Arts, it is likely that someone in the neighborhood, an art dealer or a resident, had put the painting out onto the street for the taking. Or that the painting's owner had passed away and no one in the family wanted to keep it. Where better to leave an unwanted painting than in the art-centric 6th arrondissement? I agree with Lucien's logic, thank him for his help and head to Gilbert's gallery.

Arriving across the street, I peer from afar into the gallery's windows. There are, thankfully, no signs of life or light within, and feeling safe, I approach to have a closer look. The eerily deserted space reveals several recognizable Kupers hanging on walls and stacked up against them. Like *The Girl in Red*, they seem abandoned, lost in time.

Although it's hard to make out the details, the canvases are characteristic of the Kupers I saw online at Lipp and in the catalog Gilbert gave me—each canvas a "portrait" of a commonplace object painted thickly, emerging from a muted, heavily impastoed surface. Sometimes Kuper includes the object—an old paint brush, a spoon—but from a distance it's hard to tell whether the objects are there on the canvas (assemblage) or represented in thick paint. Either way, I feel the deep pull of these images and a connection to Yuri that I hope to sustain once home.

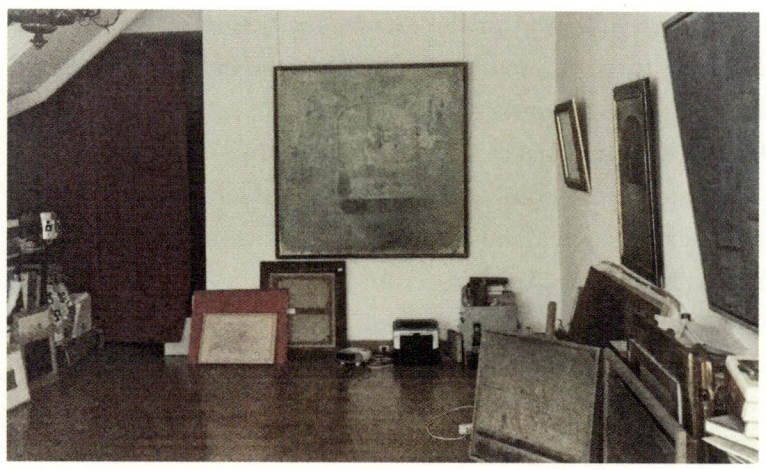

A Yuri Kuper painting through the window at Gilbert's gallery

Back at the apartment, I take another look at Yuri's work in the Pushkin Museum catalog and carefully read the introductions by Peter Selz and Robert Johnson:

> The artist recreates these objects with such complete authenticity that the aura surrounding them is preserved, or rather recreated, through artistic images.
> —Peter Selz

> It all becomes part of an assemblage communicating Kuper's almost Proustian sensibility, his remembrance of things past. He carefully collects the flotsam and jetsam of everyday life and places it in a new visual constellation, giving it a rebirth.
> —Robert Flynn Johnson

Yuri Kuper, gleaner of aura.

A final cleanup of the apartment before leaving in the morning turns my red letter day gray, the existential gray of Yuri Kuper's work and my pending Paris departure. Leaving the land of heureux hasard is always hard to do.

Later in the evening, after a dinner of leftovers and my final packing, I decide to email Robert Johnson to see whether he has heard back from Yuri and to tell him about my run-in with Gilbert. I attach an image of *The Girl in Red*, soliciting his comments for the first time, more confident now that it's worthy of his professional consideration.

The reply is immediate. Yes, he has heard from Yuri and is excited to have reconnected with his old friend. He also comments on Gilbert and speculates that the problem has to do with a suspicion that I may be trying to get something going business-wise with Yuri. "Sad but typical in the art world," he concludes. As for *The Girl in Red*, he describes the portrait as "nice" and adds, somewhat flippantly, I think, "The price was right." Johnson is a knowledgeable and ambitious collector, proud of having amassed a large and important collection of works on paper, many of them anonymous and obtained at modest prices. Perhaps there is more admiration than sarcasm in his comment.

Attached to Johnson's email is a link to the catalog introduction for a forthcoming exhibition he is curating at the University of Miami. To my astonishment, the exhibition, titled "Contemplating Character," focuses on portraits—drawings, prints and paintings from his own collection. *Heureux hasard encore une fois!*

In the introduction, which I immediately read, Johnson makes the crucial point that the power of a portrait is in the revelation of character, the soul of the sitter, more than the technical achievement of the subject's likeness. It's as if his text was specifically written to contradict any argument that the unknown identities of *The Girl*'s artist and the girl herself render the portrait aesthetically deficient and a mere art historical curiosity. The power of *The Girl* as a work of art, as Johnson might argue, does not depend on knowing who she is or who painted her, but on what she is—her soul and her character as revealed in the portrait—and on what we feel about her auratic presence as a witness to her time.

At the end of the day, late that night as I prepare for London, my gray mood turns bright red.

ABANDONED, ANONYMOUS, UNFINISHED

o

I've arrived in London via the Eurostar, from croque monsieurs to fish and chips in just under three hours, my *Girl in
Red* safe and sound in her travel satchel. As promised, an email
arrives from Lucien Godin relaying playful comments about
The Girl from one of his art-dealer neighbors:

> August 19
>
> Lucien,
>
> The story begins with a police report. I do not know
> the creator of this abandoned child.
>
> Good luck!
> FG

"Abandoned child," indeed. The canvas itself abandoned,
left on a sidewalk to be trashed or gleaned. And the young girl
on the canvas? Unknown—imprisoned in unfinished, two-
dimensional anonymity, begging with her dark, knowing eyes
to be adopted. Because of the inherent limitations of two-
dimensional reality, that symbolic task has fallen to her virtual
adoptive parent—me. Like an amnesia victim, she may never

know who she is, but at least she will have a home and someone to care for her.

I may have to take the gallerist's amusing advice and approach the police with a "missing girl" report: "All points bulle-
tin! Be on the lookout for a young girl with a red head covering;
dark, sad eyes; and sketchily clothed from neck to waist. Last
seen on canvas in 1935."

Then a second email from Lucien:

August 20

Dear John,

New episode: Continuation of the comic-detective
series . . .

I just spoke with the owner of another gallery on rue
Guénégaud.

He says he is not the child's abductor. But he regrets
it perhaps because he believes that this is a beautiful
painting. In conclusion, the trail of the kidnappers is
not good. I will continue to interview residents, but it
is necessary that you specify exactly where you found
the painting.

Regards,
Lucien

Is Lucien alluding to the Tintin comic book adventure
series by the Belgian comic book writer and artist Hergé
(Georges Prosper Remi)? In that case, I am the young reporter-
cum-sleuth, Tintin, on a new caper.

After a little detective work online, I have located a Tintin episode, *The Broken Ear,* serialized beginning in 1935 and published as a book in 1937. In it, the intrepid young adventurer and his little white dog, Snowy, hunt for a small tribal fetish figure with a broken ear, stolen from an ethnographical museum and replaced with a fake.

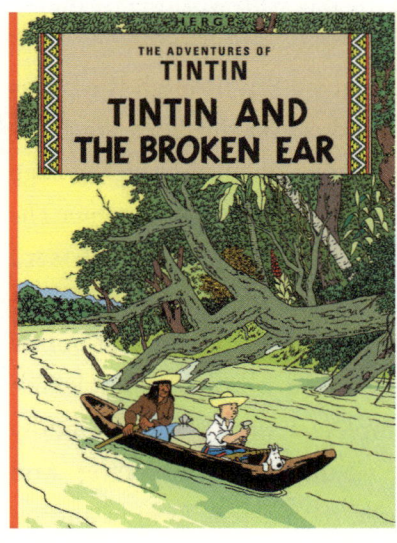

The cover of Tintin's The Broken Ear *episode*
© Hergé/Tintinimaginatio 2024

Surviving dangerous escapades, including murder and civil war in an imaginary South American country, Tintin, with the help of Snowy and a talking parrot, recovers the real fetish figure and returns it to the museum. It turns out that inside the figurine is a large diamond, the motive for the original theft, which falls into the ocean during the final skirmish for possession of it on board a ship in the Pacific Ocean. If this is the kind of adventure I'm on, I'm game. My fetish figure, *The Girl in Red*, has been found, and it has a missing signature instead of a missing anatomical feature, part of an ear. Alas, there is no embedded diamond, at least not a literal one.

I respond to Lucien that I will contact him when I've returned to California with all the details of my gleaning of the portrait. But first things first—three days at DUKES London, a small hotel in the West End's posh Mayfair district. What to do besides visit Bonhams auction house where an 1863 Antonio de Torres guitar (the guitar's Stradivari, lutherie's other great Antonio) is being auctioned off; sketch in my journal while hanging out at the delicious Wolseley restaurant on Piccadilly, around the corner from the hotel; enjoy afternoon high tea at Brown's Hotel nearby; and end the day with world-class martinis at DUKES Bar?

Seated in the hotel's cozy lobby, I flip through the pages of the *Time Out* magazine I picked up on the Eurostar, looking for interesting art exhibits. The one that jumps off the page like a flashing neon sign is titled *Unfinished . . . Works from The Courtauld Gallery*. "Brilliant!" as the British say. Heureux hasard now in London, an entire show devoted to an extensive collection of important unfinished paintings. I order a ticket online and note in the exhibit's description a quotation by Baudelaire asserting that an artist can complete a work without literally finishing it, and that it will be all the more compelling. And another quote by Pliny the Elder, the ancient Roman author, who elaborates further, saying that unfinished works are "more precious than finished ones because they allow the viewer to see into the artist's mind."

At the show, a painting catches my eye, the center section of a triptych by James McNeill Whistler, *Young Girl with Cherry Blossom*. The girl is wearing a red headscarf and is outlined in black against a neutral background behind her and the flower she caresses. It's a lovely image, but Whistler was unhappy with the painting and kept reworking it between 1867 and 1878. Finally, he decided to destroy the entire triptych and only the one panel was saved, thanks to a zealous patron who, like me with my *Girl*, saved Whistler's *Young Girl* from total oblivion.

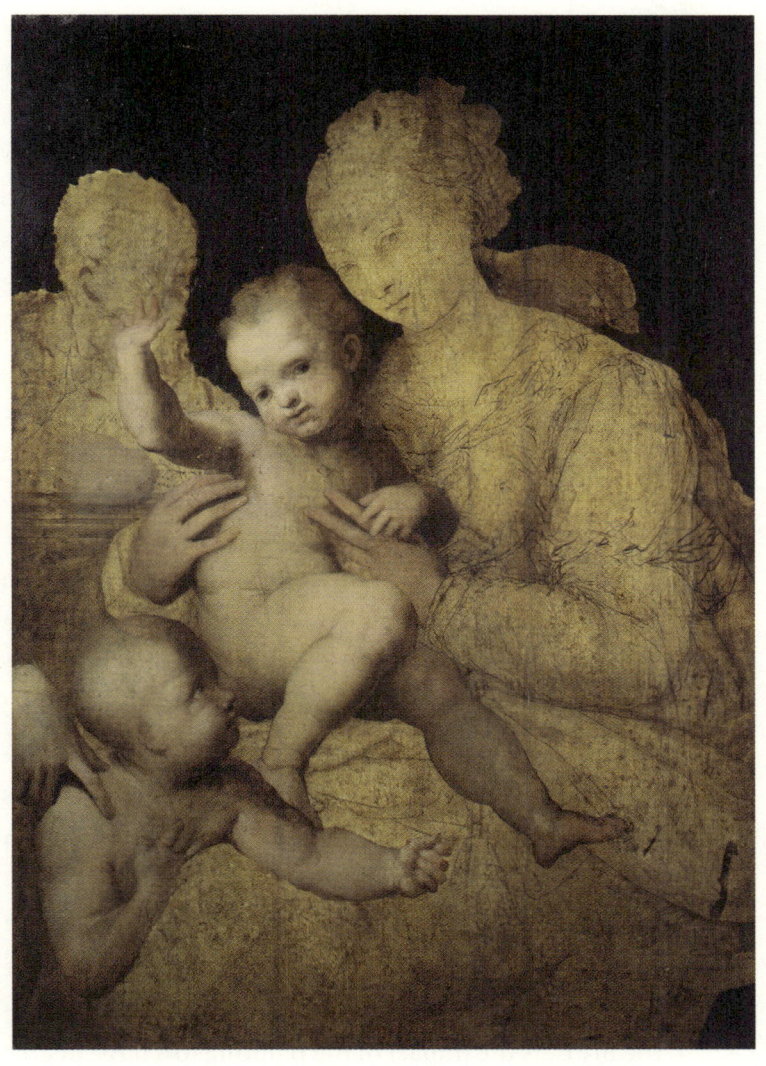

This unfinished painting by Perino del Vaga,
Holy Family with Saint John the Baptist, *c. 1528–37,*
appeared on the cover of the Courtauld's exhibit catalog.

o

The question can be posed yet again: Is *The Girl in Red* finished? If not finished, is it compelling on its own terms? After the Courtauld exhibit, and with Baudelaire's approval, my answer is a reconfirmed yes. And do we need to know the artist's identity to understand a work's intentions? Although this was not a question asked by the Courtauld exhibit directly, Pliny's quote provides a relevant answer: the unfinished work allows us to see into the artist's mind whether we know their identity or not.

I wonder if some of the power of *The Girl* would, in fact, be lost with the discovery of the identities of the artist and sitter. Unless a famous artist and/or notable subject were revealed, I think perhaps so. I can imagine, for example, being disappointed to learn that the artist, a male, was an art student who ended up a lawyer who collaborated with the Nazis in the 1940s. Or that his young sitter became, several years later, the lover of an SS officer stationed in Paris. Or that she simply lived out her life—a librarian, a doctor, a housewife—without fanfare or drama, like so many millions who survived the horrors of the 1940s. Where's the romance, the magic, the mystery in these scenarios?

The potent year of the portrait—1935—is enough to hint at all manner of possible and ominous narratives related to the failure of Europe, especially France, to stand up to German fascism in the 1930s. Is the impact of the painting to a large degree based on its boldly scrawled date alone, without any details of authorship and provenance? My answer here in London is yes, very much so.

What more, then, is there for me to know or say about *The Girl in Red*? The painting is complete; it is well done, says

Yuri Kuper; it is evocative of its time; it is mine, just as Robert Johnson has argued. Case closed. Back to Berkeley with *The Girl* and my unfinished croque survey, ready to be completed and published. But no, the case of *The Girl in Red* is not closed. I feel both compelled to continue the quest, whether in Paris, London, New York or Berkeley—and somehow chosen to do so. Tintin has not grown up and retired.

The French use the word *abandonné* to describe those who have given themselves over to something completely. This is how the late W. G. Sebald must have felt about his involvements (they lasted for years) with what is hidden about the characters he has investigated in his novels' haunting narratives. From his collection of conversations titled *The Emergence of Memory*: "Once you get hold of a thread you want to pull it out and you want to see . . . what the colors of the pattern are. And the more difficult it gets . . . the more intrigued you become, the more you know there is something buried there. And the less you want to give up on it."

"Something buried there"—like Tintin's embedded diamond. I'm beginning to understand Sebald more deeply. And Samuel Beckett's famous lines in *The Unnamable*: "You must go on. I can't go on. I'll go on."

GLEANING 101

○

Back in Berkeley with my special cargo, I remove the ragged-edged canvas from its traveling tube, carefully unroll it and pin it to a cabinet in my kitchen where I can see it as I work. After missions in Paris where most every meal is eaten out, I do more writing in my kitchen than I do cooking. It takes a while for Berkeley's gastronomic élan and my cooking chops to resurface.

With my deadline looming, it's time to finish the croque article. The almost two dozen croques I had in Paris must be categorized by price (under 8 euros, 8–12 euros and over 12 euros) and evaluated for the best and the worst. Finally, all of the analysis and ranking must be converted into sparkling prose for the magazine's hungry online readers.

But *The Girl* beckons, a siren song. On my second day back home, trying to keep up my Parisian strolling regimen, I float, jet-lagged, down to the local video store—a twenty-minute walk each way—and rent Agnès Varda's documentary *The Gleaners and I*. Putting croque work on the back burner for the evening, I watch the film, amazed and delighted. I'm particularly struck by a comment from one of the film's many fascinating, sometimes quirky, characters, the painter and collage artist Louis Pons. His "canvases" are constructed of small found objects assembled on wooden boards. "Each object," he explains, "gives a direction, each is a line picked up here and there, indeed gleaned, and which become my paintings. The aim of art is to tidy up one's inner and exterior worlds. . . . I make sentences from things."

Varda explores the phenomenon of gleaning to reveal it as a profound human construct and a more diverse activity than its narrow dictionary definition would suggest. On the basis of her film, you could describe the human species as *Homo glaneur*. When I bent down—stooped—to pick up an abandoned painting, I was performing an act no less fundamental than the gleaners stooping to pick up wheat left in the field after the harvest in Jean-François Millet's Barbizon School masterpiece *Les glaneuses* (1857), the inspiration for Varda's film.

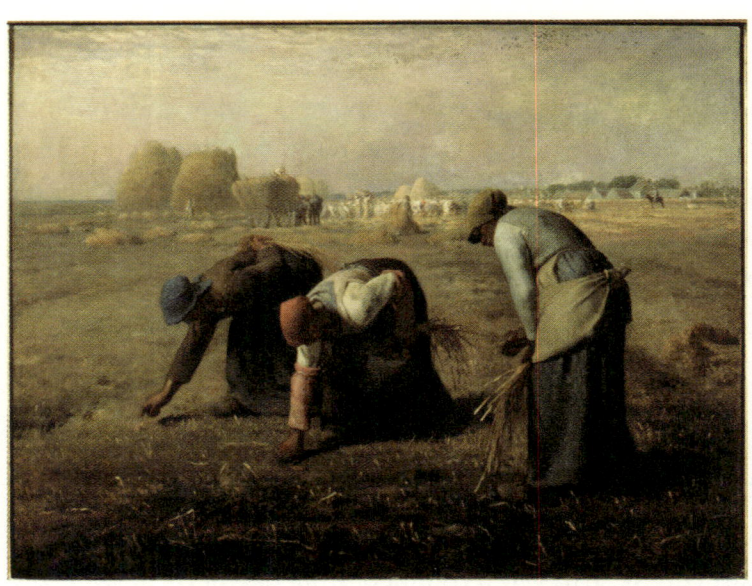

Les glaneuses *by Jean-François Millet, 1857.*
Note the gleaner in the middle with a red head cover.

o

It's instructive to point out again the obvious, that to glean is to stoop. The Paris flâneur strolls upright, detached from utility (work), seemingly disconnected from the reality around him. He doesn't consume and he doesn't stoop; he merely observes. The glaneur is literally grounded in reality, stooping low to harvest what has been abandoned.

Here's my amateur anthropological analysis: humans are able to stoop because we are, in fact, erect, descended from pre-humans who first stood up—*Homo erectus*. Our four-legged mammalian relatives do not—cannot—stoop. Therefore, they cannot, do not, glean, though they can scavenge on all fours. Gleaning demonstrates a solely human behavior that both highlights our elevated sapient humanity and connects us to our earliest hominid roots—erect, bipedal, mammalian.

Curious, though, how "to stoop" has become, semantically, class-sensitive. Peasants stoop, but the middle and upper classes "would not stoop to . . ."—fill in the blank. Prideful, elevated elites have agency. Humble, lowly peasants do not. Which is not the case in Paris, at least when there is valuable stuff to be had. Everyone, both high and low on the cultural totem pole, stoops to glean in Paris, whether it's to claim useless items like paintings or useful items like kitchen appliances, clothing, books, chairs and, of course, umbrellas! My still-lingering feelings of guilt notwithstanding, according to French law revealed by a lawyer featured in Varda's film, I am the legitimate new owner of *The Girl in Red*. An abandoned object has no legal owner until it is claimed.

It's a testament to Agnès Varda's film that it expands the meaning of the French verb *glaner* (to glean) for all time. From Varda's voiceover narration of the film: "On this type of gleaning, of images, impressions, emotions . . . gleaning is defined figuratively as a mental activity. To glean facts, acts, and deeds, to glean information. And for forgetful me, it's what I have gleaned that tells me where I've been."

Yes, having gleaned *The Girl in Red*, I know where I've been. Paris, New York, London. And now Berkeley. A globe-trotting flâneur/glaneur.

But I am struggling to complete my croque article against the constant pull of *The Girl*. I'm still more in Paris than I am in Berkeley. The article will not, it turns out, be titled "In Search of Lost Croques." The magazine's editor has nixed this title, which I had argued was perfect (not just funny), on the basis, she says, of its poor level of SEO (search engine optimization). She has devised, instead, a title that will satisfy the journal's new distribution arrangement with the media giant MSN, a title completely lacking in what I would call PIO—pun intended optimization. Her new title? "Perfect Parisian Croques: Where to Find These Rare Treasures."

It's that old publishing industry maxim—writers can't be choosers.

FRAMING *THE GIRL*
IN BLACK AND GOLD

○

I began to plan the framing of *The Girl in Red* while detaching the canvas from the stretcher bars in Paris. I imagined something elegant but not gaudy, perhaps with a cloth matting between the canvas edge and the frame to expand the size (and presence) of the piece beyond its modest dimensions. It has to fit in style and size within the picture niche of the fireplace surround of my Arts and Crafts Berkeley living room.

Then, in London, on my way home, I came across a painting by Georges Braque in the Stern Pissarro Gallery, owned by members of the great impressionist's family, some of whom have become good painters in their own right. The tiny still life—approximately 8" × 10"—was set into a black-stained wooden frame, a shallow box really, leaving exposed the raw sides of the canvas. Voilà! I was taken as much by the frame as by the work itself and decided then and there to replicate this treatment for *The Girl*.

Although a huge fan of Braque since attending his retrospective in Paris at the Grand Palais in 2013, I was seeing this painting more as an object on display than a framed *tableau* by a great master. Whether this small piece is or isn't a masterpiece is not the point, though it does have extraordinary power for its size. The framer had, I believe, consciously emphasized its status as an object—perhaps as compensation for its small scale—by exposing, almost highlighting, the edges of the canvas, with its folded corners and nail heads. I can imagine Braque himself pounding the nails into the stretcher bars to secure the raw toile. I can't say this with any certainty, but from what I learned from that retrospective in Paris, Braque seems like the kind of man and artist who would have stretched his own canvases despite his growing fame and wealth after World War II.

The framed Braque got me thinking: The edges and sides of a painted canvas can be revealing, but are usually hidden. Frames hide the edge because the two dimensional image—the work of art—doesn't usually spill over onto the edge, the third dimension, the boundary between pictorial art and not art, between the world of the painting and the world. At least, that is, until modern art made it possible for painters to involve the edge, as if to say that in fact the painting *is* an object and more than the image represented. In one painting class at Cal in the late 1960s, we would continue our work onto the stretched canvas's sides. It was radical. It was cool. We were making a statement, but I don't think we really understood what it meant, theoretically or art historically.

Painting, in an almost desperate response to photography's emergence in the nineteenth century, had become the subject of painting itself via Impressionism, Fauvism and all the radical "isms" that followed. A new radical art form that emerged in the twentieth century, inspired by Marcel Duchamp's assaults, took art off canvases and pedestals and delivered its content by other means. After Duchamp, art could be a "non-retinal" concept (Conceptual Art), or a textual/visual joke (Dada), or a real-time spectacle (Performance Art and Installation). The line between art and life blurred, and the frame was internalized in the work, so says Roger Shattuck in *The Banquet Years* (a book everyone in my art crowd was reading in the 1960s and '70s): "The frame had been overrun, and art set itself up as continuous with life."

All of this belongs to the domain of art historians, critics, and philosophers. I am simply a journalist and storyteller and a sometime maker of images. I leave the deep theory to the pros, the thinkers about art and the artists who merely think. The iconic 1963 photograph of Marcel Duchamp bent over a chess board, thinking about his next move against the naked writer and art groupie Eve Babitz comes to mind: Duchamp as Rodin's *The Thinker*. If Picasso was the greatest modern artist of the twentieth century who looked back at the nineteenth century (and earlier) for inspiration, Duchamp was the greatest postmodern artist of the twentieth century who looked forward to the twenty-first.

Notwithstanding the avant-garde's escape from the frame, inquiries into the history of art framing have proven instructive as I make final decisions about *The Girl*'s frame. Dutch frames in the seventeenth century were often black, made of woods found in furniture making and interior design. Black, as either ebony or stained wood, mirrored the black and white clothing of the wealthy mercantile class—the art collectors of the day. The Golden Age Dutch poet and composer Constantijn Huygens wrote, "An ebony frame can enrich a poor canvas, and make it look or sell as well as a good one." Yes, *The Girl* will have a black frame to enrich the canvas's modesty and to mirror the black attire of its bourgeois-bohemian Berkeley owner.

As I probe further into frame history, a curious semantic puzzle grabs my attention. The French word for frame is *cadre* (from the Latin *quadrum*, square), which also means, in military parlance, "a detachment forming the skeleton of a regiment." Curious, because the idea of an avant-garde, a term used since the fifteenth century in its strictly military sense, entered the lexicon of modern artspeak between the mid-nineteenth and early twentieth centuries to describe the overthrow of the academic art system (the Academy). This revolt had begun in earnest with Édouard Manet, followed by the impressionists.

How then, I wonder, did the vocabularies of art and war— cadre, avant-garde, even carpet bombing—become so intermingled? We say "the art of war" but what is "the war of art," and who is the enemy? We are, of course. "*Épater la bourgeoisie!*" said the French Decadent poets of the late nineteenth century.

With my head swimming in the ironies and etymological amusements of artspeak and the history of framing, I am ready to pay a visit to Barbara Anderson, a framer who works with her crew out of a sunny studio in West Berkeley. What I have appreciated about Barbara and our framing collaborations going back decades is that our strong opinions, at times not completely aligned, ultimately find a happy resolution. I am clear now that I want *The Girl* set into a shallow black box *à la Braque*. And that the sides of the canvas be revealed with the original rusty nails that were graciously returned, along with the stretcher bars, by friends visiting Paris after I had left with *The Girl* rolled up in a tube.

I show Barbara a picture of the Braque frame. "This is what I am thinking." Barbara likes the idea of a black frame and suggests a burnished gold face and cream-colored cloth for the mat. *Bon!* We are on the same page. I make my selections from the options she shows me for both the frame style and the mat.

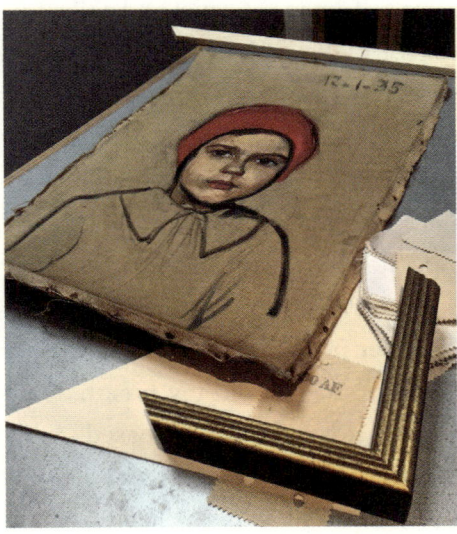

The Girl *and her framing materials*

Barbara's shop mate—the person who actually builds the frames to her specs—suggests adding a glass front. Great idea! *The Girl* will now be a painting/object preserved in a museum-quality, non-glare, UV-protected display case. A collector's vitrine. Just like the *Mona Lisa*! This is the respect (and expense) *The Girl* deserves.

I never asked Barbara for a price because I don't want it to be a factor in creating the perfect frame. Frames can telegraph not only what a collector thinks about his painting—its monetary value and art status—but also what he thinks about himself, *his* monetary worth and social status. Extravagant frames in Rembrandt's day said as much about the owners of the works as about the works themselves.

One might think that a high-priced painting by a fashionable artist should only require a simple frame, letting the work speak for itself. But that is not generally the case. Throughout history, art has been framed to the limits of the owner's bank account—and ego. In this case, a modest, low-valued painting like *The Girl in Red* placed in a high-priced frame suits my ambiguous and vaguely perverse self-image as artist and collector.

The day finally arrives for me to pick up *The Girl* at Barbara's shop, and you can cut the suspense with a mat knife. When I enter the shop, the framed painting lies on the large entry counter neatly wrapped in brown paper secured with easily removable strips of masking tape. Expressionless, a paragon of composure, Barbara slowly unwraps the package for the first viewing. How many times has she performed this same ritual for her loyal clientele? Her prices are high, but the performance is included with the frame. I hold my breath, then gasp as she holds up *The Girl*. I am more than pleased. A bit overwhelmed, in fact, by the transformation from gleaned object to collectible treasure. Bravo!

Barbara rewraps the framed *Girl*, I pay the bill, we hug Berkeley-style, and I rush home to mount the piece in its waiting niche. The elegantly carved and paneled fireplace surround in redwood and mahogany was designed by the great Bay Area Arts and Crafts architect Walter Ratcliff in 1937 to display, no doubt, an earlier owner's worthy painting. Ratcliff's splendid niche and *The Girl's* black-and-gold vitrine give the girl an elegant, perhaps extravagant, but deserving home.

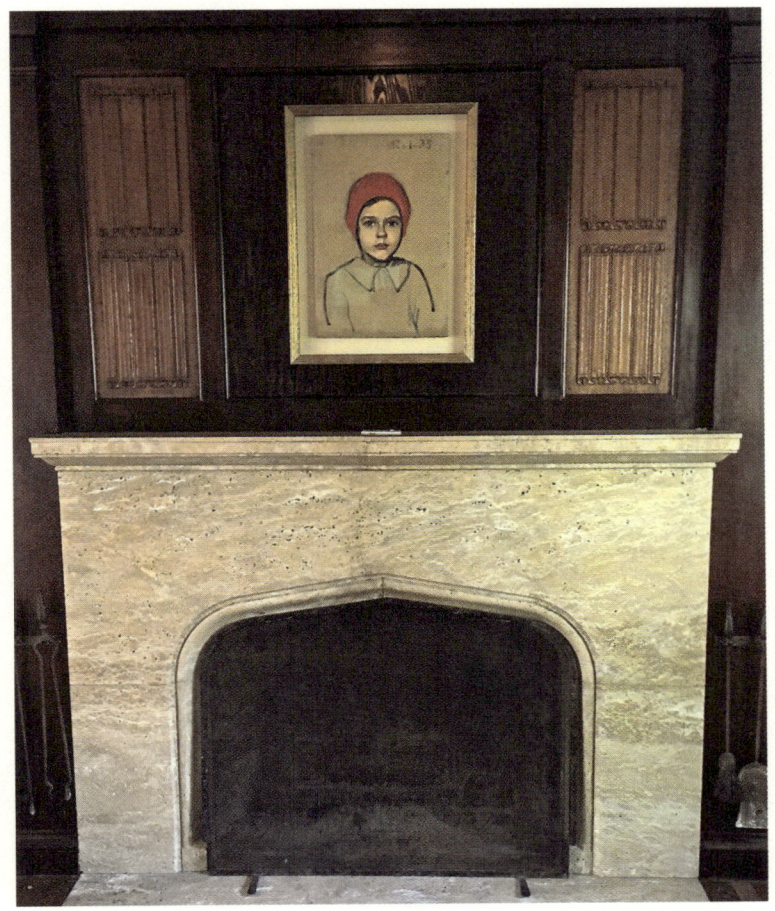

The Girl *framed in her niche*

o

THE VERNISSAGE

○

I love this story about British painters John Constable and J. M. W. Turner. They both showed pictures at the summer exhibition at London's Royal Academy in 1832, and there was a private preview for professionals only that they both attended, a vernissage in the technical parlance. These two important British artists did not get along, and sparks were bound to fly.

Turner arrived and hurriedly made a small but reportedly "deft" change to his canvas that seemed scandalous to this conservative group of painters. Adding a small daub of red paint—a buoy—to his otherwise drab seascape, the gesture dramatically finished off the painting with, it was noted at the time, an admirable combination of restraint and virtuosity. Turner then stormed off. After the uproar in the salon subsided, Constable uttered his famous line about Turner: "He has been here and fired a gun."

The word *vernissage*, common now in English, is from the French verb *vernir* (to varnish), which describes the traditional practice of varnishing a new painting to protect its surface before exposing it to the public. As varnish ages it can darken and yellow, creating either "patina" or "discoloration," depending on your point of view.

Vernissages were also used by artists to perform last-minute touch-ups, as J. M. W. Turner demonstrated, and which is amusingly presented in the Hollywood biopic *Mr. Turner*. The term has always sounded a bit snooty to me, and therefore perfect for the printed invitations to my unveiling of the framed *Girl in Red*, a modestly grand and playful celebration of her arrival in the Bay Area.

Response to the invitation has been enthusiastic. The guest list includes an artist or two, a novelist, a poet, several musicians, a composer, a philosopher, a contractor, a curator, a lawyer, and a pair of restaurateurs, one of them the caterer of the event. Your typical Berkeley crowd.

I am honoring *The Girl* at my home with all the bells and whistles of a formal first viewing of an important work, including a musical offering featuring Tessa Seymour and her guitarist classmate from Curtis, Jiji Kim, who are in Berkeley on vacation; catered victuals from our local *traiteur*, Poulet; and a professional evaluation of the portrait by Robert Johnson, who has kindly volunteered.

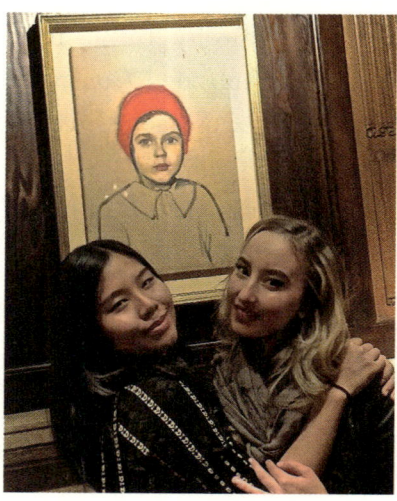

Three girls at the vernissage: Jiji Kim, guitarist (left); Tessa Seymour, cellist (right); and The Girl in Red

With our group of thirty to forty seated in the living room facing the framed *Girl* in her niche, duets are performed by Tessa on her beloved Testore cello and Jiji on a sonorous Torres guitar from my collection. Then, with our ears seduced and our appetites satisfied at the buffet table, Robert Johnson, who has just returned from mounting his *Contemplating Character* portrait show at the University of Miami, opens our eyes.

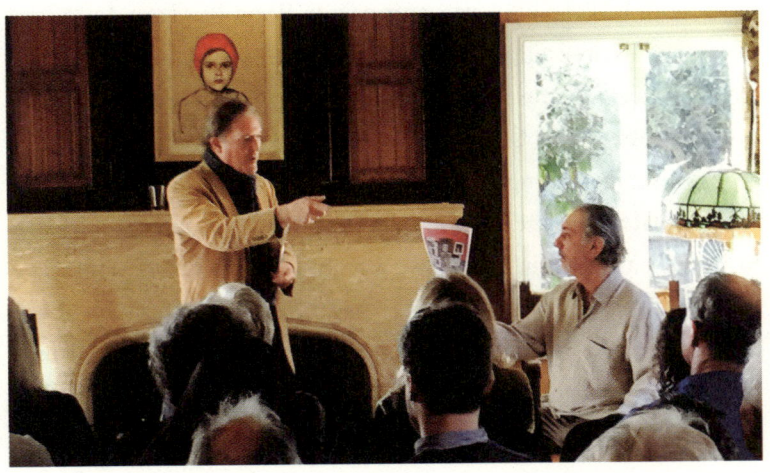

Standing in front of The Girl *and across from me, Robert Johnson makes a point at the vernissage.*

With a boyish insouciance that belies his emeritus status at the Achenbach Foundation, Robert gives a stimulating twenty-minute presentation. He speculates, quite reasonably, that the sitter for *The Girl* was likely a nervous and jittery young girl, forcing the artist to finish the portrait in one take, which explains the sketchy clothing and blank background. But then, firing his own rhetorical gun, Robert makes the bold claim that the painting is definitely finished. His proof? The date scrawled on the canvas, January 12, 1935. The artist would not have dated the canvas, he states, if the painting was unfinished. Sounds right.

More surprising to me than this assertion is Robert's admission, which I find quite flattering, that if he were to see *The Girl in Red* in a shop, he would buy it. This makes sense, of course, given Robert's fascination with anonymous images and their undervalued virtues, as proclaimed in his book *Anonymous*, which I read after returning from Paris. But I am delighted to hear it expressed in public because of what seemed to me a dismissive comment—"the price was right"—after I emailed him a photo of *The Girl* from Paris.

More surprising still is the implied compliment aimed at me, *The Girl*'s gleaner, though perhaps not a conscious one on Robert's part. In his book he pays homage to those who have salvaged lost and found images from oblivion: "This is where the individual who is willing to sift through the pictorial morass becomes crucial. Essentially dead and forgotten images can be resurrected by the process of selection. This searching out and collecting is an example of a highly personal connoisseurship. There are no art history books, auction catalogs or grand reputations to lead the way or reinforce one's decisions."

After Robert's presentation, we all head back to the buffet table, now arrayed with desserts from Masse's Pastries in North Berkeley. The comments I hear from my guests all endorse Robert's speculations about *The Girl*. I am pleased, the proud father of my "resurrected" *Girl in Red.*

A CHRISTMAS SALON
CHEZ ROBERT

o

Following the vernissage, Robert Johnson invites me to his annual Christmas party at his home in San Francisco's Richmond District. It's no ordinary holiday affaire, though the giant baked ham and whole roasted turkey are perfectly suited for such. It's part soirée, part art-world salon, and part homage to Robert's vast and eclectic assemblage of visual art and collector-level bric-a-brac gleaned through his years as a curator. I'm hoping to meet some folks in Robert's crowd with helpful suggestions for my provenance and attribution search.

You feel when entering Robert's home that you have entered a house museum filled with its celebrated owner's material obsessions—art, furniture, books, mementos. Balzac's house museum in Paris comes to mind. The paintings that line the wall of the staircase to the second floor of Robert's house are portraits of Robert himself, received, he says, in lieu of payment for writing exhibit catalog introductions for his artist friends. At the second level there are bedrooms and the designated guest bathroom where one finds yet another exhibition space, covered floor to ceiling with framed prints, drawings and small paintings. Ditto in all the rooms of the house—the bedrooms, kitchen, dining room, and front parlor. The art positioned on every available vertical surface, and several horizontal ones, contributes to a feeling of aesthetic claustrophobia, amplified by the volume of aesthetes now occupying every nook and cranny of the house. It's an invigorating claustrophobia, visual and aural.

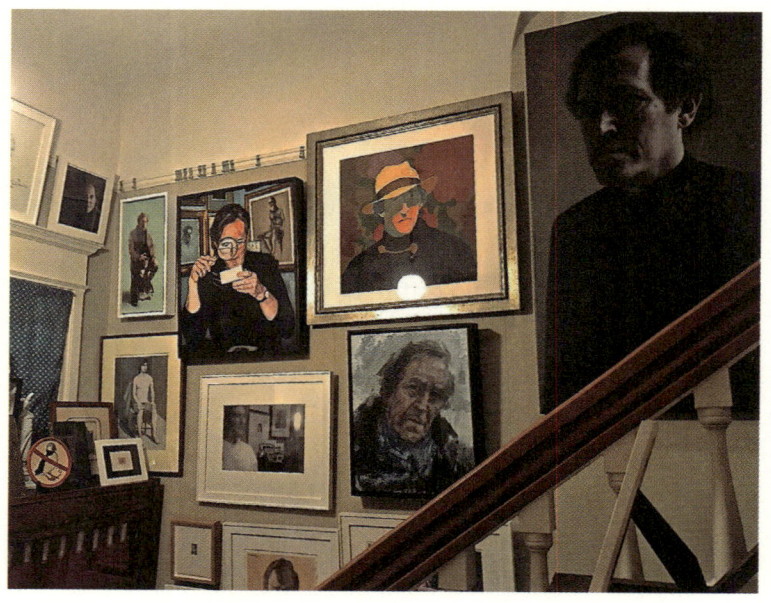

At Robert Flynn Johnson's San Francisco home,
an entry wall of portraits, mostly of Johnson himself

I know a few of Robert's guests from the East Bay, but the group is overwhelmingly Frisco, a lively mix of artists, art dealers, collectors, Robert's former colleagues at the Achenbach and diverse others, including neighbors. It's as if *The Girl in Red* has led me via Robert Flynn Johnson (via Yuri Kuper's catalog) to the very group that can truly appreciate the portrait and help reveal its secrets.

One guest, Catherine Burns, a former intern of Robert's at the Achenbach and now an Oakland-based art dealer with an international clientele of collectors, art galleries and museums, expresses curiosity about my connection to our host. Catherine and I had met recently at a Chanukah party in Berkeley and are now, by chance, nibbling side by side at the buffet table. I explain my history with Robert and the short version of my Paris discovery. When I show her the portrait on my cell phone, she is quite taken by it, reinforcing the idea, now fairly well established, that this painting is no mere flea market curiosity. I promise to ask her over to see the painting in the flesh, and she agrees to help me construct the details of a provenance and appraisal report.

But how can one ascribe a value to *The Girl in Red* with no known artist or previous ownership or sales data? Catherine will advise me on the format and terminology, if not the valuation. I will take care of that. There will be a price range topping out at the $1,000,000 mark posted in Paris. Absurd, of course, but who's to say?

I leave the party with the giddy feeling—fueled by the generous flow of wine and repartee—that *The Girl* has created an entrée back into an art world I left decades earlier. Robert's soirée has been a welcome home for me and my *Girl*, if only in my own mind.

FINISH THE UNFINISHED—
A CONTEST

o

Considering the young girl in the portrait as a real, living person, obvious questions about her arise. What was she like—her personality, interests, education, family life, dreams, joys and sorrows? The mystery of knowing nothing about her fuels my passion to know everything about her. If the painting had been finished in the conventional sense, we would know what she was wearing and where she was sitting while posing for the artist—at home, in an artist's studio, in an art school classroom? Those visual details may have helped fill in some of the blanks in *The Girl*'s story.

When I first took possession of the canvas, I began to consider how I might finish it, a kind of art prank via kitsch and pastiche. I did not know until the Courtauld show in London that this idea of finishing the unfinished was a common art practice in the Renaissance—masters deliberately leaving paintings unfinished for their assistants to complete in the master's style. An example from the Courtauld: a portrait of Michelangelo by Daniele da Volterra showing only a finished head and left hand (the difficult parts) that students and later artists would make copies of and complete with the body and background in Volterra's style.

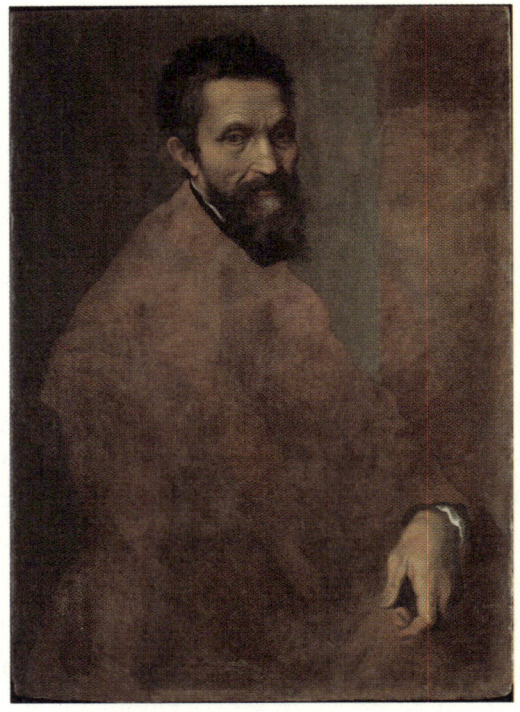

Michelangelo *by Daniele da Volterra, c. 1544*

I imagine this process now with a twist: a contest in which artists will finish *The Girl* digitally with clothing and a background of their choosing and in their own style. Although historical accuracy, in terms of setting and wardrobe, would not be required, the choices made by the artist would have to be "defended" in a written statement submitted with their work.

The contest rules would require that *The Girl*'s face and head covering not be altered, that the torso be dressed within the existing black lines on the canvas, and that the date be included as it is. There would be cash prizes for first, second and third place, and a jury of experts (artists and art-world professionals) would select the most compelling submissions.

All submissions (as high-res scans) would be posted on-line and the winning images printed and mounted alongside the original *Girl* at a participating gallery. Visitors to this show and online would be able to purchase prints of the winning entries signed by the artists, proceeds from which would offset the expenses of the contest—promotional costs, prizes, and so on. Any profit after expenses would be donated to a worthy arts organization.

As I plot all this, I am in Los Angeles visiting family and friends. It's "so LA" to think of promoting and monetizing *The Girl in Red*. I'm advised by a tech-savvy friend to orchestrate a social media "breakout" of my journey with *The Girl* with daily tweets if I want viral success for the contest and notoriety for *The Girl*—and ultimately, of course, a movie based on the book he urges me to write.

I'm sure that once I'm back in Berkeley, this impulse to promote *The Girl* via a contest will recede. My entire life in Berkeley—going on half a century now—has moderated, if not eradicated, entrepreneurial instincts inherited from a multi-generational family of businessmen. Still, given our contemporary art world's fascination with installations, conceptual art and spectator involvement in the art process, I continue to imagine ways to bring a portrait from 1935 into the present via social media. Doing something about it is another story.

PARIS, JANUARY 12, 1935

○

If the only thing I really know about *The Girl in Red* is the painting's date, and somehow, by some cosmic twist of time, I'm living simultaneous lives, then and now, I want to know more about what happened in Paris on that day, January 12, 1935.

"Painters don't date paintings if the date is unimportant to them," writes novelist and essayist Julian Barnes in his book *Keeping an Eye Open*. Why did *The Girl*'s artist render the date so prominently and yet withhold a signature? At the vernissage in Berkeley, Robert Johnson judged the painting finished because of the date. But he didn't speculate on the meaning of the date and its boldness of scale.

Perhaps the scrawled date *is* the artist's signature, and this particular day in 1935 can be viewed as the painter of the canvas; as if the individual wielding the brush is merely a channel for all that is happening on this day in Paris, in the world and, of course, in the artist and model too. Isn't this what representational painting is—a picture of everything all at once on a two-dimensional surface? A photograph freezes the moment with a mechanical lens—a snapshot. A painting allows the viewer to experience in the surface of the painting a more expansive and evolving time and place "as it happens." Or, as the French novelist and art theorist André Malraux put it, "A

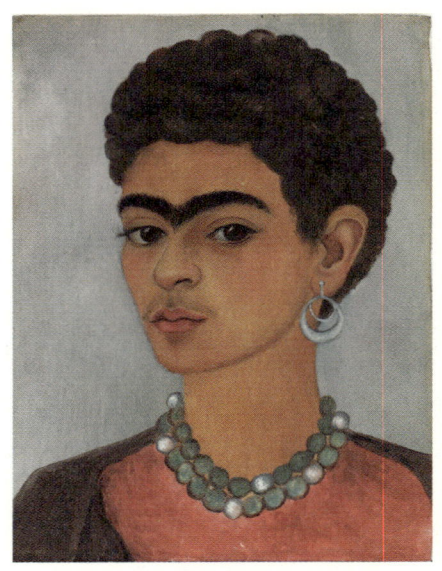

Self-Portrait with Curly Hair *by Frida Kahlo, 1935*

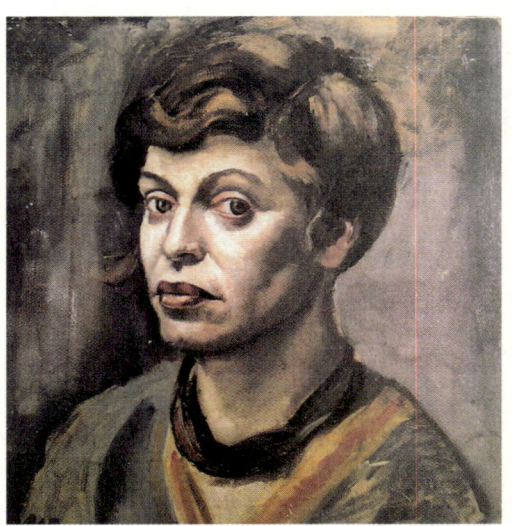

Self-Portrait *by Elfriede Lohse-Wächtler, 1930*

work of art is an object, but it is also an encounter with time."

It has also been said that a portrait is the "face of history," not merely of the subject. I have come across two such portraits from the 1930s, both self-portraits, that graphically and emotionally support this notion: Frida Kahlo's *Self-Portrait with Curly Hair* from 1935, a year after her breakup with Diego Rivera, and the "degenerate artist" Elfriede Lohse-Wächtler's 1930 *Self-Portrait*.

Lohse-Wächtler was force-sterilized by the Nazis in 1935 and never painted again. In 1940 she was euthanized. One senses a ghostly horror in her pale-white face and terror in her eyes. As for Kahlo's self-portrait, it has been suggested that her short curly hair represents her rage at Rivera's betrayal. Evidently, he loved her long flowing hair (more than her?), which she defiantly cut short after the breakup.

The idea of a face reflecting history relates to the rhetorical term *synecdoche*, where parts stand in for wholes (a "hired hand" is a worker). It's associated with metonymy ("the crown" is the king) and metaphor, where two different things are used for comparisons (eyes are the windows of the soul). These terms are all related and sometimes hard to distinguish. The portrait of *The Girl* reveals a place and time beyond her—history. In her full red lips I see budding sensuality; in her closed mouth I hear her silence; in her eyes I see the sadness of the world she sees. With her red head covering I see a young Marianne, the spirit of France. And in the canvas's bold black date I feel the looming catastrophe of WWII and the coming Nazi occupation of Paris.

So, what exactly was going on in *The Girl*'s world, in Paris on January 12, 1935? Newspapers from that day tell us it snowed so heavily that city workers were dispatched to clear important public spaces, such as Place de la Madeleine. They used shovels and coarse salt to melt the heavier drifts.

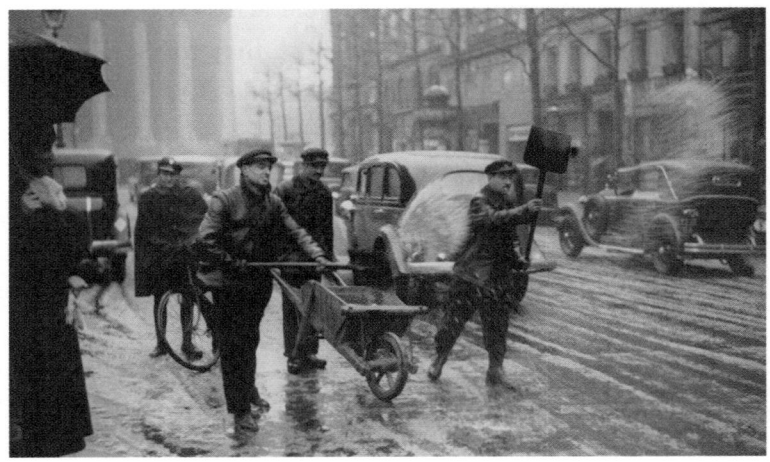

Clearing ice on Place de la Madeleine,
January 12, 1935

It was a Saturday, and young children, dressed warmly in hats and boots, romped in the streets, no doubt building snowmen, throwing snowballs and, not surprisingly, catching cold. Two children playing outside in the cold (*le froid*) are depicted in the evening newspaper, *Le Petit Parisien*, in an ad for a children's throat syrup, *Sirop vert-cadets.*

One of the children in the ad seems to be wearing a cloche, a tight-fitting, brimless, bell-shaped hat fashionable in the 1920s and '30s (resembling our American beanie). The genders in the image are vague, but boys didn't wear cloches. The young girl in *The Girl in Red* could very well have been one of these kids. Was she late for her portrait appointment that day because she stayed out too long playing with her friends, causing the artist to stop short of a finished portrait? Or did the artist stop because the girl was restless, as Robert Johnson believes, anxious to join her friends who were waiting for her?

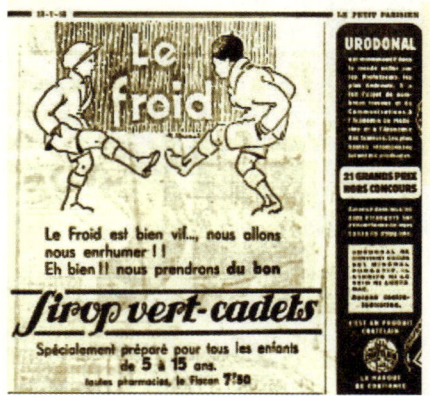

This ad for a cough syrup appeared in a Parisian daily on January 12, 1935.

While snowstorms blanketed Paris on January 12, political storms were brewing there and all across Europe. As the *Petit Parisien* banner headline for that day proclaims, a critical plebiscite was scheduled for January 13. This would determine the fate of the Sarre, a coal-rich German region bordering northeast France, administered by the League of Nations after the end of World War I. Joseph Goebbels, the Nazi minister of propaganda, was in Gdansk, Poland, on January 12, and noted in his diary, "*Saarkamph* [Sarre battle] climax. It's good that it's coming to an end tomorrow. That's unbearable. But our victory is certain and great."

As Goebbels predicted, the population of the Sarre overwhelmingly supported reunification with Germany, an important step toward World War II. Hitler's operatives had succeeded in manipulating public opinion within the Sarre, using brutal tactics to neutralize left-wing, pro–League of Nations elements in the voting ranks.

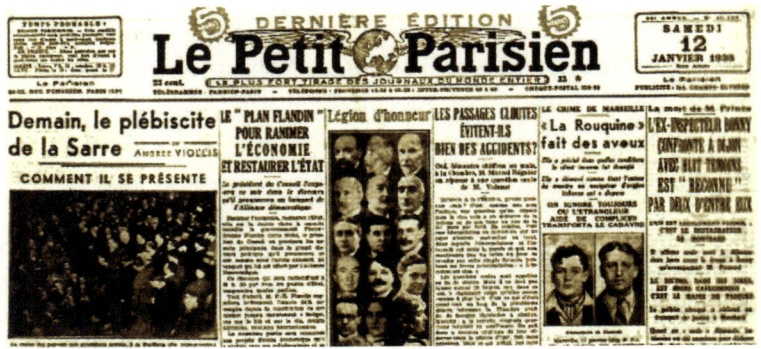

The major headline for a daily newspaper in Paris on
January 12, 1935, reads, "Tomorrow, the Sarre plebiscite."

Many in Europe believed that the return of the Sarre to German control would satisfy Hitler. In Paul Myers's historical novel *Paris 1935: Destiny's Crossroads*, Hitler is quoted as saying, "As I said after the Sarre's return to Germany last spring, Germany has no further claims on France." But Hitler's real goal was to remilitarize the Rhineland and open Europe up to German advances and control, and 1935 was the turning point from diplomacy to war, a "crossroads" as Myers puts it.

The fate of Europe as it suffered from the lingering economic devastation of a global depression in the 1930s rested in the hands of men in France and England with fading names such as Laval, Hoare, Eden, Baldwin, and Léger. These are the characters, portrayed in *Paris 1935*, who failed to contain Hitler. The year 1935 was also a crossroads for Italy's Mussolini, who would soon pounce on Ethiopia, and for Spain's Franco, who was about to ignite the Spanish Civil War.

The political storm clouds gathering over Europe in 1935 appear to have descended on Paris's snowbound avenue Foch, as revealed in another photograph published on the eve of the plebiscite. This was Baron von Haussmann's broadest and most elegant street installed during his reconstruction of Paris beginning in the 1850s. From the Arc de Triomphe to the Bois de Boulogne, rich Parisians would promenade in their carriages along the chestnut tree–lined avenue between the Bois and the Place de l'Étoile.

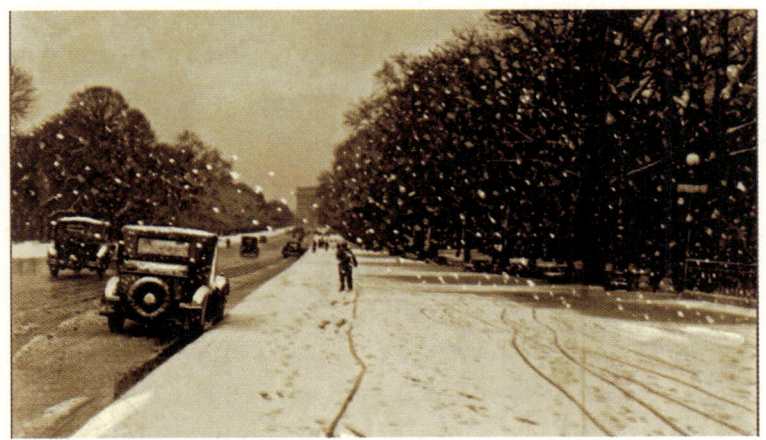

Avenue Foch, January 12, 1935

The avenue has had several names since its creation during the Second Empire, the first being avenue de l'Impératrice (Avenue of the Empress). After World War I the name was changed to avenue Foch, in honor of the French hero of that war, Général Ferdinand Foch.

Soon after the fall of Paris in June of 1940, the Gestapo set up shop at 84, avenue Foch. The street was renamed yet again, unofficially: avenue Boche—*Boche* being an old derogatory term for Germans, especially German soldiers, etymologically related to "block head" or "cabbage head." The street was also known as the Street of Horrors because of the screams coming from the torture rooms on the building's sixth floor.

Deportations of Parisian Jews to concentration camps were organized after 1940 in an office located nearby.

According to Joseph Goebbels's diary shared with me by Carla Shapreau, an attorney at UC Berkeley's Institute of European Studies who documents and returns Jewish-owned musical instruments stolen by the Nazis, he visited Paris in October of 1940 along with Air Marshall Herman Goering, just after the Occupation. While the Gestapo was rounding up Jews, Goebbels was enjoying the city and recording his impressions: "Paris. The old magic of this wonderful city, where the pulsating nightlife has returned. Lots of military. I stroll through the streets with Goering. A huge sensation. Then I do some shopping."

Goebbels, the Nazi flâneur!

Between 1935 and the end of the German Occupation, what happened in the life of the girl in *The Girl in Red*? Was she a Jew who suffered the ghastly fate of an Anne Frank? Or did she live through the Occupation like so many Christian Parisians, going about the business, more or less, of everyday life?

By the end of the war, the girl would be, presuming she had survived, eighteen or perhaps twenty years old, starting out an adult existence in a city cannibalized by Nazis. Paris did slowly come back to life, led in large measure by the arts and the left-leaning polemics and politics of the avant-garde, a narrative that has helped shape Francophile passion for Paris to this very day. This is perfectly showcased in the Hollywood film *An American in Paris*, with Gene Kelly in the role as the American GI–cum–aspiring artist. What's missing from the 1950s Hollywood version of the story, though, is the darker theme added to the Broadway version I saw in New York in 2013: the

GI's love interest, a young French dancer, has been hidden from the Gestapo by a wealthy Parisian family whose butler was the girl's Jewish father. Once you've seen the play, it's hard to watch the sanitized Hollywood version, though Gene Kelly's dancing is always a thrill.

Whatever the real story behind the canvas and the girl captured on it, I believe strongly that *The Girl in Red* carries the weight not only of the snow that buried Paris on one particular day over three-quarters of a century ago, but of the entire history of that terrible time.

THE GIRL FROM PARIS MEETS
THE BOY FROM BRAZIL

o

When I show the image of *The Girl in Red* to Sérgio Assad, a Brazilian composer and classical guitarist and one half of the acclaimed Assad Brothers duo, he seems surprised, almost stunned.

Sérgio, a handsome, bearded man in his sixties, is the newest member of the guitar faculty at the San Francisco Conservatory of Music (SFCM), and we are getting to know each other. Ever since meeting him and swooning over his performances with his brother, Odair, I've thought of them, jokingly of course and never publicly (until now), as "the Boys from Brazil," the title of a Hollywood sci-fi thriller about German boys (future führers) cloned from a single cell extracted from Adolph Hitler. In the case of the Assads, they are indeed "clones," but from a very musical cell taken from their beloved father, their first teacher and a brilliant musician in his own right.

Over dinner at a Brazilian restaurant near the conservatory, just after the spring semester has started, I tell Sérgio the story of finding the painting in Paris. When people are about to encounter the painting for the first time, my assumption is still, despite all the favorable responses to date, that it's going to seem to them amateurish, a piece of "Sunday art" or an unfinished student exercise. But then, when they see it on my cell phone or on Facebook or, especially, in person, they are surprised, and judge the work to be by a very talented student, at the very least. Sérgio's reaction is even more enthusiastic and more perceptive than most.

After quickly studying *The Girl* on my cell, he takes the phone in one hand, turns it toward me and places the edge of his other hand over half of the screen, covering the left side of the girl's face. "Look at the right side of her face," he says, in his Portuguese-scented English. "She is much sadder and older on this side. There are signs of suffering and a little bitterness and regret." Sérgio then switches the phone to his other hand and covers the other side of the face. "Now look at her left side. Younger and naïve."

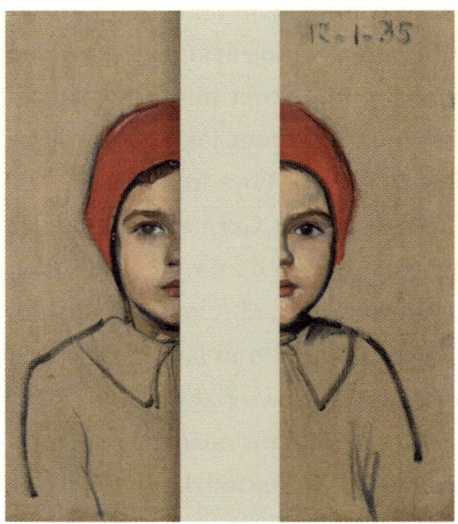

Sérgio had me look at a bifurcated Girl in Red: *the right side of her face (on the left) and the left side of her face (on the right).*

I agree with Sérgio, amazed at the sensitivity of his interpretation. "This is exactly what I am looking for," I tell him. "I'm documenting every dimension of *The Girl in Red*, and every reaction, especially the most interesting ones." I pause, then continue: "Like yours."

As I'm talking to Sérgio, it comes to me, and I blurt out, laughing, "You have just given me another chapter in my book!" By this time, more than six months after finding the painting, the idea of a book about *The Girl in Red* is emerging. Sérgio laughs now too, though I sense he is still not quite sure what I am up to—and not quite sure about *me* either. He knows me as a guitar collector and knows about the relationship of my collection to the conservatory's guitar department, but not much else, including my work as a writer and artist.

"You see," I continue, pushing aside my empty plate, "it doesn't really matter who threw out the portrait, or who painted it or who the sitter is." Lowering my voice and bending forward toward him, as if confiding a secret, I tell Sérgio, "My story is really about the search for answers that may never come, a journey with an unknown destination. And you are now part of it."

Sérgio smiles and nods his head in approval. "This is good," he says.

What I don't tell Sérgio is that I had already noticed the disconnect in *The Girl*'s left/right facial affect. But I haven't explored any further in this direction. Now, thanks to Sérgio, I'm eager to do so. After paying the bill and saying goodbye, I rush home to look in my library for a book by Jan Diepersloot, a brilliant scholar and writer who was socially connected to my Colby Street commune. His hybrid political/anthropological tract *The Tao of the Species* contains, as I remember it, a photoanalysis of Richard Nixon's face that reveals a radically bifurcated (left/right) and deeply pathological psychology.

Locating the book, I confirm my memory. A composite photo of the left side of Nixon's face—taking the left side and flipping it over to create a whole face—appears to support Harry Truman's observation, quoted by Jan: "Nixon was a mean, vindictive son of a bitch." On the right side, Nixon's composite image is, in Jan's words, "dazed, retarded, depressed."

These composite images of Nixon are instructive and painfully hilarious and seem to bear out Sérgio's perceptive analysis of *The Girl*. But is this the pseudoscience related to physiognomy, or "face reading," that dates back to Greek times and resurfaced in the twentieth century with Hitler's stereotyping of the Jews? Perhaps. But as I prepare for bed, I am determined to subject *The Girl* to the same analysis.

Over the next several days, I work on the project with a graphic artist. I'm anxious to see how *The Girl* will correspond to Sérgio's insight and Jan's technique. The results are remarkable. The composite images of *The Girl* show two different girls, just as Sérgio described. The right-side composite shows an older, sadder, more knowing girl. The left-side composite reveals a less developed, naïve young girl. And it all makes

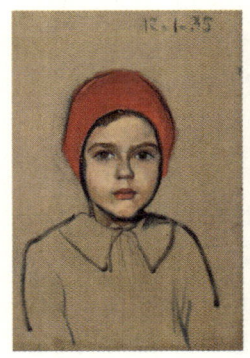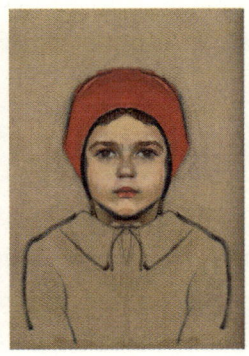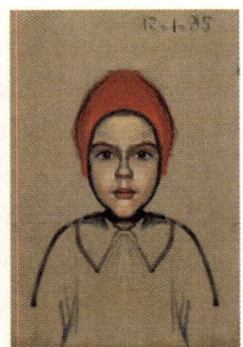

The original portrait (left), the right-side composite portrait (middle)
and the left-side composite (right)

perfect sense based on neuroscience's "lateralization of brain function" principle—that the left hemisphere (analytical, detail oriented) controls the right side of our faces (and bodies), and the right hemisphere (emotional, wholistic) the left side, though both hemispheres work together in their own way.

Although relegated to the domain of pop psychology in decades past, left/right-hemisphere theory has been making inroads in recent years, back into the sphere of science proper, thanks to neuroscientists such as Ian McGilchrist, as exhaustively documented in his extraordinary book, *The Master and His Emissary: The Divided Brain and the Making of the Western World*. But whether or not my (and Sérgio's) analysis of *The Girl* makes scientific sense, I marvel at the girl the artist has captured on canvas—both of them.

Following this exercise, it dawns on me that Sérgio himself might be better understood in this same context—one half of a pair of contrasting performers as viewed next to his more extroverted younger brother, Odair. To confirm this hunch, I locate online an image of Sérgio and Odair from the cover of one of their CDs, *O Clássico Violão Popular Brasileiro*. And there it is! To Odair's right, Sérgio looks sensitive, introspective (left-brain analytical, the duo's composer and arranger). On Sérgio's left, Odair looks younger, cockier (right-brain emotional, the duo's flamboyant virtuoso). These are the faces, the personae, that the brothers project into the world.

I next run into Sérgio several weeks later at a bar near the conservatory, the Sugar Lounge on Hayes Street, where the SFCM guitar faculty often meets after classes. "I'm writing about you," I tell him, "for a book about *The Girl in Red*."

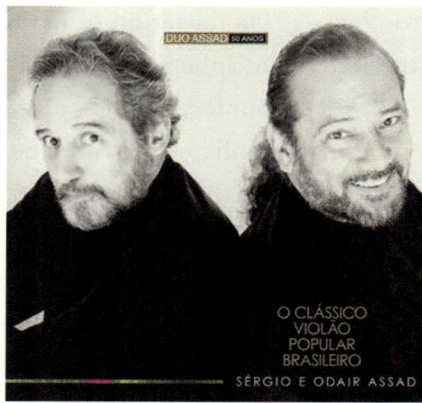

*The Assad Brothers
on a CD cover:
Sérgio (left) and
Odair (right)*

He stares at me vaguely. "And not only as a guitarist and composer," I tease, "but as an art critic."

Sérgio smiles broadly, without knowing, I'm sure, what I am talking about.

Sipping on a martini, I remind him of our earlier conversation about *The Girl* and his observations. "You see, your insight into *The Girl*'s two contrasting facial affects makes absolute sense. After all, you are one of two halves of the Assad Brothers duo, almost attached at the hip to your brother since childhood, right?"

Sérgio nods and again stares at me, dubious no doubt, waiting for the punch line.

"Consciously or not," I continue, "you and your brother have presented yourselves to the world as two opposing halves of a complementary musical whole. A singular duet combining light and dark, power and sensitivity, energy and wisdom, and . . . " Before I can finish delivering the goods, Sérgio looks away, distracted by Larry Ferrara, another faculty guitarist who has just entered the bar.

Cut off now from their collegial repartee, I giggle to myself. The punch line I never get to share with Sérgio will become a chapter title in my book: "The Girl from Paris Meets the Boy from Brazil."

NON FINITO REDUX

○

When I read about another museum showcase of unfinished art, the Met Breuer's exhibition *Unfinished: Thoughts Left Visible*, opening in March of 2016, I made a hotel reservation and jumped on a plane to New York.

I suppose that in the museum world, as with book publishing, moviemaking and the like, when a theme catches on, it makes the rounds. The Courtauld Gallery's *Unfinished* show dazzled me last summer with the works on display and its catalog quotes by great artists on the virtues of unfinished paintings. But the heureux hasard of discovering that London exhibition was even more important than its content, convincing me to stay on my journey. Now, I am less excited but no less curious about what else can be said about unfinished art at a second major venue.

I note on arrival at the Met Breuer a Rembrandt quote boldly posted on the wall at the entrance to the exhibit about an artist's control of the decision that a work of art is finished—when, says Rembrandt, "the Master's intentions have been realized." The master is always right, of course. Except that even masters can change their minds. Many great artists have modified their works after completion. Art history is full of colorful stories about this, and J. M. W. Turner's moment at the Royal Academy of Arts in 1832 is a prime example.

However, these changes are at the artist's peril, according to Eugène Delacroix. He points out in another wall quote at the Met Breuer, "One always has to spoil a picture a little in order to finish it." Turner's example seems to argue against this warning. So does the example of Balthus (Balthasar Klossowski de Rola, 1908–2001), who often changed his finished works. This wildly eccentric and controversial painter, in an age of abstraction and surrealism between the two World Wars, delivered retro levels of figurative form and Renaissance finish to his erotic (some say deviant) portraits of prepubescent girls. These caused a huge scandal at a show in Paris in May of 1934. So scandalous, in fact, that Balthus decided to stop painting for a time before returning in 1935 to portraiture in the traditional style, I read, of the eighteenth-century artist Joseph Reinhardt. One story goes that Balthus touched up all the paintings hanging at an important show at a Parisian gallery in the 1950s because the light in the gallery was so unflattering to them. It was evidently easier to change the paintings than the lighting. Finished becomes re-finished.

It seems clear, then, that a work of visual art, finished or not, is not created as a fixed event in time with a set duration—a beginning, middle and end. As is, say, a meal at a restaurant—when you are done, the plate's empty, the meal is definitely, unambiguously *terminé* or, in Italian, *finito*. In the culinary arts you can have seconds, never again firsts. Creating an oil painting is, then, more like a journey, an explorer's voyage across an ocean with an unknown destination, duration and arrival time. Picasso, in a film about the making of *Guernica*, says, "A painting is not thought out and settled in advance. While it is being done it changes as one's thoughts change."

The critic Robert Morris, speaking of Marcel Duchamp's work in the exhibit's catalog, asserts: "The notion that a work is an irreversible process ending in a static icon-object no longer has much relevance." The finish line for a work of art is never predetermined or time-limited and can be, even at the end, ambiguous. This contemporary idea of art as process, and how the theme of the unfinished fits into our postmodern context, is the element of the Met Breuer show that has exceeded, it seems to me, the more historical focus of the Courtauld exhibit. Again from the Met Breuer's catalog: "The unfinished has been taken in entirely new directions by modern and contemporary artists . . . who alternately blurred the distinction between making and un-making, extended the boundaries of art into both space and time and recruited viewers to complete the objects they had begun."

Making art as journey.

To truly understand the current art-world fascination with the unfinished, I've gone back to its earliest expression in Western art—the Renaissance. The art term *non finito* applies to the Renaissance Italian style in sculpture of allowing a part of the original block of stone to remain visible, as if the image were still encased in, or emerging from, its marble block. This was Michelangelo's inheritance from Donatello, explains Jeremy Angier, in a 2001 article titled "The Process of Artistic Creation in Terms of the Non-Finito." Angier references Michelangelo's *Captives,* meant to decorate the tomb of his patron, Pope Julius II: "How strangely appropriate that these figures remain encased in their marble blocks, as though Michelangelo had intended the world to witness his own creative torment in bringing his art into being. Never before had works of art so clearly revealed the process that made them, or provided such incontrovertible evidence that the piece was made by the hand of a mortal man under the duress of the creative state."

In painting, the same principle applies. Leonardo da Vinci's *Head of a Woman* (*La Scapigliata*), or, as it's nicknamed, *Lady with Disheveled Hair*, is similar to other non finito works by the artist. More than a sketch (pigment is used), it's less than a fully conceived portrait. As the Met Breuer's label notes, there is intentionality in the contrast between the wild sketchiness of the hair and neck and the refinement of the face. Much like the refinement of *The Girl*'s face contrasted with the sketchiness of the torso.

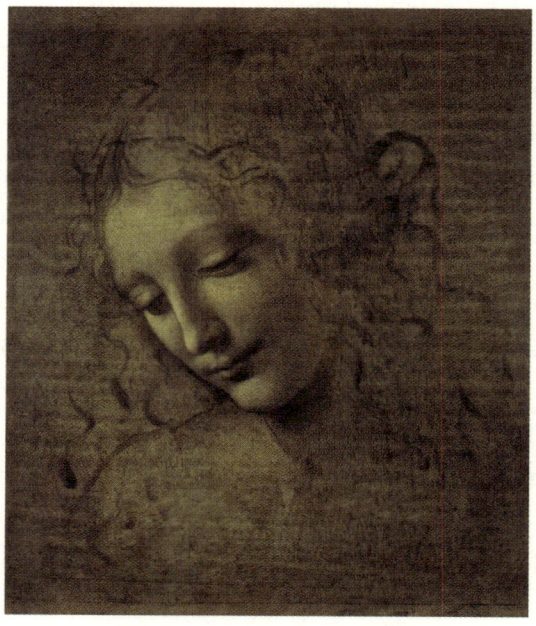

Head of a Woman (La Scapigliata)
by Leonardo da Vinci, 1505–1508

o

At the Met Breuer exhibit, I have spiraled back to the question I asked when I found *The Girl in Red* last summer: Had the artist finished the portrait of a young girl? After the Courtauld show and Robert Johnson's talk at the vernissage, I concluded yes. Now, I say yes and no—because there is no way that one can definitively penetrate the mind of the master or apply some external set of rules to determine the status of a work as finished or not. And maybe there is no reason to do so. From the master's point of view, the question is irrelevant, since they can say yes today and no tomorrow. Maybe only the art market cares one way or the other because it can price a finished work higher than an equally or more brilliant unfinished one.

Finito, non finito, maybe finito? The late, great painter Barnett Newman gets the final word on the subject, yet another quote on the wall at the Met Breuer: "The idea of a finished picture is a fiction."

II
THE JOURNEY CONTINUES

2016

Berkeley · London · Paris ·
London · Paris · Berkeley

BACK TO PARIS WITH A
POSTER AND A PLAN

○

The timing of the Courtauld show in London seemed uncanny, lending a sense of inevitability to my attendance last year. After I returned to Berkeley and saw the announcement of the Met Breuer's show in New York, it was, again, as if I were being directed by some unknown force—fate, the gods, heureux hasard. Perhaps just obsession, a deep impulse set in motion and driving me forward, as Lucian Freud describes the motivation to make art: "The painter's obsession with his subject is all that he needs to drive him to work." I've never been one to jump on an airplane to fly cross-country to see a museum show, or anything else. I am now.

But what of my own work, the documentation of this journey I'm on and its brewing literary by-product? Where will my obsession take me next? I have determined to end my provenance search in Paris on the one-year anniversary of *The Girl*'s arrival in my life. Somewhat arbitrary, I know, and open to the shocks of heureux hasard that erupt out of the blue and throw me off course. But I like the symmetry of a one-year project, a frame, like the stretcher bars that form the edges (and limits) of a painter's universe. As the master of my work (like Rembrandt), I have determined the final finish of my work in time and space, date and place: Paris, July 26, 2016.

The plan is to arrive in Paris in late June following a stop-over in London. This will give me almost a full month in Paris with eighty posters—Wanted posters (*les avis de recherches*) sent from Berkeley—to be placed all around *The Girl*'s ground zero. The posters are in French, and the bold "WANTED" headline is followed by a request for information about the painting shown. My email address appears at the bottom.

I have no foodie mission in Paris this summer. Just a month of poster posting and the hope that *The Girl*'s story will be revealed—its artist, sitter and provenance.

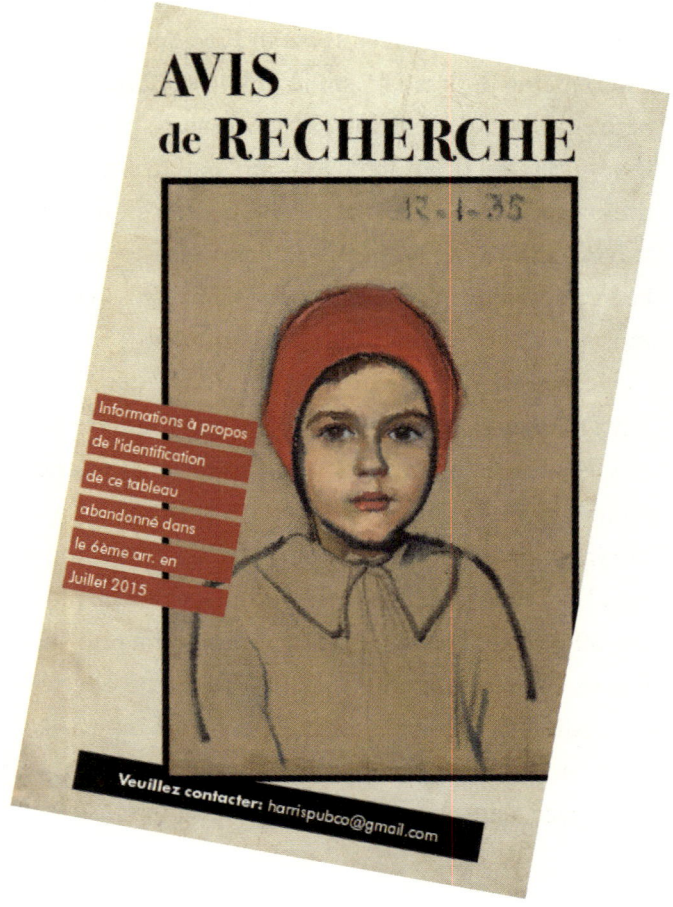

THE GODS MUST BE SURREAL

o

When stopping in London before my annual Paris *séjours*, I stay for several days, usually at DUKES London, a hotel embedded in Victorian architecture and charm. The area's art galleries, bookshops, and afternoon tea salons are all grand, and the vibe historic British. But more important, there is the Wolseley, the casually elegant watering hole I can't wait to return to.

I once ate at the Wolseley nine times in five days to research an article for my magazine about the delicious magic of the place and about artist Lucian Freud, who had died in 2011. Freud adopted the Wolseley late in life as his go-to dinner venue. One Wolseley server I talked to during that binge remembered how the late, great artist—perhaps the greatest portrait painter of the twentieth century—would wad up little pieces of paper, moisten them in his mouth and, from his vantage point at his favorite table 32, fling them out into the restaurant's cavernous central hall. Spitballs! Childishly silly behavior from an artist who, using paint, explored the most private and darkest secrets in his models' silent faces and naked bodies. His more genteel grandfather, Sigmund Freud, used only his clients' words to plumb their depths.

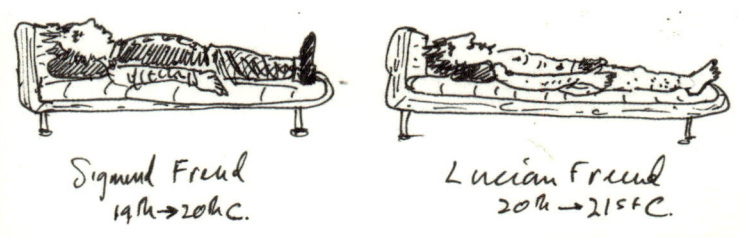

A sketch from my journal for a cartoon,
"Sigmund Freud vs. Lucian Freud," 2012

It's not surprising that German-born Lucian loved the Wolseley with its Eastern European and German dinner specialties alongside its British and French fare. The menu lists no fewer than three variations of *schnitzel*, two made of veal, one of pork. In the morning at the Wolseley, it becomes English "full breakfast" time: eggs, grilled tomatoes, bacon, bangers, beans and toast. Good food in a fabulous Art Deco pavilion built originally for a car manufacturer, Wolseley Motors Limited. A place to be seen if you're a VIP, and a place to see them if you are not.

After breakfast at the Wolseley today, I stumble jet-lagged out into Mayfair's shopping district, bounded by Piccadilly to the north, Green Park to the west, the Mall to the south and Haymarket to the east. I seldom breach these coordinates on my brief stops in London, at least on foot. Peering into the window of Peter Harrington, a vintage bookshop on Dover Street, I am gobsmacked by what I see. (I hesitate to use this pretentious bit of Gaelic slang—gobsmacked—common now with my literary friends in Berkeley, but here in London it feels appropriate.) In full view is a book titled *Unfinished Portrait*. Maybe it's jet-lag delirium, but I almost keel over, laughing out loud like some sad, undermedicated wretch collapsed on the sidewalk.

Composing myself, I enter the shop and ask to see the book. Turns out it's a first edition of an Agatha Christie novel, one of several written under the pen name Mary Westmacott. Published in 1934, it's Christie's semiautobiographical account of Celia, a woman who, distraught following a divorce, is about to commit suicide while vacationing on a tropical island. An artist named Larraby comes across her and intervenes. He's a portrait painter.

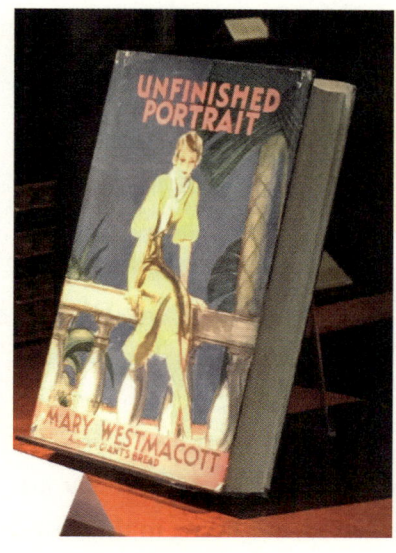

Agatha Christie's pseudonymous novel Unfinished Portrait *in a shop window*

Should I buy the book, I ponder, a souvenir of this latest eruption of heureux hasard? I don't even have to read the book, just frame the vintage cover to hang in my office. But the price is dear, and I decide to pass on it. Then, the next day, at another secondhand bookshop, this one devoted to art books and art criticism, I pick up a volume of Denis Diderot's *Salons*, a collection of journal-like entries on art and philosophy. I'd read about Diderot in relationship to Paris café history; he was one of the Enlightenment intellectuals, along with Voltaire, who helped brand the café in Paris as chic after its arrival from Turkey in the late seventeenth century.

As I thumb through the book, out falls a typed staple-bound essay, a college paper by a student named Edna, dated January 7, 1971. The title is "Diderot the Art Critic: His Influence on Greuze and Neo-Classicism." Clearly, the Diderot book had belonged to, or was used by, this student for her class Rococo 18 C. Art History, as the paper's cover references. Edna must have forgotten to remove the paper from the book when she unloaded it.

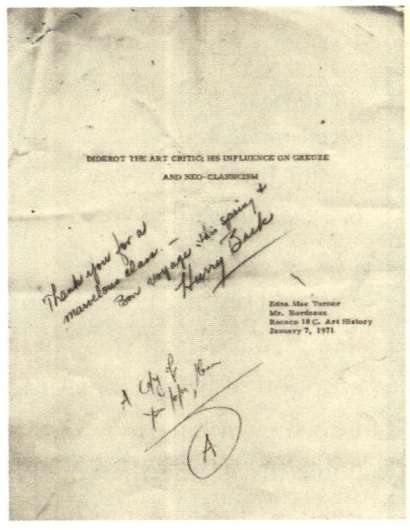

*A student paper on
Denis Diderot from 1971*

Sitting down on a chair in the shop, I'm more excited to read the essay than the book. The first sentence reads, "Denis Diderot (1713–1784) was the most important eighteenth-century writer on art and a precursor of the modern-day art critic." His favorite artist of that period, according to the essay, was Jean-Baptiste Greuze, now almost forgotten, but famous in his day for his portraits.

Another shock. Everywhere I turn are references to portraits or portrait artists. Luckily, I'm already sitting down. It feels as if I am being notified by the gods that my stay in Paris this summer will pick up where it left off last year. First the Agatha Christie novel, now a random student essay emerges from out of nowhere. I'm reminded of that hilarious film from 1980, *The Gods Must Be Crazy*, about a tribal hunter-gatherer in South

Africa who discovers a Coke bottle dropped from an airplane and believes it to be a gift from his tribe's gods.

I don't know whether the gods are crazy, but they are decidedly surreal.

Edna's paper, awarded an A by the teacher, a Mr. Bordeaux, looks much like the ancient undergraduate essays from Cal I've saved from this same period: the slightly crumpled and yellowing typing paper, the tarnished staple, the faded pencil of the professor's comments. More patina. More power.

One can speculate on the relationship between this student and her professor based on her note scrawled on the cover: "Thank you for a marvelous class. Bon voyage this spring & Hurry Back." Edna underlined and capitalized "hurry back." Reading between the lines, one wonders if there was more going on here than just a "marvelous class." If I weren't heading to Paris where my Wanted posters await me, I'd stay in London and search for Edna, assuming she is still alive, and uncover her story. Who knows what kind of obsessive journey that would launch?

UNLIKELY COMPLICITIES

○

I first met cellist prodigy Tessa Seymour and her mother, Kerstin, at the French Hotel café in North Berkeley's legendary foodie epicenter, the so-called Gourmet Ghetto. The eleven-year-old would sometimes hang out at "the French" with her mother and warm up before being taken to her morning music classes at the Crowden School nearby. Her Bach cello suites, pieces I love and struggle with on the classical guitar, wowed our café crowd.

Then, a decade later in New York, and after Tessa and I had seen Gustav Klimt's *Woman in Gold* and had our apple strudel at the Neue Galerie's café, we paused in the hallway just outside the café in front of a full-sized, framed print of the portrait. I took Tessa's picture and teasingly told her she was a "girl in gold." Two days later, in Paris, I found *The Girl in Red*.

I now see *The Girl in Red* as the symbolic offspring of Tessa Seymour and Adele Bloch-Bauer. *The Girl in Gold* + *Woman in Gold* = *The Girl in Red*. This perhaps fanciful equation emerges as I reread a book here in London from my art school days, André Breton's 1928 surrealist novel, *Nadja*, a semiautobiographical account of an actual relationship with a young woman (sometimes referred to by Breton as a girl) he meets in the streets of Paris.

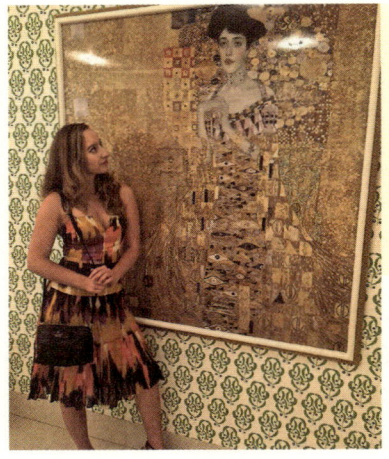

Tessa Seymour checks out a full-sized reproduction of Woman in Gold *outside the Neue Galerie's Café Sabarsky in 2015.*

In the book, Breton makes the case for surrealism as not merely an art form but a lifestyle. He speaks of "unlikely complicities," not in the criminal sense of the word, but as a conspiratorial force outside his conscious awareness, which guides him: "Facts which when I am alone permit me to enjoy unlikely complicities, which convince me of my error in occasionally presuming I stand at the helm alone." One can read in Breton's comment Carl Jung's concept of synchronicity, which had a profound effect on Breton and the French avant-garde. Breton believes in the fluid nature of identity—his—and how our unique "self" is built up from "the prejudices I acknowledge, the affinities I feel, the attractions I succumb to, the events which occur to me and to me alone."

When Breton meets Nadja, her eyes capture his attention: "What was so extraordinary about what was happening in those eyes? What was it they reflected—some obscure distress and at the same time some luminous pride?" All of this illuminates my journey with the ever-mysterious *Girl in Red* and, in turn, brings Breton's *Nadja* vividly to life in a way it never was back in the day.

Nadja is quite real to Breton when they meet, but she begins to devolve into a "ghost" as he gets to know her better. He soon drops her because she is, he realizes, quite insane and belongs in a sanatorium. Nadja continues to haunt Breton's waking and dreaming life, he says, even more so through her absence than through her presence. My gleaning of *The Girl in Red* follows the reverse course: a ghostly girl on canvas—though very real in 1935—has captured me with her eyes, though the facts of her existence remain unknown and perhaps unknowable. As Breton might put it, *The Girl* is reshaping my identity—"the attractions I succumb to."

I've finished another book here in London, Nobel laureate Patrick Modiano's 1997 hybrid novel *Dora Bruder* (autofiction, actually—part memoir, part fiction). The book was given to me just before I left for London by a Berkeley friend, the author, playwright and radical feminist philosopher Susan Grif-

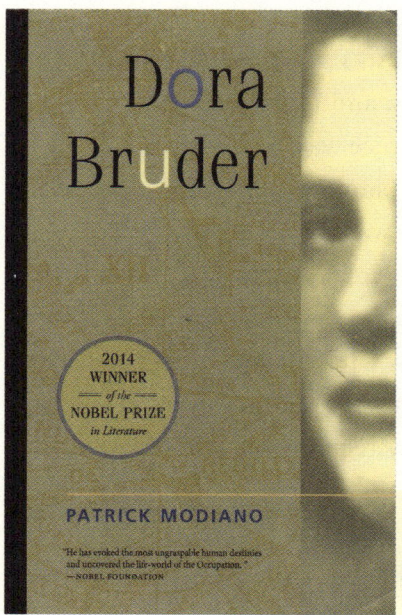

fin. *A Chorus of Stones* and *The Book of the Courtesans* are two of her best-known works. My search for the artist and provenance of *The Girl in Red* reminds her of Modiano's search for information about another Paris girl, Dora Bruder, who went missing in 1941 during the Nazi Occupation.

On the cover of Modiano's novel, a photo of Dora

"All of Modiano's books," Susan explained to me over cups of tea at her Berkeley Hills home recently, "are in the form of a search, the ones I've read. You have been searching for the story behind a painting of a lost girl. But she is only lost to the culture, not to herself. She knows who she is, but she is vulnerable. You can see it in her eyes." Susan smiled when she said all this, as if putting it in italics or quotation marks, letting me know it's important.

My relationship with Susan has its own surreal magic. When we met in the 1990s through our mutual friend Leonard Pitt at a dinner party at my house, we discovered that her adoptive father in Los Angeles, the artist and African art dealer Morton Dimonstein, was my mother's art teacher and had sold her the African pieces Susan noticed in my living room. I now suspect, without solid evidence, that Mort and my mother had been lovers. Susan agrees that it's possible. At my bon voyage afternoon tea, Susan recalled a dinner party sometime in the 1960s at my mother's house. (I was not present.) She had gone with Mort and his wife, Gerry, and remembers my mother as "very vivid, commanding in a nice way."

Susan corrected herself, smiling ironically: "Nice is not the right word. In an *attractive* way."

Our virtual brother/sister relationship has grown deeper over the years, filling a void left by my brother's death at forty-three from AIDS in 1988. Now I have a gay sister and literary confidante who, by connecting *The Girl* and *Dora Bruder*, has sparked a breakthrough in my relationship with the painting, and with her.

In Modiano's book, Dora arrives in his life a bit like the arrival of *The Girl* in mine—neither one in flesh and blood, as with Breton's real-life Nadja. Modiano comes across an old missing person's notice for a fifteen-year-old Jewish girl sought by her parents during the first years of the Nazi occupation of Paris. The notice appeared in the New Year's Eve edition of *Paris-Soir* in 1941 and was gleaned by Modiano in 1988. He soon uncovers another fact about Dora: her name appears on a list of deportees to Auschwitz in 1942. This discovery launches Modiano, deeply troubled by France's shameful collaboration with the Nazis, on a ten-year mission to uncover Dora's story and restore her narrative. Along the way, he tells his own story, blending all with fictional elements.

Both Modiano and Breton convert chance encounters with a girl—one in print, one in the flesh—into ruminations on the deep personal implications of the strange events described in their narratives. While I don't aspire to the literary heights of *Nadja* and *Dora Bruder*, my "chance" encounter with *The Girl in Red* is likewise deeply personal to me. Her story is becoming my story, her absence my presence, her mysteries my revelations.

What can be said of this motif—three older male writers (two autofiction novelists, one auto-nonfiction journalist) obsessed with a "lost girl" in Paris? This begs for a psychoanalytic critique, and a feminist one too, and I brace for both as I had in Paris last summer after my social media postings. Sharing with Susan via email from London my ideas about Breton's *Nadja* and Modiano's *Dora*, she suggests that my search for facts about *The Girl* is not an external search but an internal one—a search for my "inner lost girl," an impulse to reclaim my suppressed feminine side.

This comment launches an exchange about my journey in Jungian terms, the idea of *The Girl* as an anima projection out from the shadowy world of my unconscious via an objet trouvé—a sad, abandoned young girl on canvas. This is, no doubt, a simplistic application of Jung's theory of the anima (the collective image of the female in a man's unconscious), and Susan cautions me that his insights were colored by his male prejudices: "The repression and separation of qualities thought male or female also distorts them," she explains. "Women viewed as 'gentle' and 'without courage' becomes submission"—just one example she offers. These caveats about Jung are well taken. It would require full-on Jungian analysis to come to terms with my *Girl* as an anima projection. Nevertheless, it represents *my* interpretation from *my* psyche at this stage in *my* journey with *my Girl*.

Whatever the ultimate meaning of *The Girl's* arrival in my life—Jungian, Freudian, feminist, surreal, or, who knows, extraterrestrial—Susan's "inner lost girl" trope does align nicely with an amusing observation by Alain de Botton, again from his clever lecture on Stendhal and love. According to the notoriously foppish Bloomsbury Group aesthete Lytton Strachey, Stendhal had, de Botton reports, the inner emotionalism of a twelve-year-old girl. De Botton goes on, somewhat tongue in cheek, of course, and without elaborating, to apply Strachey's quip to himself. One would like to hear more about de Botton's inner twelve-year-old girl, but he stops short. Again, as with his humorous comments on Stendhal's *The Red and the Black*, I feel that I'm in good company. My inner twelve-year-old girl has been found.

All the speculation about the meaning of *The Girl in Red* in my life tends to obscure the stunning possibility that the real girl in the painting could conceivably be alive today. She would be about ninety years old now if ten in 1935. Is she, was she,

Jewish? Is she, was she, French? Or Russian, as some have suggested, based on the details of her sketched clothing and her red head cover? Did Modiano's Dora, born in 1926 and nine years old in 1935, pass my girl in the streets of Paris in the 1930s? Could they have attended the same schools, played in the same parks, dated the same boys? And Breton's Nadja—actually Leona Camille Ghislaine Delacourt, born in 1902 and about twenty-five years old when Breton met her in Paris—she would have been about thirty-three years old in 1935. Did she pass Dora and my girl in the streets, cafés and parks of Paris after being released from the sanatorium Breton mentions?

Three lost and found girls, quite likely living in Paris at the same time, remembered in the narratives of three men caught in a web of unlikely complicities they feel compelled to explore.

POSTING *THE GIRL*

○

On my arrival at the apartment in Paris after a surreal week in London, the first thing I do is open the waiting package of posters and tape one to the tall mirror over the mantel in the salon where I had placed the found canvas last year after bringing it back to the apartment. I'm like an old dog marking his territory. We, *The Girl* and I, are back.

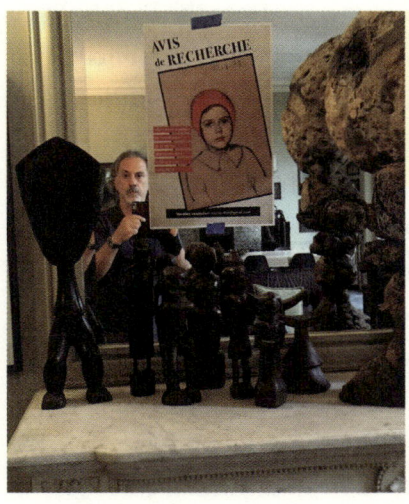

A selfie with the poster taped to the salon's mirror

Wandering through the apartment's rooms, eyeing my swap mates' eclectic inventory of paintings, prints, sculpture and framed photographs, I imagine they are doing the same in Berkeley. Everything here seems just as I had left it last summer. The wall color is that somber chalky greenish gray I've heard described as *château gris*, the traditional color of old French woodwork. It shows off art well, as if one were strolling through a flower garden on a gray day, and the colors pop.

The first few times I stayed here, the art, photos and miscellaneous *objets* displayed on walls, tables and shelves felt like images and collectibles from another life—someone else's paintings and drawings; someone else's framed photographs of children, grandchildren and older relatives; someone else's bric-a-brac. Now, several visits later, there is something oddly familiar, almost familial, about it all—a parallel universe to mine in Berkeley. Even their books have become my books. I discovered W. G. Sebald's haunting *Vertigo* here, and I've reread my host's well-worn copy of Gertrude Stein's clever romp, *The Autobiography of Alice B. Toklas.*

There are three floor-to-ceiling windows in the salon that look out over blvd. Saint-Germain, which runs river to river in a sweeping three-and-a-half-kilometer arc from the Pont Sully to the east, near the Île Saint-Louis, to the Pont de la Concorde in the west. The apartment sits in the approximate middle of this arc. Heavy gray metal shutters cover the windows—true of all the apartments in this Haussmann-era building—that protect the room's aging and creaky but quite beautiful wooden floors, the contemporary upholstered furniture and the framed art from the intense sun that rises in the early morning over the stately eighteenth-century building across the street, the Ministry of the Environment.

There have been times, when I am alone here, that the grayness produces in me a mood I call *existential gris.* I feel at these moments like a ghost in an old château. But this summer I am not alone. I have a companion to keep me company, eighty of them, in fact—a pile of *Girl in Red* posters. And I have a mission to keep me busy, *comme d'habitude*, albeit not a foodie one—to place the posters in shops and cafés and on walls and kiosks from Saint-Germain-des-Prés to the Latin Quarter around ground zero.

The French text of the affiche translates as "WANTED: Information related to the identification of this painting abandoned in the 6th arr. in July 2015." Perhaps this is a futile undertaking, but like Modiano in *Dora Bruder*, "I send out signals, like a lighthouse beacon in whose power to illuminate the darkness, alas, I have no faith. But I live in hope."

I am hopeful.

I think about Robert Johnson's challenge to my Paris project in an email exchange just before my flight to London: "You have the work, a thoughtful little girl. You have the date it was done, January 12, 1935. You do not know who made it. You do not even know if it was made in Paris or even if it is French (but one can assume it is). Embrace the mystery . . . otherwise you are implying that the work is somehow lacking."

I agree with Robert, whom I have dubbed the Apostle of the Anonymous. I do embrace the painting as it is, without benefit of provenance and official art-world status, let alone commercial value. *The Girl*, finished or not, lacks nothing. It is complete. But I am not. Something is pushing me forward, as it has from the beginning. I reply to Robert, "I am a journalist not an art critic or curator. I tell stories."

A journalist's obsession? A detective's caper? An art lover's passion? Patrick Modiano's "mania"? All of the above. Yet my mission has become more than a search for the story *behind* the painting; it's also about what's *in front* of the painting, and in front of me as we make our way, hand in hand, toward an uncertain destination.

The next poster I take from the pile is earmarked for Café

de Flore, where I will head after my ritual glass of champagne and dose of church bells at the Deux Magots. Flore's tall wall next to its heavily trafficked spiral staircase to the secluded second level, where, it must be noted, Sartre and de Beauvoir wrote together during World War II, is always chock-a-block with posters advertising current plays, concerts, gallery exhibits, and the like. It's an ideal location for the first poster placement. The Deux Magots doesn't have this same setup for les affiches.

Tightly rolling up several posters, I place a rubber band around them, carefully insert the roll into my satchel along with a spool of Scotch tape and head down the apartment's dramatic stairwell four flights to blvd. Saint-Germain and the short walk to the Deux Magots.

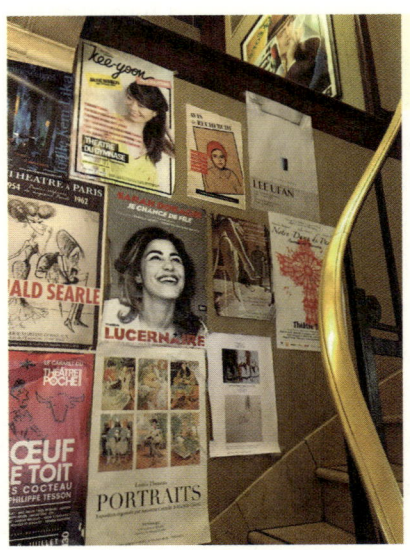

The poster at Café de Flore

After champagne and bells on the corner terrace, I make my way to Café de Flore. Getting permission to put up a poster proves easier than I expect—they speak English at the cashier's desk next to the staircase and are accommodating. I tape a poster to an available spot on the wall halfway up to the second floor and then head back down to a table for a café crème, in full view of the poster.

Nursing my crème, I have the feeling that my budding poster project is already *tout fini*. It doesn't seem to matter what will come of all the other postings that follow. For the moment, a glorious moment, it's enough to just sit near *The Girl* on display in the gallery of public opinion. It's as if I'm the artist of *The Girl in Red*, and the canvas is being shown in Paris for the first time. An artist's dream come true!

No doubt the poster will be seen at Flore by hundreds, if not thousands, of customers headed upstairs to the second-floor restrooms for the relief that follows their crèmes and *café Américains*, champagne coupes and bottles of *eaux minérales*. Yes, there is voluminous relieving going on in Paris, and it's not just the dogs on sidewalks and in parks marking trees and benches.

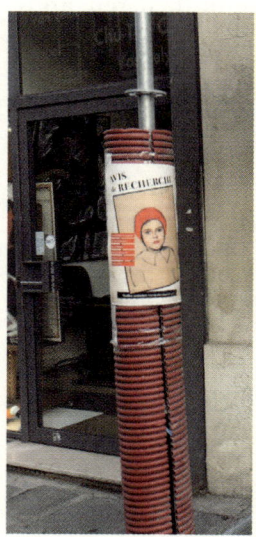

The Girl outside 35, rue Guénégaud

Leaving Flore, we, *mes affiches et moi*, stroll along blvd. Saint-Germain to rue de Seine, then past La Palette on rue Jacques Callot to ground zero at rue Guénégaud. There is construction scaffolding at the entrance to no. 35, and I tape a poster to one of the support poles. I note other postings in the area and their means of attachment—various types of tape and glue for walls and kiosks, and staples for wooden surfaces. I visit a few art galleries, too, and rehearse in my mind the French phrases I will use when I approach the proprietors for permission to post *The Girl*.

The week before leaving Berkeley, I worked with my French teacher on how to request permission in various scenarios. Still, I am nervous. The French can be abrupt, if not rude, when approached without sufficient politeness (*"Bonjour monsieur"* or *"madame"*) or with bad French. I am prepared for rejection. To test the waters, I venture into Galerie de l'Europe on rue de Seine, which is showing the work of a contemporary French artist, Fanny Vanoye. I like what I see displayed in the window. Mme. Vanoye herself sits at a reception table, having rented the gallery, I learn, to show her colorful abstract work. Her English is good, and I present a poster with a brief overview of my story and mission. My rehearsed French lines will have to wait.

Expressing admiration for *The Girl*, Vanoye agrees to mount the poster in her gallery back home in Île d'Yeu, an island just off the Vendée coast in western France. She then invites me to return the next day to continue our conversation during her lunch break when she won't be so consumed by visiting friends and potential customers.

We are off and posting, *La Jeune Fille en Rouge et moi.*

MEETUP WITH PICASSO
AND BALZAC

○

Almost a week into my postering project, the biggest thrill so far, along with posting at Café de Flore and at ground zero, is attaching the *avis de recherche* to the wall next to the gate at 7, rue des Grands-Augustins in Saint-Germain-des-Prés. It's one of the most celebrated addresses in French art and literary history, linked to both Pablo Picasso and Honoré de Balzac. There is a plaque mounted at the gate with a dedication to Picasso, who lived in this *hôtel particulier* from 1936 to 1955. Standing in front of the gate, I feel the power of the site pulling me into the neighborhood's history, which dates back to the thirteenth century and the birth of the "liberal arts" at the nearby Sorbonne University, in the heart of the Latin Quarter.

I feel a bit like a Picasso groupie, and have been since childhood. His mythology is more powerful to me than his misogyny. I still have a copy of the entire *San Francisco Chronicle* edition with the front page headline announcing Picasso's death on April 8, 1973. And I've toured his Château de Vauvenargues near Aix-en-Provence where, in 1958, he moved in to be near Cézanne's favorite subject, Mont Sainte-Victoire.

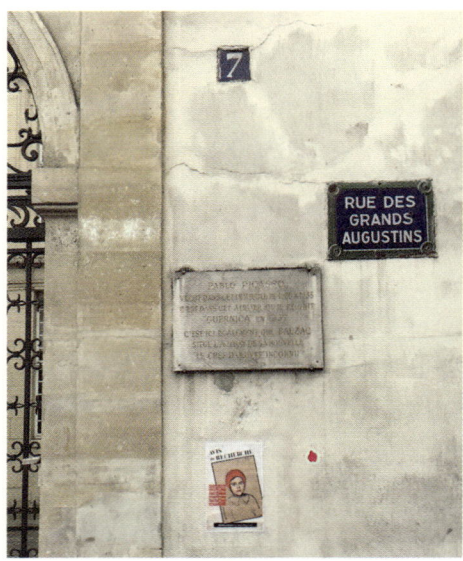

The poster outside 7, rue des Grands-Augustins. The plaque above the poster notes that this was the address where Picasso painted Guernica.

Picasso moved into the Grands-Augustins residence after a one-year hiatus from painting beginning in 1935. The break was brought on, the story goes, by the artist's self-doubt and romantic chaos, having thrown over one woman for another—Marie-Thérèse Walter for Dora Maar—something Picasso specialized in on and off canvas. During the hiatus, his obsessive focus was on journal writing and poetry, to mixed reviews from his literary and art community. André Breton was, however, a big fan of Picasso's poems and compared him to Stéphane Mallarmé. But there was more at play here than Picasso's personal chaos and literary talent. Europe was descending into political chaos, and Picasso struggled with this melancholy state of affairs. In a 1935 interview with Christian Zervos, published in the Greek art critic's magazine, *Cahiers d'Art*, Picasso refers to the mood of the times as *"misère morale."*

By 1937, following the outbreak of the Spanish Civil War and the vicious aerial bombardment of a small Basque town, Guernica, Picasso had bounced back, refocusing on painting in his new Grands-Augustins studio. Appalled by the stories he read in the press about the Fascist massacre, and with a commission from the Spanish government, he began working on what would become his greatest achievement, *Guernica*, to be shown at the World's Fair in Paris that year.

There was magic for Picasso at no. 7, the address of a character, the painter François Porbus, in Balzac's novella *Le Chef-d'Oeuvre Inconnu* (*The Unknown Masterpiece*), an allegorical tale that explores the subject of mimesis in pictorial art—representing or "bringing to life" on canvas the artist's subject. Seeing himself in Balzac's artist protagonist—the aging Maître Frenhofer who was obsessed with reproducing on canvas his courtesan and model, Catherine Lescault—Picasso was delighted to be living at this address discovered by Dora Maar. He had already illustrated a deluxe edition of Balzac's novella in the 1920s, and now he would be living in rooms associated with Balzac's Frenhofer.

Picasso had met Maar, then a photographer, on the set of Jean Renoir's 1935 film, *The Crime of Monsieur Lange*. Their affair was launched soon after at the Deux Magots. These "unlikely complicities" of time and place—Saint-Germain-des-Prés in 1935—continue to startle me. Could the artist of *The Girl in Red* have been living in this neighborhood, mere blocks away from ground zero and the great Pablo Picasso? I hear the theme music from TV's *The Twilight Zone* strike up in my mind's ear.

I have read Balzac's novella twice now, and its introduction by the art critic Arthur Danto more than twice, in an effort to understand the profound effect of the story on some of the greatest artists—Picasso and Paul Cézanne, among others—who followed Balzac's generation in painting's magical quest:

"bringing reality to life . . . the problem and the promise of pictorial art," says Danto. This at a time when painting styles began to shift from traditional mimetic representation to a cascade of modern and postmodern "isms": Impressionism, Cubism, Surrealism, Expressionism, Abstract Expressionism and Minimalism, all in reaction to the nineteenth-century challenge of photography.

The Balzac tale has had a powerful effect on artists outside the visual arts as well. Two films based on the novella—one by the French director Jacques Rivette (*La Belle Noiseuse*, 1991) and one by the Spaniard Fernando Trueba (*The Artist and the Model*, 2012)—are among the greatest films ever made about artists and their obsessions. Although the films are very different, both artists portrayed (one a painter, one a sculptor) are, like Balzac's Frenhofer, dealing with age and the decline in their capacities, and, as with Frenhofer, the unexpected surge of new energy and inspiration brought on near the end of life by the arrival of a beautiful young model. (As I write these words here in Paris, I can hear the tsk, tsks back in Berkeley, as when I began posting on social media the first chapters of my journey with *The Girl in Red*.)

In Balzac's story, Frenhofer is struggling with what he thinks will be his greatest painting. He cannot find a suitable model for executing some of the final anatomical details of his subject, his beloved Lescault, who had died before the painting was complete. When a young artist friend, Poussin (based on the real-life artist Nicolas Poussin), offers his beautiful young lover to Frenhofer as a model in exchange for the privilege of seeing the master's *inconnu* (unknown) masterpiece, Frenhofer accepts.

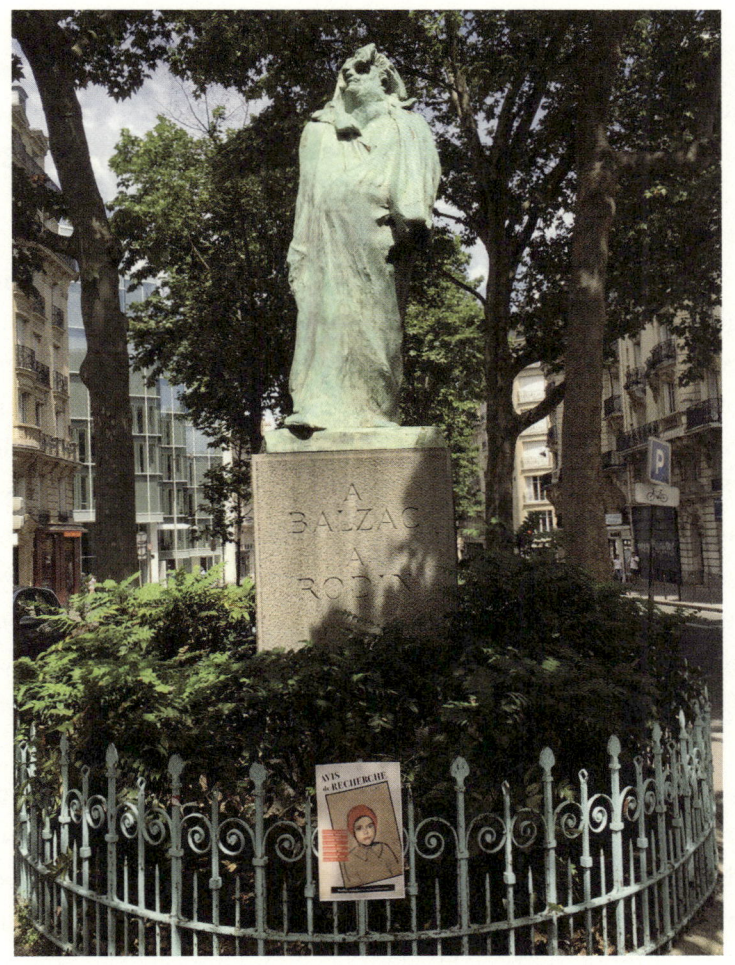

The Girl *posted at the* Monument to Balzac, *1892–1897,*
on blvd. Raspail in Saint-Germain-des-Prés

Poussin and the third major character in the book,
François Porbus (based on another historical artist, Frans Pour-
bus, but Balzac changes the spelling), are called in to see the
picture after Frenhofer's short, evidently successful session
with the model.

"My work is perfect!" says Frenhofer.

For Poussin and Porbus, the painting is a blur of tangled lines and blotches of wild color, with only a partial but recognizable foot emerging from the chaos at the bottom of the large canvas. In other words, not only unfinished—a total disaster.

Poussin exclaims, "There's nothing on his canvas!"

The two younger artists, admirers of Frenhofer as the greatest painter of the late seventeenth century, believe he has gone mad. For Frenhofer, the picture is the finest achievement of his life. It isn't just a representational portrait in oil on canvas, he explains. It's a *real woman*. He has brought her to life. While this may be an old man's crazy talk, the story seems to suggest, also, the idea of a genius who sees something the younger and less talented artists don't, as with Cézanne and his repetitive and obsessive Mont Sainte-Victoire paintings that few understood in his lifetime, and Picasso with his game-changing *Les Demoiselles d'Avignon* in 1906, which was also misunderstood (even by Matisse) and hidden from view for years.

At the end of Balzac's novella, Frenhofer, after overhearing his friends' criticisms, acknowledges his failure to bring his dead lover back to life on canvas. His humiliation is just too much to bear, and that night, after everyone has left his studio, Frenhofer destroys all of his work and himself. He is found dead the next day.

Arthur Danto, who started out as an artist (woodblock prints) before turning to philosophy, then art criticism for *The Nation* magazine beginning in the 1980s, describes Balzac/Frenhofer's masterpiece as possibly the first truly modernist painting, albeit in literary form. It's impossible to suggest, as Danto makes clear, that Balzac had Impressionism in mind, let alone

Cubism or Expressionism. But Cézanne and Picasso must have seen themselves in Balzac's hero, an artist who so believed in the magic of his art and its ability to represent reality that he could say to his dubious friends, "You're in the presence of a woman. And you're still looking for a picture." Perhaps Frenhofer was also an object lesson for Cézanne and Picasso. Balzac's artist succumbed to doubt at the end of his life. Cézanne and Picasso did not.

Outside the gate to Picasso's residence, I wonder about my obsession with *The Girl* and consider the absurd possibility that this is all some grandiose Frenhoferian aberration, the confusion of a girl portrayed on canvas with a real girl. But there is method in my madness. As I attach my poster to the wall just below Picasso's plaque, suspecting that the concierge of the building will tear it down that same day, I believe that I am both violating and embracing the historic narrative embedded at this address. If only for a day or two, I have placed *The Girl in Red*, and myself, into that narrative.

TENDING TO

MY ATTACHMENTS

o

I'm discovering how attached I am to my attachments. I seem to regard each poster mounted on a wall or kiosk, or in a café or shop window, like a newborn child a parent anxiously checks on in the middle of the night. It's as if I've forgotten about the original purpose of the posters, to uncover facts about *The Girl in Red*. Instead, the postings are becoming some sort of installation piece documented in words and images.

There have been no responses to the postings to date. If none are forthcoming, my project may yet succeed on this secondary aesthetic level—the collected texts and photo documentation of a month in Paris, bringing a yearlong Tintinian treasure hunt to a close. On a more psychological level, everything I fail to learn about *The Girl in Red* is something I am learning about myself and my relationship to art. And to failure. The expression "It's the journey not the destination that counts" may be literally true (one never actually finds the Holy Grail), but it's a cliché that fails to convince some who are following my quest, and at times, me.

I think there is also a bit of separation anxiety associated with my "attachment attachment." In the case of an infant, when the parent leaves the room, the child imagines they will never see the parent again, which causes panic and crying. From the other side, when the parents come to the room in the middle of the night, it's not because they imagine the child is gone but because they want to assure themselves that the child is alive, or just to admire their new loved one, the miracle of a child, *their* child. I am responding to my posters as both child and parent—I want the poster to be there *and* I want to admire it.

At Café de Flore again, I have positioned myself at a table in full sight of the poster. Flore is close by my apartment, has free Wi-Fi, and is convivial, with great people-watching credentials. I prefer it to the more formal, more luxurious Deux Magots. Mostly, now, I come because I am the very proud father of my newborn! Yesterday, I took a selfie with the poster reflected in the giant wall mirror as I looked down on the stairway from just outside the café's upper-level *toilettes*.

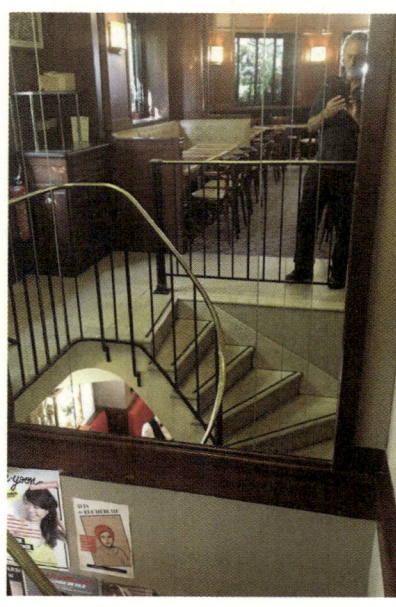

Through the upper-level mirror at Café de Flore, a selfie with the poster at lower left

Although the coffee is not very good at Flore (nor at most traditional cafés in Paris), if you melt into your café crème the little wrapped chocolate square that comes on the saucer, you can cut the bitterness of the inferior robusta coffee beans by turning your crème into a mocha. A little sugar helps too. Yesterday, a very hot July day, I did this, and then poured the concoction over a glass of ice cubes that I had requested from the accommodating garçon. My mediocre crème became a tasty and refreshing iced mocha. It's not on the menu, of course, and if it were, it would be double the already high price of a crème. Is this the kind of practice that gives American tourists a bad name in Paris, or is it a food writer's prerogative? Confession is good for the soul.

While enjoying my mocha and my view of *The Girl*, I receive an email from my cousin Stuart in Los Angeles commenting on my postering project, which he is following on Facebook: "Cousin John, you need to get a life!" he teases. A retired interior designer, he is now a full-time painter and a full-time teaser. I have a life, I respond, just not one that takes place within the four walls of an art studio as his does. Paris is my studio, a flâneur's studio. "Got it," he says.

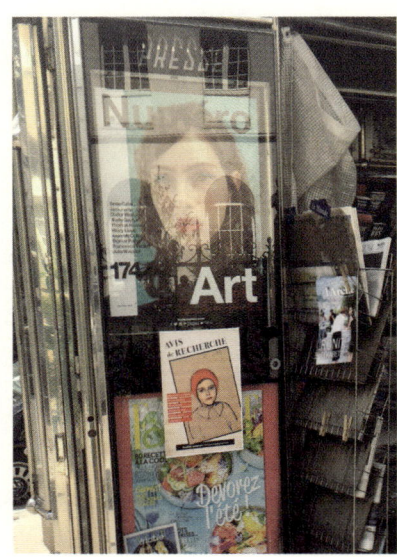

A poster mounted over an ad on a kiosk door on blvd. Saint-Germain

Close by Flore, at a newspaper kiosk facing the Ukrainian church on the corner of rue des Saints Pères and blvd. Saint-Germain, I am surprised to find an affiche that is still up several days after posting. I had placed it on one of the folding glass doors after the kiosk had closed up in the evening, not realizing that the next morning the poster might be hidden by the doors in their open, folded position. Luckily, that is not the case. An advertising affiche inserted in the plastic holder behind my poster has been changed out, but my poster is still there, suggesting that the operator has seen it and decided to leave it. I could have thanked the fellow, purchased a magazine I don't really want—or just tipped him—but I'm afraid that calling attention to my poster might backfire.

Let sleeping posters, like sleeping dogs and sleeping babies, lie.

RUE VISCONTI, BONNARD,
AND MORE BALZAC

∘

This day of flâneuring and posting begins with another visit with Fanny Vanoye at Galerie de l'Europe. Her gallery is so close to ground zero that I pass it almost daily and stop in to say hello. I ask her to pose in front of one of her canvases while holding a poster of *The Girl*. I note the similar orangey reds in her painting and the poster. She agrees.

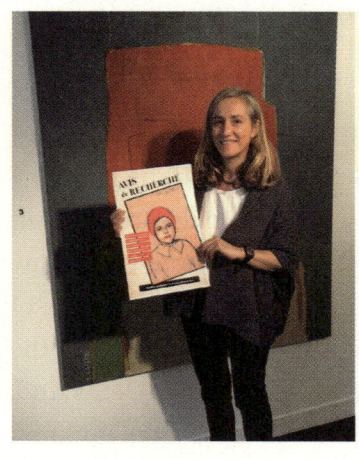

The artist Fanny Vanoye at Galerie de l'Europe in front of one of her paintings

The kind of painting Fanny does—abstract, gestural, improvisational—was barely on the horizon in the Paris art scene of 1935. Her influences came a generation later, from the 1940s through the 1970s, among them, she says, Twombly, de Staël, Kiefer and Soulages. She describes her art in a flyer available at the gallery: "My painting . . . is the result of a multiplicity of moments; it is not like a regular process. . . . And at a certain unpredictable moment the unexpected happens. It is like a number of steps to the unknown that comes to an end when the created work meets my sensibility."

Yes, "steps to the unknown." The emphasis on process over a preconceived result is, again, an important theme in contemporary art. And a perfect metaphor for the Parisian flâneur, the artist of the streets, the first modern artist who travels without a destination. And for my journey with *The Girl in Red*.

Fanny's sensibility is totally consistent, also, with certain ideas about the distinction between art and craft. The craftsperson knows what they are doing; the artist often doesn't until a work is finished, and maybe not even then. Craft may be necessary for great art, but it's not sufficient. One can speculate that the artist of *The Girl in Red* began their task with no final outcome in mind, stopping short of a "finished" painting when the image had met their sensibility, just as Fanny describes her process (and Rembrandt his).

But what can be said about the style of *The Girl's* artist? What were the influences? By 1935, Cubism, followed by Surrealism, was dominant in Paris. But there is nothing remotely cubist or surrealist about *The Girl*. The only thing surreal about *The Girl* is her emergence in my life, and just about everything that has flowed from it. Perhaps our mystery artist was one of the holdouts for an expressive realism working in Paris in the 1930s. One might guess that they looked back to Degas and, especially, Manet, whose broad brush strokes, black outlines, flattened perspective and everyday subject matter—including the scandalous use of prostitutes as models—made him arguably the first modern painter.

Pierre Bonnard might have been a more contemporary,

albeit indirect, influence for *The Girl*'s creator. Another holdout for figurative art during the '30s, Bonnard paid a price for it, being considered by some as passé, frivolous and merely decorative. Picasso was quoted saying nasty things about Bonnard in the 1940s, that he was the end of an old idea about art—not modern or, as we might say today, edgy. Matisse, however, came strongly to Bonnard's defense, created a close relationship with him and hailed him as a genius. Bonnard's reputation has steadily grown ever since. I think Picasso couldn't really "see" Bonnard because no major painter of the period that I'm aware of was less Picasso than Pierre Bonnard. Bonnard was not a destroyer, like the bullfight-loving, some would say woman-hating Spaniard. Bonnard was pure lover. He was French.

A Bonnard retrospective I attended at San Francisco's Palace of the Legion of Honor, just before leaving for Paris this summer, was a huge affirmation of Bonnard's greatness, and my first real in-person exposure to his work. A painting on display dated 1935 caught my eye (of course), *Table Corner*. It's described by Julian Barnes in *Keeping an Eye Open* as "one of the most discreetly alarming pictures of the century." Avoiding the dramatic distortions of Picasso, it's a painting on the edge of realism in more ways than one. The barely identifiable objects resting near the table's corner appear to be leaning, about to fall off. A tiny wooden chair lies almost horizontal on the ground (or is it floating?) below the edge of the table. Yet despite its sense of chaos—vertigo is more like it—the painting is formally harmonious, and in true Bonnard fashion, the colors are vivid and lush. This picture is far from merely decorative—it's gorgeous, very French, and literally edgy.

I focused even more on Bonnard's self-portrait from 1904,

a non finito work, with loose brushwork that is more radical than that in *The Girl in Red*. A self-indulgence, says one Bonnard critic, a not fully realized work, but I get the impression that Bonnard knew when to stop with this piece, at the point where Delacroix's warning kicks in: finishing a work of art can do harm to what is right about it.

On the other hand, it has been said that Bonnard never felt that his paintings were finished, would work on them sometimes for years, and in one case, surreptitiously touched up a painting on display in a museum. Bonnard spoke for himself in his work, no matter what his critics said, and I know of no other modern artist who has spoken more vividly, more intimately, and more expressively than Bonnard.

After reiterating her promise to put up the poster of *The Girl* in her studio back home, Fanny and I say our goodbyes, and I continue my stroll along rue de Seine toward the river and rue Visconti where I had posted an affiche a few days earlier. More an alleyway than a street, the narrow, three-hundred-year-old rue Visconti, a survivor of Napoleon III's urban renewal, connects rue de Seine to rue Bonaparte, virtually at the entrance to the École des Beaux-Arts. The street's residential history is chock-full of colorful characters and intrigue, but what struck me when I began to dig into it some years ago is rue Visconti's relationship to Balzac. The author lived and worked as a printer at nos. 17 and 19 beginning in 1826. He failed as a printer there, though his shop, taken over by the son of a former lover, would later print Stendhal's *The Red and the Black*.

Serializing my adventures with *The Girl* via social media—much as Balzac had done with his novels and articles in newspaper supplements known as *feuilletons (feuille* is

French for "leaf")—connects me to Balzac's literary strategy, if not his literary talent and output. Feuilletons offered witty, concise, ironic and personal articles to feed a growing middle-class hunger for general entertainment, not just news. I've modeled my social media postings about *The Girl* on the feuilleton, as first drafts for the longer pieces that may appear in a book.

Rue Visconti also triggers my identification with Balzac's love of fine food (gluttony, actually) and the hard-to-believe fifty-cup-a-day coffee addiction that killed him, according to biographer Graham Robb. That's "identify with," not "matching of." But that's another feuilleton.

It's curious to me that for years now, I've gravitated to rue Visconti, long before the Balzac connection emerged. It's not as if there is much to see on the street, a fairly deserted and claustrophobic residential stretch with only a few nondescript shops and galleries in its architectural mix. The street is so narrow that the artist Christo and his wife, Jeanne-Claude, were able to close it off in 1962 with his installation *Wall of Oil Barrels—The Iron Curtain*. Eighty-nine wrapped and painted barrels created a fourteen-foot-high barricade that blocked the street for eight hours, obstructing most of the traffic through the Left Bank. But I come to rue Visconti to feel, not to see. There is something deeply embedded in this urban geography, something both familiar and strange, like going back in time to a place I knew in a former life, perhaps in Balzac's Paris. If I were to live in Paris full-time, rue Visconti would be my own ground zero.

Arriving at the corner of rue de Seine and rue Visconti, I'm delighted to find that my poster has survived, and startled by another poster placed alongside, virtually touching it. It's an affiche for the opening of an exhibit by a Russian painter working in Paris, Ekaterina Aristova. The painting reproduced on the poster is a portrait of a young female with a blue head covering. I'll call her *The Girl in Blue*. The two posters mounted side by side remind me of Millet's *Les glaneuses*, two women working next to each other, one wearing a red head covering, the other a blue one. I must meet this Ekaterina Aristova and get her take on *The Girl in Red*. Did she herself place her poster next to mine? I'll go to the opening and find out.

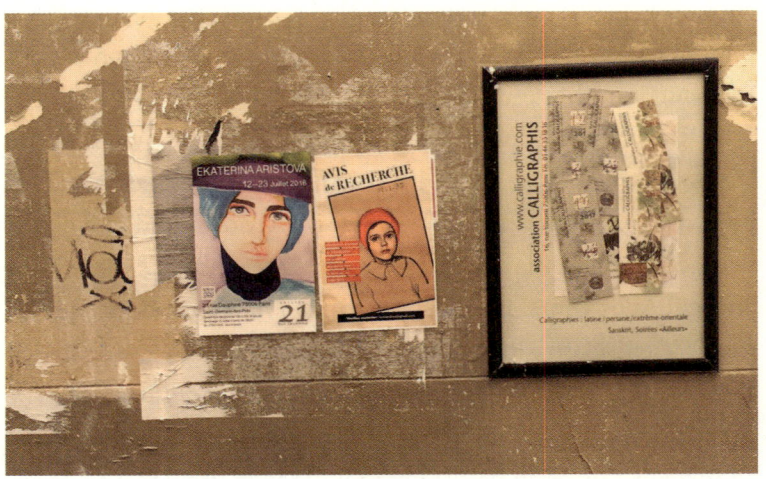

The Girl in Blue *joins* The Girl in Red *on rue Visconti.*

o

FIRST CONTACT

o

A poster mounted on blvd. Saint-Germain near Café de Flore, across the street from Brasserie Lipp, was tagged today. This is the first unsolicited response to the poster, though of little apparent consequence.

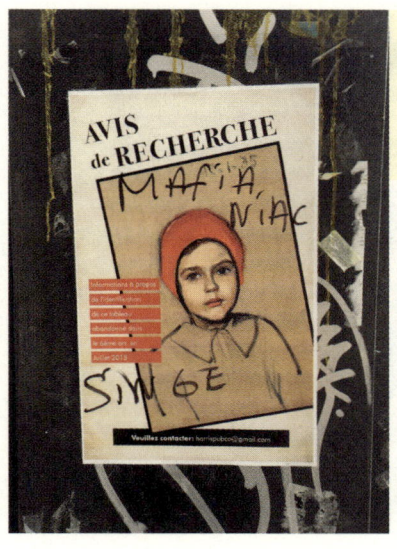

Tagged on blvd. Saint-Germain, the poster covers up the graffiti on the kiosk behind it.

The tag's three elements are:

MAFIA
NIAC
SINGE

Carefully removing the poster and replacing it with a fresh one, I bring it back to the apartment for further analysis. Googling NIAC, I turn up the National Iranian American Council, a lobbying group that supports good relations between the two countries. Some call it a pro-Iranian front, but no need to go there.

The bottom word in the tag is challenging. Is the letter an *N*? Is this someone's name? What's the language? In English, *singe* means "to burn." In French it means "monkey," and in an obscure French translation, it refers to corned beef. It's not a word in Farsi, according to a Persian friend. I imagine corned beef made with monkey meat, but no need to go there either.

Is there any reason for this tag beyond the poster being an available surface to mark? Did the tagger think *The Girl*'s head cover was a Muslim woman's hijab? Michael Ondaatje, the Canadian writer, has said, "Everyone has to scratch on walls somewhere or they go crazy." True. And paradoxical because graffiti can be interpreted conservatively as a destructive social act by someone *already* crazy. The lines and tags blur.

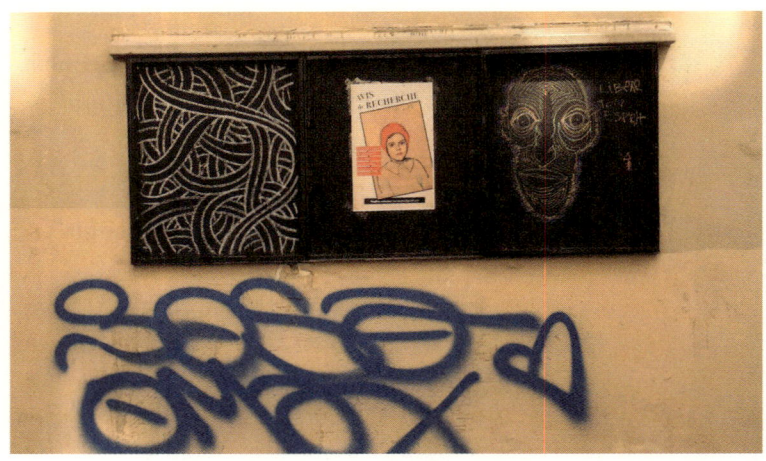

Surrounded by graffiti on rue Jacob

I send a photo of the tag to a friend in California who spent a lot of time when young as a graffiti artist. He writes back: "The placement of *SINGE* at the bottom makes it possible it is some kind of moniker, but this is not the work of a graffiti artist in the normal sense, who would typically have a more refined style of handwriting, repeating his *nom de plume* over and over again. I would guess it was just an opportunistic passerby, perhaps with a political agenda, someone who carries around a marker like a Sharpie or Marks-a-Lot."

The tagged poster will go into the archives of the Girl in Red Poster Project, the first response to my posting mission. I hope not the last.

POSTER IN THE POUBELLE

o

It was inevitable that an aroused merchant or resident would rip down a poster from one of my more aggressive, perhaps invasive, placements and toss it in the poubelle. I am surprised by how hard I take it.

The French language can make anything sound sweet, like *toilette* for toilet. Poubelle is the language's relatively new and unintentionally ironic Anglophonic term for trash can and trash—which I like to translate as "beautiful poo." The word actually derives from the name of the man who popularized the use of containers for domestic garbage collection in late nineteenth-century France—Eugène Poubelle.

I had placed a poster on a narrow vertical strip of wall between the door and display window of a vintage print and poster shop on blvd. Saint-Germain, just a few steps from the entrance to my apartment building. It was about 9 p.m., and darkness was falling. In the shop window were two very large posters on display, one advertising a Brigitte Bardot film, *La Parisienne*, and the other, an old Paris travel poster showing the amazing view through the smaller Arc de Triomphe du Carrousel outside the Louvre, all the way to the Arc de Triomphe de l'Étoile at the Champs Elysées. The display was dramatically illuminated, and the juxtaposition of the vintage posters and my *Girl* gave me a thrill, just as Bardot had given me and the entire world a thrill in the 1960s.

I took a photo.

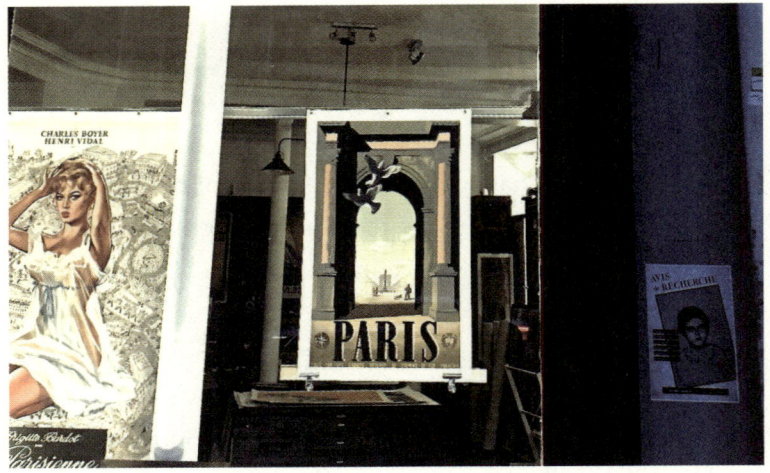

At a vintage poster shop at night, my poster at right in the darkness

Back at the apartment, I discover that in the shot the poster is almost totally shrouded in the growing darkness. I will have to go back to try again. Then, in the morning, approaching the poster shop as I head out for my "first coffee" at Le Saint-Germain, my *café du coin* (corner café) on rue du Bac, I see an empty space where the poster had been. I pause, crushed, taking in the void, the first teardown.

Continuing on blvd. Saint-Germain toward the café, I pass a corner poubelle and there she is, peering up at me through the transparent plastic liner. Stunned, I am taken back to the painful sight of my severely jaundiced firstborn son all bundled up, isolated and pathetic, staring out from behind the glass window of the newborn intensive care unit. Should I salvage this crumpled poster and add it to my Paris poster archive? I take a photo and continue walking. It will still be there, no doubt, when I return from breakfast.

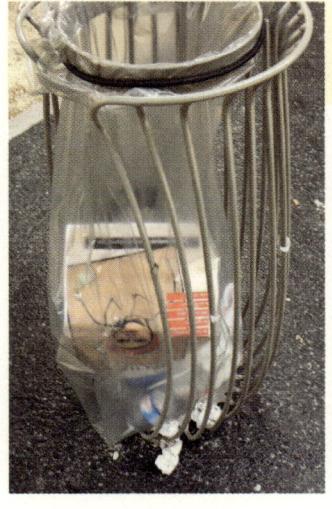

Poster in the poubelle

Somewhat restored after my *petit déjeuner*, heading back toward rue de Seine for more posting, I decide to leave the trashed poster where it is and not repost at the same location. But I anxiously survey previous posting locations now, expecting the worst. I'm relieved to see that all the posters are still up, safe and sound.

Once back in the area of galleries and shops that radiate out from either side of rue de Seine, I begin to post, aware that I'm still taking each placement too seriously. "Get a life," my cousin said in his email after the first posting at Café de Flore. I think about how a soldier might feel when, close up, he witnesses for the first time a comrade fall in battle. I have not fought in a war, or even been close to one, so I have no clue. I don't mean to sound insensitive (or conceited), but I'm an *artiste* not a warrior, and like Mark Twain dodging the Civil War, I dodged the Vietnam War. In truth, though prepared to claim conscientious objector status, I was rejected at my physical in 1969.

The attachments in my life, work and politics are pacifistic and internationalist, not martial and nationalistic. So I steel myself against the pain of inevitable losses and vow to keep my focus on the routine task at hand—posting, not pouting.

RITUAL CROQUES

o

For lunch today at La Palette, about two weeks into my mission and just a few days before the wild and wonderful citywide Bastille Day *fête* that will swallow Paris on July 14, I will order croques, this time in honor of *The Girl*, not out of professional duty. The entire day is dedicated to the official return of *The Girl in Red* to Paris (symbolically via mechanical reproduction) almost one year after her emergence out of the shadows of art history.

Fanny Vanoye is joining me at La Palette along with a few of her friends to share in the celebration. One of them, Francesca, a French teacher from New Jersey, is visiting Paris with her students, some of whom will join us at the table. It's not exactly a cult of *The Girl in Red*, but I'm feeling the love today and a wave of energy generated by Bastille Day vibes already in the air. The apparent failure of my mission to uncover *The Girl*'s provenance (no responses to my poster from or about the previous owner of *The Girl* after dozens of postings) seems, at least for the moment, unimportant.

I pass out posters to everyone at the table and tell my story. One of Francesca's students, Jessica, gets quite excited about *The Girl*. She believes she resembles her, especially the lips, she says, and vows to dress up like *The Girl* back home and send me a photo for my project archives.

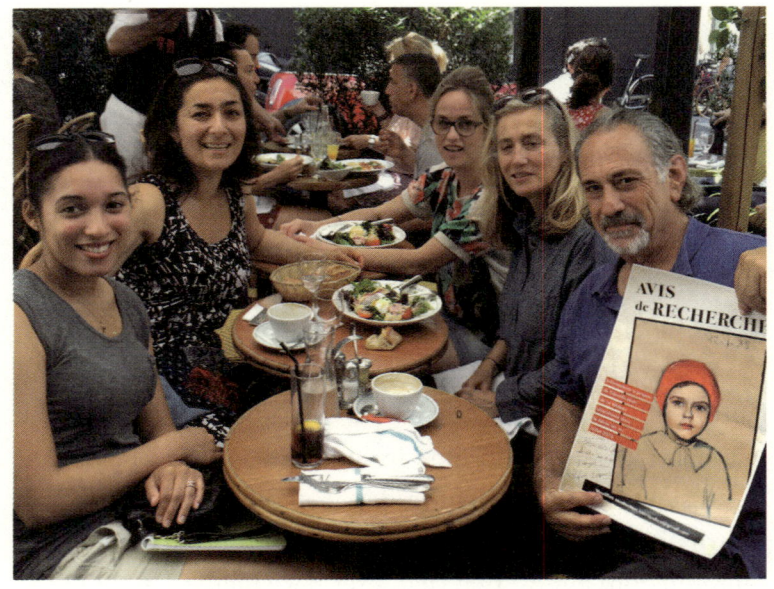

I am with Fanny Vanoye and friends at La Palette.
Jessica is at the lower left.

Jessica is not, however, the first real girl to identify with *The Girl*. Soon after I posted the portrait online last summer, a New York friend, the jazz guitarist Steve Khan, got a response to his sharing of my post from his friends the trumpeter Randy Brecker of Brecker Brothers jazz fame and his wife, the saxophonist Ada Rovatti. Their seven-year-old daughter, Stella, made herself up like *The Girl* and stood in front of a neutral background. They took a photo and sent it to Steve, and he passed it on to me with their approval after putting a Photoshopped frame around it.

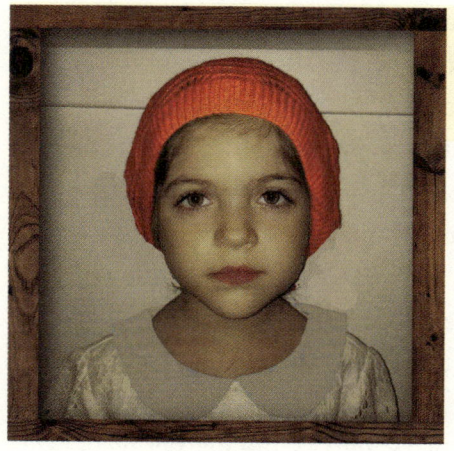

Following my brief presentation to Fanny and her friends, I order croques for the table (my treat), and, exactly as last summer, they arrive open faced on rustic Poilâne bread and without discernible (or tasteable) béchamel sauce. I say nothing to my guests about this anomaly because today is not about critical eating or, as I like to call it, left-brain analytical eating. It's about emotional, right-brain eating. The croque is our ritual food, like matzo at Passover or the wafer at Holy Communion. Only the most obnoxious foodie (or food critic) would judge the taste or texture of the matzo or the wafer at their respective sacraments.

After feasting and farewells, I venture up the street to rue Guénégaud to place yet another poster near the doorway at no. 35, on the wall just above the exact spot, ground zero, where I found *The Girl*. The poster I had already taped to the scaffolding on my first day back in Paris is gone, along with the scaffolding. This posting won't last either. I'm OK now.

I had invited Lucien Godin—the resident at no. 35 who reached out regarding *The Girl* to his neighboring galleries last year—to the lunch, but was informed by his partner, Anne, that he had passed away several months earlier after a short and unexpected battle with cancer. I was deeply saddened by the news. As I stand in front of Anne and Lucien's front door now, I speak out loud, "Farewell Lucien, and eternal thanks to you for your help with *The Girl in Red*. Rest in peace."

I had wanted Anne to join our group in Lucien's place after hearing the news, but she was not available. We made a date to meet at Le Bistrot Mazarin, just steps from her apartment, before I leave Paris, to discuss a plan for continuing the poster campaign after I'm gone. In honor of Lucien, Anne says she will take his place in my search.

Heading home now along rue Guénégaud, I stop at Galerie Arnoux to request permission to tape a poster near their door. I show the poster to two gallerists, but neither recognizes the image. They both love *The Girl* and are happy to have me post it. They promise to get in touch if they find out anything.

Attaching the poster, I stand back to take a picture when a fellow in a cowboy hat walks up to read the text. He must be a tourist, because I can't recall ever seeing a Frenchman wearing this type of Western-style hat. I can imagine the great Jean-Paul Belmondo wearing one in some French New Wave film, but a quick search of the web on my cell comes up blank. Belmondo once said, "Every Frenchman dreams of making a Western." His signature hat is a *borsellino*, the Italian version of the fedora worn all over the world. And by me. Further checking online for images of French cowboys reveals that those working in the south of France today wear fedoras while herding cattle. This doesn't compute. Imagine Roy Rogers in a beret.

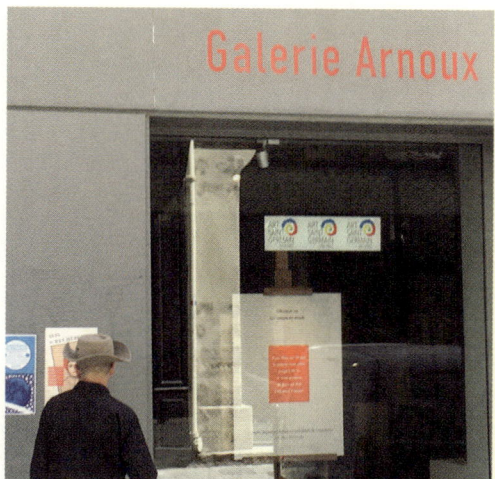

A gentleman in a cowboy hat reading the poster's text outside Galerie Arnoux on rue Guénégaud

Almost giddy now, riding high on ritual croques and sidewalk serendipity, I leave a trail of posters all along my route home.

DASHED HOPES AND
MINI-CROQUES

○

After a postritual nap in the comfortable red leather armchair in the apartment's guest quarters, I start preparations for yet another croque-centered celebration, a gathering with friends in the grand salon. Peter Jackson, a chef acquaintance visiting from Berkeley, has agreed to make several styles of croques for an *apéro*—a French happy hour—in honor of *The Girl*'s return to Paris. I had suggested to Peter via email that we make a variety of croques and cut them into little hors d'oeuvre–sized pieces as I had them last year at the bar at La Closerie des Lilas, one of Ernest Hemingway's favorite cafés. We will serve them with wine and assorted mixed drinks along with olives, cheese and pâté.

Peter had worked in several acclaimed Bay Area restaurants from the 1970s through the '90s, most notably at Jeremiah Tower's legendary San Francisco bistro, Stars. With Peter agreeing to focus on the humble croque, the results are guaranteed to be masterful, traditionally correct, and tastier than anything I had sampled last year for my croque monsieur survey.

As it turns out, the highlight of the evening is not a traditional croque but a hybrid version Peter has devised using French Comté cheese, milder than the usual Gruyère, and some expensive truffled Italian ham that we bought together at the Bon Marché, along with a loaf of pain de mie. With just a light schmear of béchamel on top of the lightly pan-toasted croques before they went under the broiler until golden brown, they are sublime. The French croque has never had it so good, or so Italian.

One of my guests, a gay American expat, laughingly labels this truffled improv a *panini in drag*. "A macho Italian grilled ham and cheese," he goofs, "dressed up in a silky, saucy béchamel." Everyone cheers.

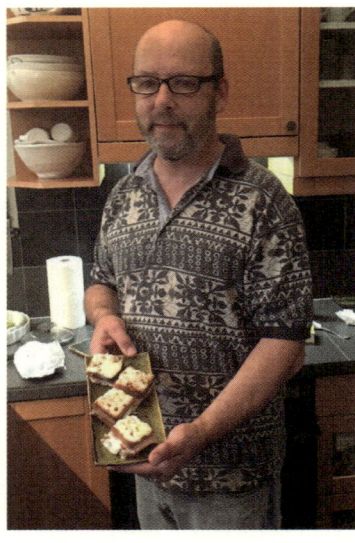

Chef Peter Jackson's perfectly toasted mini-croques

After bidding our guests adieu, Peter and I discuss a repeat performance back in Berkeley to prepare recipes I can publish online as a follow-up to my *Zester* magazine article. We wash the dishes, and off he goes. I am exhausted, and, as often happens after I celebrate—no matter how delighted I am by the event—my mood goes somber. Alone now in my château, existential gris turns gray-blue.

It dawns on me as I prepare for bed, perhaps as a bit of consolation for the washout so far with poster responses, that I don't have to eat another croque, ever—professional croques or ritual croques—a sandwich that, if truth be told, I have never truly loved, not being a huge fan of the default Gruyère cheese and its aged and slightly bitter nuttiness the French obviously adore. I am, finally, fed up with croques! Peter's variation on the Closerie des Lilas format will stand as an exception that I will gladly serve at future apéros, in Paris or back home.

Sinking into bed, the day's festivities fighting against the ennui of dashed hopes, I word-play the idea that the nuttiness of my adventure in Paris will end up, like Gruyère, with a bitter aftertaste. Humor buffers depression. I remind myself yet again with an affirmation mantra: it's the journey that counts, it's the journey that counts, it's the journey that counts. But where will this journey take me next? I fall asleep before I can make a guess.

MY *MONA LISA* VERSUS

THE *MONA LISA*

o

Approaching my one-year anniversary with *The Girl in Red* and the end of my Paris mission, I've decided to squeeze in a visit to the Louvre for a viewing of Leonardo da Vinci's *Mona Lisa*. Seeing her "in the flesh" will be instructive, reinforcing what some might describe as the negligible art historical (and monetary) value of *The Girl in Red*. I consider this visit my duty as a journalist-flâneur, a report from the source, the home of perhaps the greatest portrait in the history of portraiture.

I have seen Leonardo's *Lisa* more than once, but today's exercise is not really about "seeing" her, which is nearly impossible in any case, given the crowds in front of it, the distance one must stand from it, and the thickness of the armored glass that covers her climate-controlled shrine. No, this viewing is for the purpose of a comparative analysis—*my Mona Lisa* versus *the Mona Lisa*. An absurd task, perhaps, like comparing an American ice cream sundae (simple and, at its best, delicious) to a French *bombe glacée* (complex and, at its best, epiphanic).

It's obvious that *The Girl in Red* cannot be judged on anywhere near the same aesthetic grounds as Leonardo's Renaissance masterpiece, given the extraordinary refinement and complexity of the portrait (both the central subject and the background), the techniques he invented and applied to the painting, and the many years of painstaking work that went into its many layers (physical and conceptual). The genius of Leonardo that appears to exceed mere mortal talent places the *Mona Lisa* into a pantheon of high art well beyond *The Girl*'s reach. Agreed, though *The Girl*'s twentieth-century artist, in their defense, would not have aspired to Leonardo's level of technical refinement given modernist criteria for expressive portraiture.

As objects, however—*objects* of art, not objects of *art*—there is a lot about these two paintings I can compare, extending beyond narrow aesthetic considerations, a task better suited to professional critics and art historians. I am thinking of myself today as, say, a passionate art history student assigned by his professor to write a compare-and-contrast essay, or a travel magazine stringer in Paris researching a story about the *Mona Lisa*.

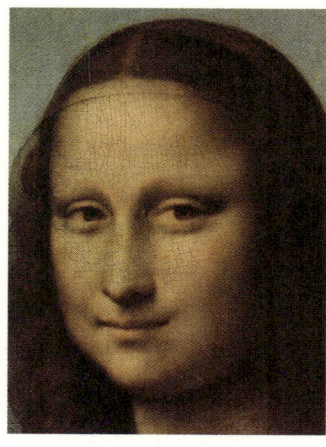 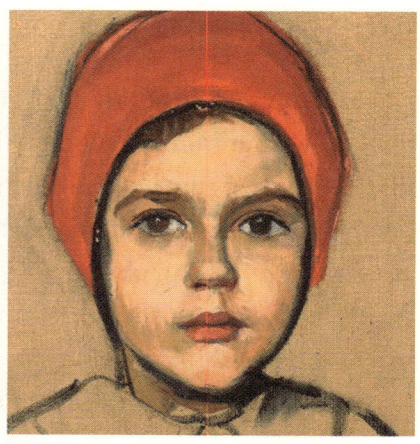

The Mona Lisa (*close-up*)   *My* Mona Lisa (*close-up*)

En route to the Louvre, a flâneur's stroll from my apartment across the Seine via the Pont Royal, I consider the aura of my anonymous lost and found *Girl in Red*. She is in Berkeley, of course, but her aura is embedded in my memory. How does the potent pictorial presence of my simple portrait compare to that of the most celebrated portrait (and possibly the best-known face) in history, *La Joconde*, as the *Mona Lisa* is known to the French (based on the surname of Lisa's husband, Francesco del Giocondo, who commissioned the portrait)?

It's important to note, though not a new note, that the extraordinary fame and value of Leonardo's painting—an insured value today of a billion dollars or more—exploded following the scandal involving the painting's theft in 1911, four centuries after it was created. Picasso and his friend the poet Guillaume Apollinaire were suspected by the police. Picasso had to suffer the humiliation of appearing in court, but he was not held. Apollinaire did go to jail, but for his involvement in the theft from the Louvre of Iberian relics, not the *Mona Lisa*.

My anonymous and not-even-a-century-old *Girl in Red* carries no known historical baggage or notoriety, let alone scandal—none at all except for my Facebook postings last year and whatever else may follow from my activities this summer and beyond. The late film critic and author Parker Tyler explored the idea of scandal in the arts in his 1964 book, *Every Artist His Own Scandal*. One can imagine today a sequel: *Every Work of Art Its Own Scandal*. The *Mona Lisa* would be chapter 1.

The stories (sometimes scandalous, sometimes just silly) that swirl around Leonardo's portrait heighten the effect of the painting's most expressive pictorial elements: her direct gaze, her enigmatic smile, her gossamer veil and her dramatic Tuscan background—an underappreciated dream-like setting. The stories seem to trump these pictorial particulars.

My French teacher, another Lisa, Lisa Taylor, recalls reading that Leonardo's model, the twenty-four-year-old Lisa Gherardini, didn't want Leonardo to finish the portrait because she feared that after selling it, he would forget her. This apocryphal legend purports to explain the *Mona Lisa*'s enigmatic expression—the "*Mona Lisa* smile." On one side of her face (the left, with her slightly upturned mouth), she appears happy to be sitting for Leonardo, and on the other side (the right, with her slightly downturned mouth), unhappy to have the portrait finished.

Taylor's story presents just one of many fanciful factoids that follow in the *Mona Lisa*'s art historical wake, reinforcing her "exhibition value," as Walter Benjamin would describe it. Some of these make Taylor's tale seem rather tame: one purporting to prove that the *Mona Lisa* is really a portrait of Leonard's assistant and lover, the young boy Salai; or that the two dissonant sides of *Mona Lisa*'s face reveal the composite portrait of Salai and Leonardo himself; or that there are magical symbols embedded in the paint.

Sigmund Freud had his own idea about the *Mona Lisa* smile, described in his book *Leonardo da Vinci: A Psychosexual Study of an Infantile Reminiscence* (1910)—that it matches the smile on Leonardo's mother's face after he suckled on her nipple. In Freud's interpretation, the *Mona Lisa* is a portrait of the mother based on Leonard's repressed erotic attachment to her. Now that's scandalous! And to my mind, an example of Freud taking Freudianism too seriously.

The real-world *Mona Lisa* scandal relating to its theft in 1911 by the dim-witted Italian patriot, Vincenzo Peruggia, is better documented. Before the heist, Leonardo's portrait was greatly admired, but not yet worshipped. It hung on a wall among all the other Renaissance paintings in the Louvre and was praised by most critics as one of the finest portraits ever painted. There was good reason—mostly aesthetic—why it was coveted by kings and emperors (King Francis I and Napoleon). But after the theft, and with the help of print technology (the "gift" of mechanical reproduction), it became a publicly worshipped image reproduced in newspapers and art books, and on postcards, one that would eventually be appropriated by such artists as Marcel Duchamp and Andy Warhol for their artistic and parodic purposes. The *Mona Lisa* became the most talked about and joked about, reproduced and caricatured, visually quoted and parodied art object (and face) in history.

Although the Mona Lisa's face has become the butt of countless art jokes, one in particular is worth underscoring. When Marcel Duchamp drew a mustache and goatee onto the *Mona Lisa* on a postcard (*L.H.O.O.Q.*, 1919), it was a Dadaist desecration almost as sacrilegious in art historical terms as placing a crown of thorns on Christ. Just as there would be no Christianity without Christ's crucifixion, many postmodern art trends and movements would be inconceivable without this violation of the *Mona Lisa* (the symbol of classic feminine beauty)— combined with Duchamp's other pranks, especially his submission of a store-bought urinal, which he titled *Fountain* (1917), to an American gallery exhibit. (*Fountain* was rejected and actually lost, but that's an art scandal for another magazine article: compare and contrast Leonardo da Vinci and Marcel Duchamp as geniuses who changed art in their time and for all time.)

As I manage a glimpse of the *Mona Lisa* today through the crowds, I have the thought that she is no longer an objet d'art at all, the reverse of Duchamp's trick of posing everyday objects as works of art. She has been transformed from an everyday art object—a painting—into the holy relic of some new postmodern religion. Walter Benjamin's ideas about cult value (private works controlled by elites) transitioning to exhibition value (works on display in museums for public consumption) and then on to mass-produced (aura-free) democratized images based on technology (photography and cinema)—this progression didn't anticipate the power of aura to persist as a parody of itself. A brand.

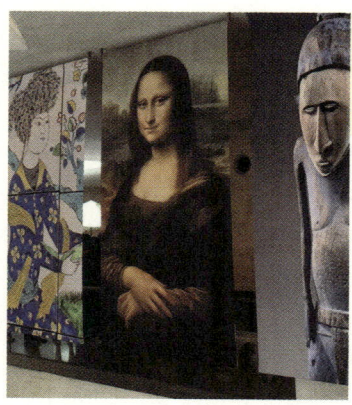

A large Mona Lisa *banner at the Louvre*

As I see it today at the Louvre, the authentic, original, auratic *Mona Lisa* is being purchased and consumed by its audience, not felt. This view is influenced by what the neo-Marxist cultural critic Guy Debord, the late founder of the Situationist International movement in the 1960s, labeled the "spectacle," the simulation of reality we swim in today, a sea of mediated, branded images. In this sense, the Louvre is a church that has enshrined the spectacle of the art world, and the *Mona Lisa* is its most sacred idol.

Meanwhile, back in the mundane art world, my scandal-free and spectacle-free *Girl in Red* remains in private hands, mounted in its owner's home where any visitor can walk up close and look deep into her eyes. Her lips are sealed and she speaks only through her eyes, and only with questions: Do you feel what I feel? Where am I going, and what will happen to me? Who will I become when I grow up? There is no enigmatic *Mona Lisa* smile. Lisa Gherardini is smiling, I believe, because she has no questions. She's a young, confident, and well-married bourgeois woman, and she has all the answers—or so I imagine after years of looking at her in all her guises, from cult object to museum exhibit to printed reproduction to, now, church icon.

There was always a note of scandal about the *Mona Lisa*, even in Leonardo's day. Women of that time, especially young women on canvas, were not supposed to make eye contact with viewers, especially male viewers. Modesty prevailed. Models weren't even supposed to smile. This same air of scandal applies to Johannes Vermeer's *Girl with a Pearl Earring*, unknown after Vermeer's death in 1675 until she reemerged at the end of the nineteenth century. Known now as the "Mona Lisa of the North," the painting's subject makes direct eye contact with the viewer, which, along with her slightly open mouth, was considered immodest. For my twentieth-century portrait of another young female, an innocent child, this is not an issue. But after the scandal of Édouard Manet's *Déjeuner sur l'herbe* (1867), everything changed. Manet's model is not only confronting the viewer head-on; she is a naked prostitute who appears to offer the male viewer an opportunity, or, depending on your interpretation, withholds one.

It will take another few hundred years to see what will become of *The Girl in Red*, the object and the painting. Will she, like her much older Renaissance sisters, enter our cultural spectacle? Will she be displayed in a museum-church, worshipped by adoring crowds? Will her image be appropriated for online catalogs filled with branded "merch"—posters, coffee mugs and T-shirts? Will she become known as the "Mona Lisa of Berkeley?" Stay tuned.

Finally, my compare-and-contrast essay must consider *The Girl*'s capitalist commodity value in relation to the *Mona Lisa*. Will *The Girl* soar in value as she ages and attracts notoriety, if not scandal? Was it "a good investment" when I picked her up? This consideration of art as financial investment obscures for some observers the truest value of art. According to the gallerist Michael Findlay (Acquavella Galleries in New York) in his book *The Value of Art*, a work's market value is only one indicator of its cultural relevance. As he explains, "Treating works of art as no more than financial instruments robs them of their potential to achieve or maintain popularity through exposure and discussion and thus inhibits what helps them increase in social and commercial value." My *Mona Lisa* and I say, "Amen."

STRING THEORY IN LONDON

o

Although my big plans for Paris this summer didn't include a second trip to London, I am eager to return now to escape the shockingly dark mood that has descended on the City of Light. This has followed a terrorist truck attack that killed dozens in Nice on Bastille Day. I had no premonition of the attack when I bought my Eurostar ticket. I had simply wanted a break from Paris and posters before packing up and heading back to California.

There is another motive for a quick trip across the channel—to see Karen, a photographer and writer I met last summer en route home from Paris with my precious rolled-up *Girl in Red*. Karen, who had a strong reaction to seeing *The Girl*, was away on vacation when I came through London en route to Paris this summer, and we have agreed to meet up if I should come back before returning home.

An attractive Brit in her early forties with a good eye for art and a charming British accent, Karen was introduced to me at a preview at Bonhams auction house where I had gone last summer to see a Torres guitar being offered for sale. James Westbrook, a musicologist friend at Cambridge and an authority on guitar history and Torres, had authenticated the guitar for Bonhams and wanted me to see it before it disappeared into some collector's closet. Karen was taking pictures at the auction's reception, and I invited her for drinks at my hotel (DUKES) afterward and to see *The Girl*, which I had briefly told her about while at Bonhams. She was eager to see it.

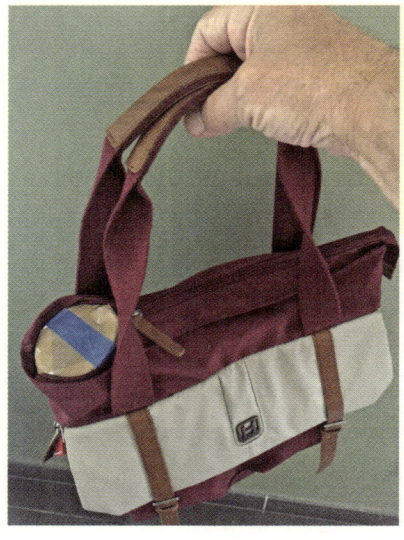

Transporting The Girl *to London in 2015, where I showed it to Karen*

After I explained the full story of the painting over martinis, we went upstairs to my room. I carefully removed the canvas from its shipping tube, slowly unrolled it and held it up. Karen gasped. I must have really wanted to impress Karen, because opening up the tube and unrolling the fragile canvas seemed risky to me. It was worth the risk. The portrait looked, Karen said, very much like her deceased younger sister—the shape of the face and the dark, penetrating eyes. Karen showed me a picture of her sister on her cell phone. There was indeed a likeness, more so even than with Jessica at La Palette and Stella in New York. A veritable doppelgänger.

Karen's reactions to visual stimuli are, she explained that night, powerful and often scary, caused by her severe pareidolia, an optical condition that produces a parade of objects seen within random abstract patterns mostly found in nature. I had never heard the word *pareidolia*, nor about its rare pathological presentation that hovers on the cusp of physiology and psychiatry. Karen becomes overwhelmed by the power of the images she sees, the quantity and the content. Seeing *The Girl in Red* didn't just remind Karen of her sister; it brought her back to life.

It's not unusual for humans to see animals, human faces, even angels and saints for the religiously inclined, in puddles, cloud formations, tree canopies and the like. All without drugs. Leonardo da Vinci had his students make drawings based on images seen in the cracked plaster and stains on his studio walls. Heightened pattern recognition, as in Karen's case, is influenced by higher-than-normal levels of dopamine in the blood, according to what I've now read, and it can be associated with schizophrenia.

On a species survival level, pareidolia relates to our hard-wired ability to identify the faces of the people we know and depend on. Imagine a baby not recognizing its mother's face when she looks down at it. And vice versa. Object relations theory in psychoanalysis is based on this visual, emotional and biological bond between mother and child that is so crucial to the healthy development of the child.

I, along with most visual artists, exhibit a fair amount of this pareidolic capacity, but Karen's case is extreme and, she acknowledges, pathological. It causes her to see hundreds of images all at once in clouds, trees, puddles, rock outcroppings and streets crowded with people. Just about anywhere she looks, at any time, she can be flooded with images that are often, she says, religious or spiritual in nature, and sometimes quite disturbing. The angels and demons she sees are real, not surreal, and they actively engage her in communication that overwhelms her if she cannot, somehow, make peace with them through, she says, "an inner dialogue." Unfortunately there is no medical treatment for these pareidolic visions, according to Karen's eye doctor, but I suspect a doctor of psychiatry would have some other suggestions (drugs come to mind).

What I learned last summer from Karen and in several follow-up emails has led me to wonder whether my engagement with *The Girl* has elements of pareidolia. If so, there is a big distinction between Karen's extreme case and my aesthetic version: Karen's experiences are involuntary and emotionally overwhelming, whereas I am volunteering for my assignment, submitting freely to *The Girl*'s power as a real object in time and space (or, possibly, from outside time and space). I may be enchanted by what I see in *The Girl* (hypnotized by it, as Yuri Kuper describes the power of a good painting), but unlike Karen, I'm not incapacitated. *Au contraire!*

Karen may not be a willing victim, but her quest to understand her condition and, she hopes, control it has forced her to consider the fuzzy edges of physics and, in particular, quantum theory, string theory, and the possibility of alternate dimensions and multiple universes—the multiverse, as it's been identified by contemporary physicists. Karen has never explained to me how her pareidolia might be connected to these radical theories other than to say that they are. Back with her in London, I want to know more.

I am obviously predisposed to consider Karen's "alternate dimensions" given my childhood with a delightful but "paranormal" mother. It's not a big stretch for me to consider that *The Girl in Red* was thrown in my path more than merely metaphorically. And not only on that one day a year ago in Paris when I first discovered her but simultaneously in 1999. That's the year I purchased *L'Italienne*, Picasso's lithographic reworking of Victor Orsel's painting, *Young Italian Woman*. Was that purchase linked to my found object in some alternate space/time dimension? Was my impulse to bring home my *Girl* related to Picasso's impulse to take home Orsel's girl? Ever since finding the *Girl*, I have noted that the faces of *L'Italienne* and *The Girl* have common pictorial qualities and resemblances, but thought of these as mere coincidence. Not now, not in the land of heureux hasard.

The thought that I'm traveling back and forth between two time zones, 1935 and the present, has led me to propose a third—1999. These considerations may be closer to the phenomenon of apophenia than pareidolia. Apophenia describes the spontaneous perception of meaningful connections between unrelated phenomena—say, between *L'Italienne* and *The Girl in Red*—that is, between 1935, 1999 and the present.

With pareidolia one sees objects that are not there. With apophenia one sees, and often exaggerates, a relationship between objects that *are* there. One researcher describes apophenia and artistic creativity as two sides of the same coin. I would add to this that the extreme edge of apophenia is psychosis and the extreme edge of creativity is genius. Most artists inhabit a world somewhere between these two extremes when in the creative grip. I fall somewhere along this continuum, probably smack-dab in the middle, leaning toward one extreme or the other. Never (or seldom) all the way.

It was my hope that seeing Karen again would yield a glimpse into the relationship she sees between pareidolia and quantum mechanics, string theory and all the rest. And this might elucidate a metaphysical dimension to my relationship with *The Girl*. More important, though, and to be honest, a brief romantic liaison with the woman I "found" in London last year, just weeks after finding *The Girl in Red* in Paris, might brighten my grayish post-poster mood.

So, with plans set for a dinner date with Karen, I arrived at DUKES by taxi from St. Pancras station, passing the site of one of Frédéric Chopin's London residences located at 4, St. James's Place, just a few doors from the hotel. There is a blue commemorative plaque marking the spot. Chopin had left Paris to escape a cholera outbreak and revolutionary turmoil in the streets (the Revolution of 1848) and to find students and concert venues, which in Paris had evaporated with the violence.

It's ironic that I've come to the same street in London where Chopin spent time, both of us fleeing Paris during dark days. It's more than ironic that DUKES is located, I suddenly realize, at 35, St. James's Place. *Heureux hasard à Londre, comme toujours!*

I'm not suggesting that a terror attack in Nice is comparable to a revolution in Paris, nor that Chopin and I have much in common other than our shared Polish heritage and a love of Paris and music. Furthermore, Chopin played the piano, and I play the guitar, two very different instruments. Guitarists do love to quote Chopin, who once said, "Nothing is more beautiful than the guitar, except, possibly two." I don't see that as much of a compliment. It would be like saying to a soprano that her voice is beautiful, but two would be more so. I am suggesting, however, that my arrival in London portends well—romantic magic with Karen and culinary magic at the Wolseley, where I've been able to reserve Lucian Freud's table 32.

Wrong! The food at the Wolseley is, as expected, sublime, especially my favorite dish there, the slow-roasted Seven-Hour Lamb with Flageolet Beans and Rosemary. But there is no flirtatious repartee with Karen, zero hints of romance to follow, and no talk of *The Girl*, pareidolia, or multiverses. Karen picks at her food distractedly, talking on and on about the truck attack in Nice. So much for my pleasant break from a bleak Paris.

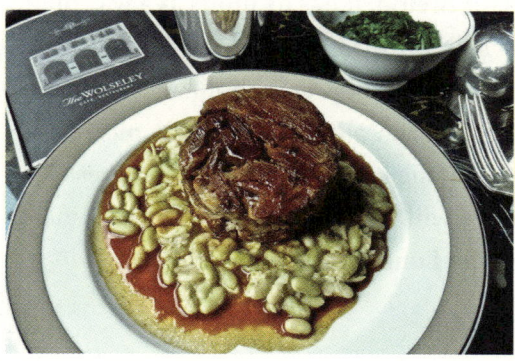

Seven-Hour Lamb at the Wolseley, one of their signature dishes

What Karen sees in the televised images and newspaper photos of the truck involved in the Nice attack is not what the media is portraying, she argues. In fact, she doesn't believe it happened at all and offers arguments to support her claim based on a careful analysis of the photographic record she has compiled. Her view of the tragedy—more apophenia, in this case, than pareidolia—is that the French government has staged the whole thing to justify its noxious policies against Muslims. She points out to me in newspaper clippings, among other visual and textual data she pulls from her purse, that the truck shows no evidence of blood on the bumper or dents in the body, which surely it would have if it had violently struck and killed so many pedestrians. What she does "see" in the visual record is a French conspiracy. All I see by the end of our meal is her wild conspiracy theory and a plate of mostly untouched Wiener Schnitzel with Thyme-Roasted Carrots.

While I can't categorically reject Karen's account of the terror attack, I can categorically reject *her*. There is a painful comparison I now see between Andre Breton's surreal Nadja and my real Karen, and as in the case of Breton, alarm bells ring. Surrealism is illuminating, often intoxicating, as an art form, and sometimes in the form of erotic and aesthetic attachments. But for me, as for Breton, it has its limits as a way of life.

Karen and I part awkwardly after dinner—no visits to my bedroom back at DUKES, nor any French air kisses or California hugs or vows to see each other again. Just a nice British handshake and talk of staying in touch about my progress with *The Girl*. But I doubt we will. String theory has met its match with conspiracy theory in London.

THE ÉCOLE DES BEAUX-ARTS SAYS *NON*

○

Back in Paris, I am facing the reality of looming failure. But only in the literal sense. From the outset of my provenance mission, I have had at best modest hopes for success; at the same time, I've truly believed that whatever the results, whatever form they took, they would be as illuminating as any facts about the painting that might emerge. From the perspective of flânerie, there is no such thing as failure.

The historical flâneur takes in the spectacle on his urban rounds and extracts images for his own purposes, often for the creation of art and poetry. He experiences the city as it is, finds it mysterious or absurd or flawed or even criminal, but always fascinating, even magical. And this is how I've viewed my journey, much as Baudelaire describes the artist-flâneur in his essay "The Painter of Modern Life": "The lover of pictures who lives in a magical society of dreams painted on canvas." *The Girl in Red* is a dream on canvas I have lost and found myself in.

Flâneuring my way to the École des Beaux-Arts, noting the surviving posters here and there along the way, I imagine placing posters all around the school's cluster of Beaux-Arts buildings, engaging the venerable art academy in much the same way as I've engaged the San Francisco Conservatory of

Music with my vintage guitars. I could suggest that their students compare the Paris art scene of the 1930s to that of today, and to address questions about how art has transitioned from modernism to postmodernism, from realism to abstraction to the conceptual, and, perhaps, back again. Using *The Girl*, we could create a dialogue between past and present, old and new.

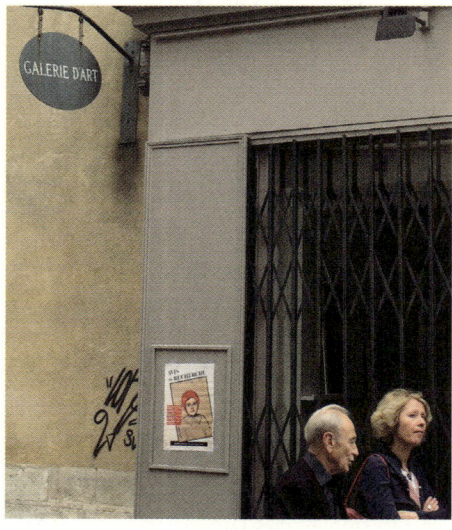

Near the École des Beaux-Arts, the poster is still up in a gallery's empty exterior display frame.

Perhaps the real motive for an engagement with the École is to enlist the students and faculty in a final neighborhood search for the story of *The Girl in Red*: dozens of young artists combing the neighborhood for clues as to the painting's story, interacting with shopkeepers and residents of Saint-Germain and the Latin Quarter. A treasure hunt with prizes—gift certificates at local art supply shops and croque monsieurs at La Palette for those who come up with information. What grand prize am I prepared to offer for the answer to the question, "Who painted *The Girl in Red*?"

Much of the sprawling complex of structures that make up the École, situated between rue Bonaparte and Quai Malaquais, is, surprisingly, open to the public. The courtyard off the rue Bonaparte entrance to the École is teeming with activity today, and as I enter the spacious glass-domed interior courtyard, students are milling about. One student is installed in a glass cubicle DJing an audio program of some sort on his computer. Students listen with earphones while seated around the enclosure on the courtyard's beautiful stone floor. Others just watch the action from afar.

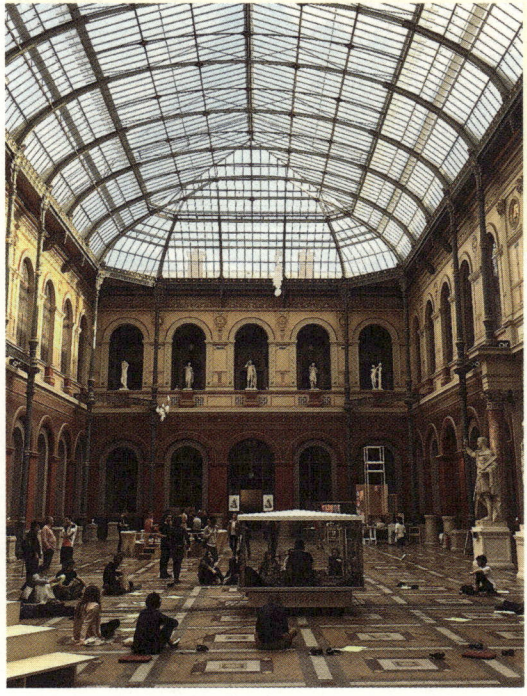

Student action in the glass-domed courtyard at the École des Beaux-Arts

Sans permission from the École, I hesitate to put up posters on the school walls, interior or exterior. It's one thing to post on a commercial or residential building, but an educational institution feels off-limits. Instead, after my self-guided tour, I head back to the apartment and reach out to the administration via email. My message is in English, addressed to three administrators whose names I've taken from the school's website. I present a short description of the proposed project and request permission to mount the posters around the school over the next few days, before I leave for

California. I include attachments showing the painting and the poster.

Silence. I resend the email the next day, asking only that I hear back, even if the project has been rejected. Whereupon a member of the administration notifies me that the campus is soon closing for the summer and that I would do better to approach galleries in the neighborhood for feedback about the painting and its history. "Good luck," "Yours truly," etc., etc. All in somewhat sketchy English.

Not giving up, I respond, asking the gentleman whether he would put me in touch with someone who handles the school publication or newsletter, if there is one. Perhaps, I suggest, they would be interested in publishing a story about a lost painting from 1935 found in their neighborhood. I would purchase ad space to reprint my avis de recherche with a short descriptive text.

No reply. I don't know how Rodin felt after three rejections from the École des Beaux-Arts. One is hard enough. I've read that Manet wanted to deliver a speech calling for the elimination of the school. Ditto me. But the flâneur in me decides to move on.

FULL CIRCLE AT LA PALETTE

○

With my remaining posters and Scotch tape I make my rounds. Only three days to go in Paris, and there are walls to baptize and missing posters to replace. In for a dime, in for a dollar. Or, in this case, in for a sou, in for a euro.

Approaching La Palette, from the corner of rue de Seine and rue Jacques Callot, I am startled to see Gilbert. He is seated at the power table, the table I was sitting at with Yuri last summer when Gilbert went on his tirade. There is a café crème positioned in front of him, and he is reading a newspaper.

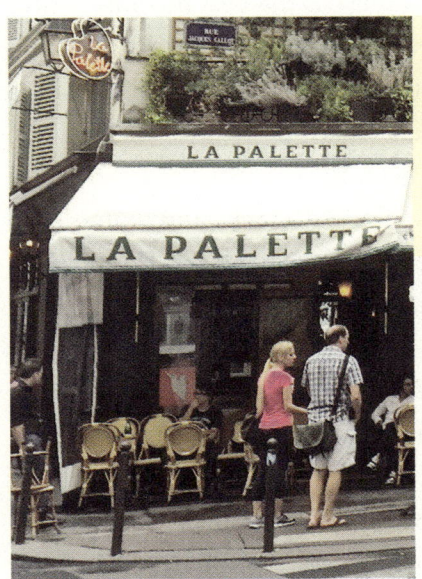

Café La Palette from the corner of rue de Seine and rue Jacques Callot. The café's empty power table is at the very left.

I have seen Gilbert several times since arriving in Paris this summer. He has always been with someone, either standing on the sidewalk or seated in a café. And, as with the first sightings of him with Yuri last summer, he is always doing the talking. This time Gilbert is alone, silent. I pause and consider my options: play it safe and keep walking or risk engaging with Gilbert.

Robert Henri, the American Ashcan School artist and teacher, observes in his book *The Art Spirit* (1923) that "there are moments in our lives, there are moments in a day when we seem to see beyond the usual. . . . Such are the moments of our greatest vision." But he also warns young artists about the fickle, sometimes hostile nature of critical opinions: "You pass people on the street, some are for you, some are not." Gilbert is my critic. I have passed him on the street, and he is not for me.

On the other side of the divide, Martha Rose Schulman, a cookbook author and fellow *Zester* magazine contributor, was not at all ambivalent last year when we met at Café de Flore for lunch. After hearing my Gilbert story, she urged me to get closure with, and closer to, Gilbert as the best possible source for information about the local art scene and clues to *The Girl's* provenance. It would be worth the risk, she advised. Now I have my chance. This is my Robert Henri moment to see "beyond the usual." I approach Gilbert.

Dressed casually in a sport coat, slacks and loafers—no socks—Gilbert is the quintessential Left Banker. He looks up from his paper as I reach the table and stares blankly, possibly not recognizing me, or not wanting to. (I'm dressed Berkeley bohemian: black tennis shoes, black jeans, a black sweater.)

"Bonjour" I say in a friendly tone. "Do you remember me?"

Gilbert does not respond, just looks at me and shrugs his shoulders. I can't tell if that means yes, no or maybe. Or, more likely, Who cares?

"I'm the guy you met with Yuri Kuper last year at Brasserie Lipp," I continue. "John." I pause and add, "from Berkeley." Then, with a bit of snarky impulsiveness and a smile, I add, "You didn't like me."

Something between a grimace and a smirk breaks Gilbert's stare. "Maybe I recognize you," he offers, "but I don't really want to talk."

Gilbert holds his newspaper half open, as if to say he is only in pause mode. He doesn't repeat my name with aggressive emphasis—*John*—as he had last year at Lipp and on the phone afterward. Or "asshole" as he had at La Palette in front of Yuri the next day.

"Well," I continue, still friendly-like, "I just want to say hello and hopefully arrange to see some of Yuri's paintings at your gallery. But I assume the gallery is closed now for the summer."

"It's always closed," he responds glumly.

Yuri had hinted in our correspondence last year after his return to Moscow that Gilbert's rage stemmed from troubles with his gallery and a difficult divorce.

"Perhaps you will let me in for just a few minutes?"

Gilbert stares again, considering his response. "Maybe if you walk by and see me sitting in the gallery. Maybe. But now I just want to sit here and read my paper."

He opens the paper fully and I walk away.

It's strangely satisfying to face this fellow, as Martha had predicted. Although some of the tension between us has faded, I feel certain it is our last encounter—closure, not closer. I don't think that going to his gallery will produce a positive result, though I would love to see the Kupers close up, to inhale their aura.

Gilbert's gift to me last year of Yuri's Pushkin Museum catalog and the catalog's connection to Peter Selz and Robert Johnson are, no doubt, the limit of Gilbert's involvement in my story. But like him or not, as a gallerist he represents one of the driving forces behind the cultural engine that runs the art world, a cog in the machine I've encountered along my journey's path:

Artist—makes art: Yuri Kuper

Dealer—displays and sells art: Gilbert

Curator—manages collections and creates exhibitions: Robert Johnson

Museum director—oversees exhibitions and acquisitions: Peter Selz

Critic—writes about art: John Berger

Collector—acquires (or gleans) art: Me

This structure and its players may seem old hat given the emergence of art as a global investment instrument and the merger of art trading and art making with information age technologies (NFTs, AI, etc.). New cogs in the machine include art advisors and "family office" wealth management services for collectors, and the art authentication and provenance experts who provide a kind of due diligence lubricant between the cogs. But I know little of this brave new world of art, made up of a relatively small global network of insiders who control the art we see, what we pay for it and, even, what we think about it.

I did, however, get a delicious taste of this new "artworld" (a term coined by Arthur Danto) in London in 2008 when I was taken in a chauffeur-driven Bentley to Damien Hirst's notorious Sotheby's auction—"Beautiful Inside My Head Forever"—featuring his whole animals (sharks and cows) pickled in formaldehyde-filled tanks. My guide, the scion of a Chinese billionaire art collector, was an old friend of my then girlfriend. After dining at his splendid Belgravia mansion, a meal made by his Australian chef whom I chatted with about "California cuisine" (he had never heard of it), we zipped off to Sotheby's in the Bentley, if Bentleys can be said to zip. They cruise oh so silently, oh so luxuriously.

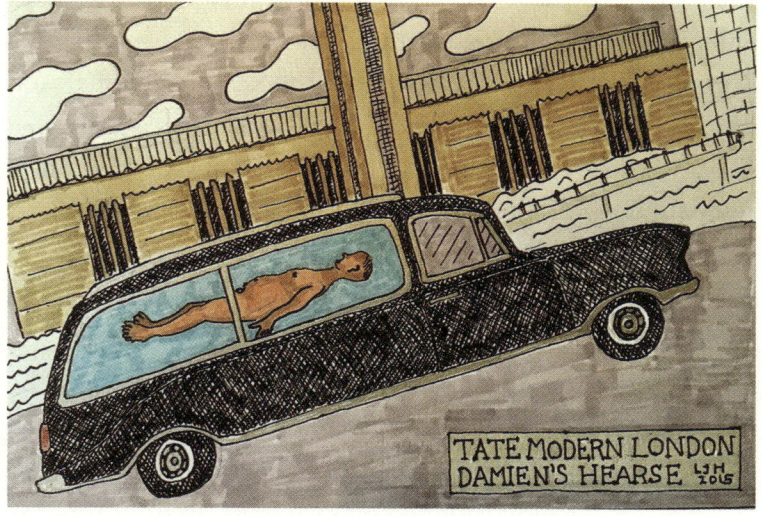

Damien's Hearse, 2015. I was so taken by Hirst's preserved animals at Sotheby's in 2008 and then again at his Tate Modern retrospective in 2012 that I eventually figured out a suitable "end game" for the artist.

This was the moment in contemporary art when a top artist—Hirst—bypassed the gallery system and sold directly to buyers (over $200 million from this sale), a huge scandal at the time and the mother lode for Hirst. I couldn't believe how intoxicating it felt at the upper end of this new art world.

Champagne before, during and after Sotheby's might have been a contributing factor.

Then, in 2012, at the Tate Modern, I had another encounter with the Hirst phenomenon. I saw his diamond-encrusted skull, *For the Love of God* (2007), which caused an art world stir almost as transformational as Duchamp's *Fountain* or Warhol's *Brillo Boxes*. Arthur Danto's first viewing of the *Brillo Boxes* in 1964 gave birth to his notorious theory of "the end of art" and launched his career as an art critic.

Similarly, the artist and theorist Johanna Drucker was transformed (scandalized is more like it) after seeing Hirst's work decades later. In her lecture at the School of Visual Arts in 2008, soon after Hirst's skull was shown at the White Cube gallery in London, she called it "amazing and shameless" and "probably the piece of work we would all most like to ignore. It is the piece of work we would like to have go away . . . that in a sense calls out and says, everything you would like to believe about what art is and how it functions isn't true."

Eye-opening and entertaining as these peeks into the contemporary art world have been for me, it's not the same art world that *The Girl* and I inhabit. Maybe we live in one of art's multiverses, the old-fashioned one we grew up in during the decades of the twentieth century that spanned *The Girl*'s childhood (1930–1940) and mine (1950–1960). These are the decades when avant-garde modernism morphed into avant-garde postmodernism, leaving me and my *Girl* stuck in the *arrière-garde*.

Of the responses to *The Girl* I've received to date from the art-world cogs on my chart, I think Peter Selz's has been the most focused and affirming. I ran into him at a restaurant in Berkeley while planning my Paris poster project. He was seated with his daughter, Gabrielle, who had just published a memoir about growing up with "Mr. Modern Art" as Selz was known from his stint as the chief curator of painting and sculpture at the Museum of Modern Art in New York before coming to the Berkeley Art Museum. Even in his late eighties, he's an elegant presence with silver hair and a charming German accent. Very much the éminence grise of our Berkeley art scene.

Selz vaguely remembered me from my stint in the '70s, working at the UC Berkeley Art Museum café, the Swallow, and from my student gig at the Cheese Board, where he was, and still is, a regular customer. Standing at his table at North Berkeley's Corso Ristorante, I told him about *The Girl in Red* and the connection I had made with Yuri Kuper and Robert Johnson. He agreed to take a look at the painting via email. His brief but potent response to my email that night came quickly:

May 12, 2016

Hello L. John,

Thank you for sending me the image of the young girl, painted in Paris in January 1935. It is a well-done portrait, painted at a troubled time—in fact, the expression of the girl seems to show anxiety. I wonder why anyone would have thrown it out?

Peter

Selz's question haunts me and will continue to. Why would anyone throw out a magical painting like *The Girl in Red*? Although I would have loved to ask this question of Gilbert, this chapter of my journey is finito.

WEB DESIGN AND
POSTER CONTROL

○

My web of posters has failed to snare its intended prey. Perhaps I have been the prey all along, caught up in a tale of my own spinning.

I think about all the spider webs that await me back in Berkeley, deposited around my home's exterior window mullions, door frames and light fixtures. Tis the season. I'll knock them down with a broom, but they'll come back, of course, and I'll knock them down again, and again. Like Sylvester Stallone's pugnacious movie hero who always bounces back, spiders are the arachnid world's Rocky Balboa.

My posters are a different story. They form a rather more fragile web. Even if I wanted to, I couldn't come close to replacing all the teardowns that accelerated with the momentum of my posting. At one location on rue de Saint-Simon, around the corner from my apartment, the posters I've mounted on an apartment building have been routinely torn down. I've responded defiantly by replacing them. Eventually I'll get the message—*Arrête!* But I like seeing *The Girl* on the route I often walk toward my first coffee.

Walls of apartment buildings are among the most vulnerable locations for posters. Concierges and residents are apparently very protective of their precious Haussmann facades.

Less vulnerable are the fat sewer pipes that run up the sides of these buildings. Posters and flyers wrap nicely around the pipes and stay securely taped at the back. Perhaps the pipes represent a safe zone, an accepted buffer between those posting and a building's occupants. If there are city rules governing all this, I'm not aware of them.

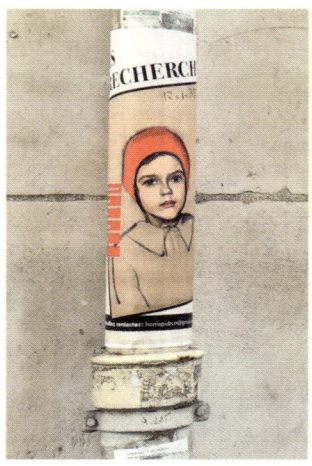

Following the teardowns, I wrap a poster around the building's waste pipe, next to an antique shop on rue de Saint-Simon.

This morning, counting down the hours before my departure, I walk up the street to rue de Saint-Simon, turn right and head toward rue de Varenne and a café, part of an international chain, Le Pain Quotidien. The coffee is smoother there than at most Paris cafés. One of the posters on this route has survived for almost a week curled around a sewer pipe. Nearing it, I am amused and amazed at what I see. Leaning against the building on either side of the postered pipe is a treasure trove of assorted discards. There are long strips of wood and metal, a window frame, a fabric-covered panel—much like the panel I found when I gleaned *The Girl* on rue Guénégaud—and a highchair! The moment is remarkable and a bit eerie, as if the gods of gleaning (and the spirit of Agnès Varda) are reaching out to honor my mission's end with a frame placed around my poster, a frame made of junk.

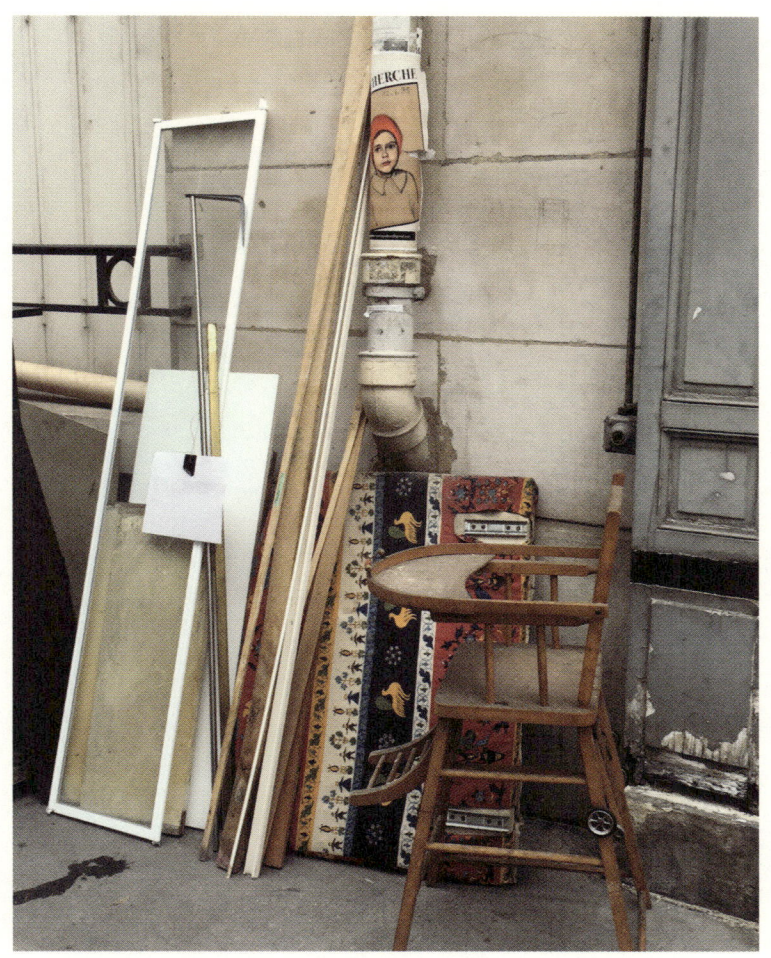

Gleanable discards appear around the poster.

o

AT THE END OF THE DAY

○

What can be said at the official one-year finish line of my journey with *The Girl in Red* today, July 26, 2016? I have known her for a year, and surely the dynamic between the portrait and this gleaner has changed. In a marriage, the one-year anniversary marks the end of the honeymoon period; the relationship starts to reveal its truth, built on the foundations of that first year.

But wait! When exactly is the proverbial end of the day? You hear this expression all the time, especially from talking heads on TV, talking lips on the radio and talking hands in print media: "At the end of the day, blah blah blah . . ." It's the current, and I think silly, version of two older idioms—"When all is said and done" and "In the final analysis." Whatever happened to these perfectly adequate phrases? Tossed into the English language's poubelle.

Honestly, I don't know whether the end of the day means midnight of the day in question, or the end of daylight. Is it a specific day's end, this day, or a day *qua* day? In the context of defining the finish point of a work of art, or a poster mission—*my* work of art—these are relevant questions. When is the end truly the end? When is finito, finito?

Only the master can decide. I will designate midnight as

the official end of this day, this journey—a mere second before tomorrow. Of course, journeys are, at the end of the day, open ended. This is true, I've learned, for the journey we call art, and especially oil painting, which is a marathon. Watercolor is a 100-meter sprint. Drawing is the warm-up exercise. For oil painting, then, with all its layers, touch-ups and varnishings, the end is not only open ended but for some artists, end-less.

Passing the midnight threshold for the completion of my journey—and its narrative—all that will be left to do is a bit of cleanup and sorting, and perhaps some culling when I get back home. In literary terms, editing. I am reminded again of the words of the artist Louis Pons, who, in Agnès Varda's homage to gleaning, proclaims: "The aim of art is to tidy up one's inner and exterior worlds."

This morning I take my poster to the Mairie du 6ème arrondissement de Paris. This is the headquarters for the area in Paris encompassing Saint-Germain-des-Prés, three other *quartiers* and parts of the Latin Quarter. It's also the office of the area's mayor (*le mairie*). I'm hoping to interest someone within Paris officialdom in my project and an article about it in the mairie's newsletter, which goes out monthly to most everyone who lives and/or works in the 6th.

This is the fine idea of Rick Tulka, an expat American artist and caricaturist I was introduced to several years ago by a historian of France and its cafés, W. Scott Haine. Rick has spent the last twenty-odd years sitting most days at the legendary artists' café Le Select in Montparnasse, drawing droll caricatures of the café's clientele, staff, and menu items, many of which illustrated Noël Riley Fitch's book *Paris Café: The Select Crowd*, published in 2007.

At the Mairie du 6ème I make some progress with Giguet, a friendly woman who works the information desk. Thanks to her, I now have the personal email address of the gentleman who is the arrondissement's *chargé de la culture et de la communication*. I will write to him tonight—before midnight—to explain the project and my ideas for an article.

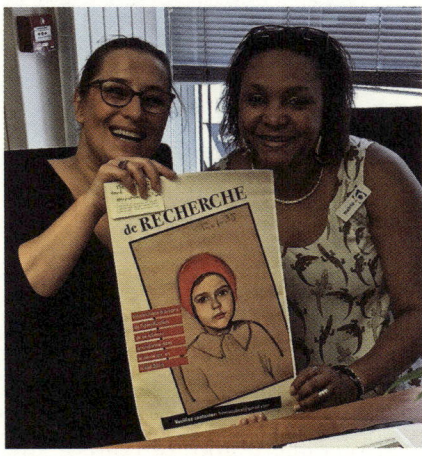

Giguet (left) and her associate at the Mairie du 6ème

I will also pass the torch to Anne, Lucien Godin's partner in business and in life. After my stop at the mayor's office, I head to Le Bistrot Mazarin to meet her, just across the street from her apartment building. Over coffee, she tells me more about Lucien—that he had been an influential architect working with the World Bank on development projects in third world countries. She will continue the work they launched together there, and she pledges to continue on behalf of my project and to keep me posted. We then cross over to no. 35, where Anne tapes a poster to the inside of the front door in her building's entrance hall. I appreciate the gesture, though I have no illusions. The trail has grown cold.

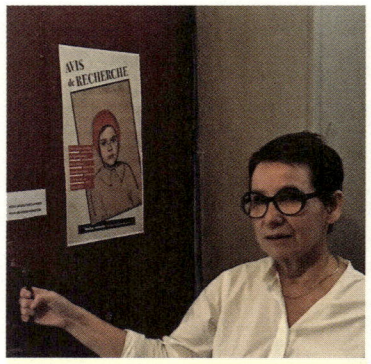

Anne, Lucien Godin's partner, poses after taping the poster to the entry door inside her building.

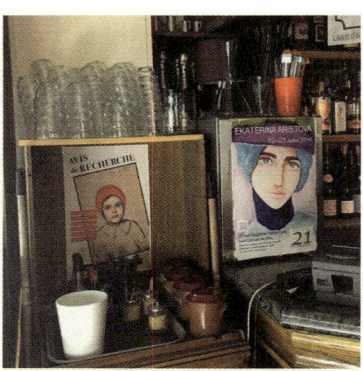

The two girls side by side at Bistro Mazarin, where I met Anne for coffee.

Weaving my way back to the apartment, I say my good-byes to the charming streets I have walked this summer: rue de Seine, rue Mazarine, rue Guénégaud, rue des Beaux-Arts, rue Visconti, rue Bonaparte, rue Jacob, rue des Grands-Augustins, rue de Saint-Simon, all the various *quais*, and, of course, my own blvd. Saint-Germain. And goodbye also to Place Fursten-berg. This is where Delacroix made his home, garden and stu-dio. Soon after arriving in Paris this summer, I taped a post-er to the sign on the entry gate to this delightful little house museum, Musée National Eugène Delacroix. It survived for several days running, unnoticed, I suppose, by the museum's security and maintenance staff. Or was it tolerated by an intrigued security guard?

The day I installed that poster, I stood back across the lovely little Place, outside a small food shop, Maison de Choux, that makes delicious bite-sized *choux* pastries (cream puffs). Munching on my small allotment, I admired how the poster dialogued with the museum sign's central image, a large fragment from Delacroix's *Women of Algiers in Their Apartment* (1834). I notice now what I didn't then, that the harem's servant girl is wearing a patterned red headscarf in the upper right corner of the image.

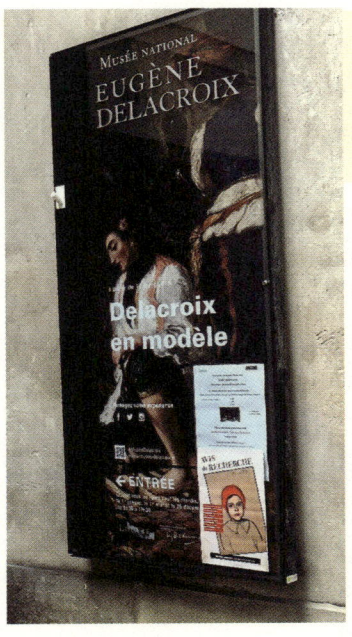

The Girl *attached to the Delacroix house museum sign outside the gate at Place Furstenberg*

Just down from the Delacroix Museum, toward rue Bonaparte, at 4, rue Furstenberg, Balthus maintained his studio where in 1935 he painted his important *King of Cats*, a self-portrait influenced, it is claimed, by Delacroix's *Self Portrait as Hamlet* (1821). One wonders if Balthus's admiration for Delacroix motivated his move to a house close to his hero's, just as Picasso's admiration for Balzac inspired his move with Dora Maar into 7, rue des Grands-Augustins, and later to the chateau near Aix-en-Provence to be close to Cézanne's Mont Saint-Victoire. Birds of a feather . . .

On this last day of flâneuring in Paris, I see no posters on any of the walls and kiosks where I have mounted them. The only survivors, save the one wrapped around the sewer pipe on rue de Saint-Simon, are inside restaurants and cafés such as Le Bistrot Mazarin and Café de Flore; in book shop windows, as at Art & Libri on rue Jacob and Shakespeare and Company on rue de la Bûcherie; and in the window of the art supply shop Esquisse on rue des Beaux-Arts. How long they will survive after I am gone, I have no idea. Soon, I suspect, it will be as if the poster had never existed, and *The Girl's* presence in Paris will fade into absence.

Back at the apartment, making my final preparations for an early morning flight to San Francisco, I am in full panic mode. The end of the day—midnight—is fast approaching. I have always found leaving Paris emotional, painfully so. After weeks, sometimes a month or more, of intense foodie research, article writing, and journal sketching, a queasy void opens and tells me time is up. The usual Paris withdrawal symptoms back home will be amplified, I'm sure, by the failure (quote-unquote) of my mission. I can of course continue the journey with *The Girl* (and no doubt will), but the truth is that despite all the clichés about works of art never being finished and masters being in charge, etc., etc., I feel I've come up against the edge of my canvas and am about to fall off, like the objects on Bonnard's table. Something is truly, achingly ending.

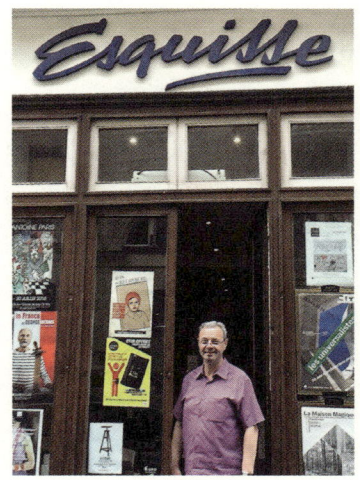

Esquisse on rue des Beaux-Arts

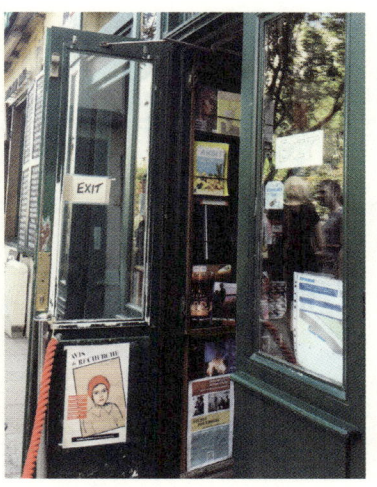

Shakespeare and Company on rue de la Bûcherie

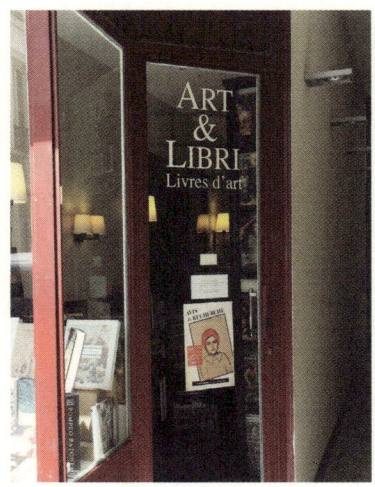

Art & Libri on rue Jacob

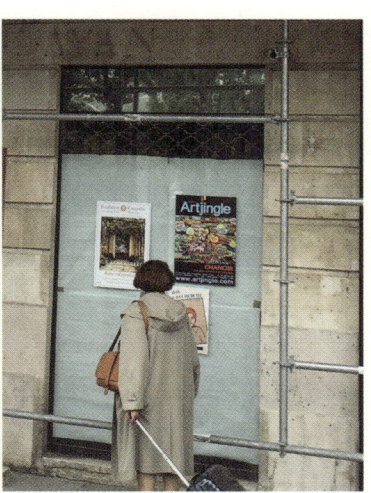

Galerie Dayan on quai Voltaire

o

III
THE JOURNEY ENDS
2016–2017

Berkeley · San Francisco · Berkeley ·
Stinson Beach · Berkeley

JEAN DUBUFFET'S

SWAN SONG

o

With Paris in the rear-view mirror, I'm licking my wounds. From Paris light to Berkeley blight, or so it always feels for the first weeks back home. It's a flâneurian thing: nothing to discover comparable to Paris's urban splendor, no medieval streets or grand boulevards to stroll, no glamorous shop windows to ogle, no haute cuisine to devour, no café culture to cultivate. It takes time for Berkeley's natural charms and San Francisco's urban glitz to reassert themselves.

The withdrawal symptoms are worse this year, as predicted. There has been no response from the mayor of the 6th arrondissement, nor from anyone at the École des Beaux-Arts. No update from Anne Godin. No pictures promised by the student Jessica at La Palette. Karen has not contacted me, not even to thank me for the dinner at the Wolseley. And Yuri Kuper is not returning my emails. They have all moved on. Why haven't I? It feels like I'm frozen in time and space—Paris, January 12, 1935—*The Girl*'s time, a dark time, not my own time.

What does it mean, the repeated appearance of that date, 1935, and the two-digit number alone, 35? It's been nothing short of uncanny from the very beginning of my journey, and continues to amaze me, and now holds me in its spell: the year of *The Girl*, and the address on rue Guénégaud where I found her; the year Picasso abandoned painting for poetry; the year of the first serialized episode of Tintin's *Broken Ear*; the publication date in German of Walter Benjamin's mechanical reproduction essay; the year the Nazis formally introduced their *rouge et noir* national flag, and many others.

In a moment of desperation, hoping for some sort of relief, I scan the internet's numerology websites and glean some interesting information. The number 35 is a component of the angel number 3535 (angel numbers are those sequences of numbers angels keep putting in front of us until we learn their lessons) and an omen of beneficial change in one's life based on "hard work and perseverance despite obstacles." OK, I like it.

Then, from an astrologer doing charts at a booth at the North Berkeley farmers' market where I've gone to stock up on fresh produce for my empty refrigerator, a shopping ritual almost as common now in Berkeley as in Paris, I learn that the number 35 adds up to 8, and there are two 35s in 3535, which gives 8 plus 8, which is 16, which when those two digits are added together equals 7, and OMG, that's a special number, a prime number, a lucky number—7. There are seven colors in the rainbow, seven continents on planet Earth, and seven days in the week, which makes the number 7 very very special. Wow!

But special how? Getting home with bags of organic greens and berries, cucumbers and carrots, onions and garlic, I'm wondering how we got from 1935 to the lucky number 7 and what it all means. I go back to the web and find this: "You'll likely keep seeing the prime number 7 if you have second thoughts about your spiritual journey. It may also pop up to give you hope and urge you to press on." Aha! Then, on a tarot site (I was now all in), I find out that when you draw the 7 card, that's the Chariot, and it means you are on a quest with difficult obstacles in your path that you *will* overcome. Yes, yes, yes!

There is hope! Except that I don't really believe any of it. I never ventured as far as numerology, tarot or astrology in my youthful esotericism. I stopped at the *I Ching*, which seemed to have intellectual integrity and was endorsed by Carl Jung. When "throwing it" back in the day at the Colby Street commune, I would occasionally encounter one of the *I Ching's* most desirable revelations, "Perseverance furthers." Isn't that also a form of hope, I ask myself as I'm scrubbing produce, in accordance with my angel number and the number 7? And suddenly time and space collapse, and I'm back in the zone of heureux hasard and Patrick Modiano's hope without faith. My post-Paris blues begin to fade.

As if on cue, entering stage left—radically left—a hero from my art past, Jean Dubuffet. He's the genius behind *art brut* (so-called raw art or Outsider Art) and a proponent of *Art Naif* (the brilliant work of "primitive" artists, some of them mentally ill). I have always felt a strong connection with his work (and theirs), perhaps more so even than with that of our own American postwar painters, the abstract expressionists, pop artists and minimalists.

A few days before I left Paris, at a bookshop near Café de Flore, I stumbled across *Anticultural Positions*, a recent collection of essays by and about Dubuffet, with a focus on his controversial portraits of the 1940s, which are new to me. Actually, the book is the catalog for a retrospective of Dubuffet's early work shown at the Acquavella Galleries in New York earlier this year. It was just too heavy to pack, and with no time to read it, I had the book shipped to Berkeley. It has arrived.

Along with Yuri Kuper's Pushkin Museum catalog handed to me so inexplicably by Gilbert last year at Brasserie Lipp, the Dubuffet catalog emerges now as a challenging bookend to my year with *The Girl in Red*. Dubuffet questions all that *The Girl* represents as a portrait, and the meaning I have taken from it. Just as predicted from my descent into numerology and tarot fantasy, Dubuffet is an obstacle on my path to overcome or, at least, explore.

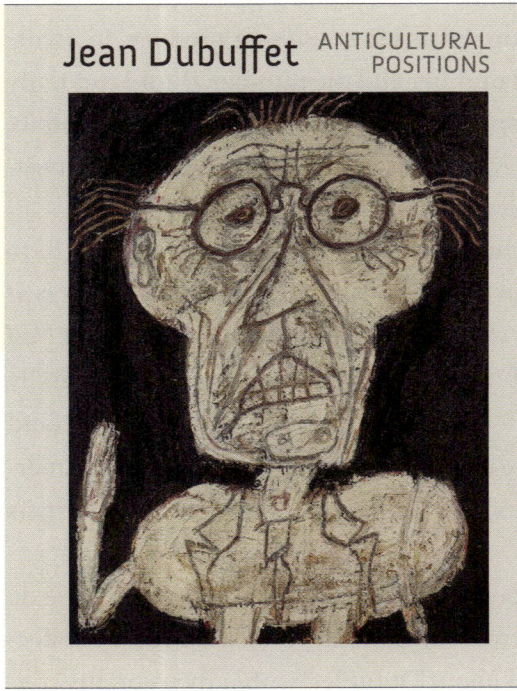

The cover of the catalog for Dubuffet's 2016 show at Acquavella Galleries in New York

On the catalog's cover is one of Dubuffet's best-known portraits—*Monsieur d'Hotel* (1947)—an anxious, even terrified man (the writer André Dhôtel) wearing glasses, with one hand raised up as if swearing an oath of allegiance. It's a distorted, grotesque mask more than an amusing caricature, which by definition must reference the actual face being depicted. This portrait is beyond reference.

It's also a long way from Dubuffet's earlier portraits in the 1930s when he was transitioning from his family's wine business to art. A portrait of his wife, Lili, from that period is what one would expect from a conservative mid-1930s modernist in Paris—a realism colored by modernism's improvisation, distortions of perspective, loose application of paint, unfinished backgrounds and, often, bold black outlines—but still representational.

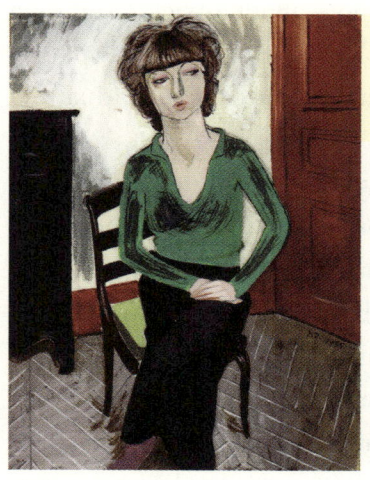

Portrait of Lili (Lili Assise)
by Jean Dubuffet, 1935

Opening the Dubuffet catalog at random just moments after it arrives, I read the following by one of the book's editors, the art historian Kent Mitchell Minturn, about a contributor to a previous exhibition of Dubuffet portraits in 1993: "In her astute contextualization of Dubuffet's portrait show, art historian Suzanne Cooke reminds us that in interwar and postwar France, painted portraits became synecdochically connected with the idea of the 'face of history' itself."

There it is again, the term synecdoche, the part representing the whole. Cooke's view supports all I have come to believe about *The Girl in Red* as a reflection of Paris, January 12, 1935—the face of history. Even Picasso said about his wild portraits of Dora Maar in the late 1930s and '40s (he called them "sort of caricatures")—"I have no doubt that the war is in these paintings I have done."

Synecdoche in portraiture is not for Dubuffet as he comes to conceive of it after 1935, and he takes the idea of portrait as caricature even further than Picasso. There is no one-to-one relationship between his portraits and history, or even between the portraits and their subjects. For Dubuffet, identity is "too fluid" to be captured in paint, like Andre Breton's fluid nature of identity described in *Nadja*. So Dubuffet goes in the opposite direction, removing history, anatomy and biography. His portrait of André Dhôtel is more about anxiety itself than about the anxious subject of the painting. As one critic puts it, Dubuffet prefers the primordial archetype to an individualized subject.

In the discourse on portraiture I've encountered this year, the question arises whether portraits truly reveal their subjects' character. Some critics, such as Oscar Wilde, have said that good portraits reveal more about the artist's character than the subject's. Robert Flynn Johnson, by contrast, believes that portraits reveal more about the subject's character than a mere technical likeness. Dubuffet is interested in neither character nor likeness. "Making portraits that are a good likeness prevents them from becoming ghosts," Dubuffet writes. He starts a portrait with some special characteristic of his model—for example, a nose or a pair of glasses (these are apersonal identifiers, not synecdochal stand-ins)—then pushes the portrait into a dimension that is "of good use." This ghost stays alive on the canvas according to Dubuffet, never losing its power to engage the viewer. Portraits as metaphor, not representation. I am reminded of Walter Pater's description of Leonardo's *Mona Lisa* as a vampire risen from the dead.

For Dubuffet, then, *The Girl in Red* would have represented all that he and his circle came to stand against from 1935 through the postwar years—the regressive nostalgia for the mimetic mission in painting. But when I face *The Girl in Red*, I can't help but feel that very synecdochal connection to history that Suzanne Cooke describes. And because there is no way to judge the likeness of *The Girl*, she remains ghostly enough to hold me in her spell.

After looking hundreds of times at *The Girl*, in both reproduction and auratic flesh, I once again try to see her with words: She is a preadolescent girl (the youthful face and undeveloped torso), seemingly vulnerable to what is taking place around her (her eyes). She is both emerging into and disappearing from history. Her prospects appear to be fading in prewar Paris (her anxious expression) precisely at the moment— January 12, 1935—when her adolescence is about to blossom (full red lips). She is the synecdochal *and ghostly* face of the history she is witness to.

Dubuffet boldly explains that the intention behind his portraits is to make paintings that are *not* paintings: "It's the moment just before death that the swan sings," he writes in his famous essay "Causette" ("Little Chat," 1947), included in *Anticultural Positions*. *The Girl in Red* is a swan song too, but at a moment just before life.

BUT A PAINTING IS A PAINTING

o

It is the mechanically reproduced copy of *The Girl in Red* that is seen wherever the avis de recherche posters have migrated after my Paris mission. I not only posted them on walls and in windows in Paris but also gave posters to friends there, and to visitors I met from London, Chicago, New York and the Bay Area, mostly at the Terrance Gelenter "Your American Friend in Paris" café salons I attended. Terrance leads tours throughout France and books apartments in Paris for his clients, bringing them together in Paris with visiting writers and artists at various cafés on Sunday mornings. I've been a guest author on a few occasions over the years.

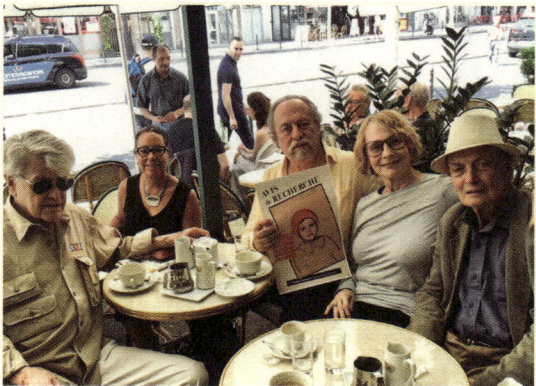

Terrance Gelenter holds the avis de recherche poster at Café Le Select, surrounded by friends and clients.

My one stipulation when handing out posters to friends is that they be framed and mounted in their offices and homes. What has been torn down from kiosks and walls in Paris, and from shop and café windows, has reappeared in private spaces around the world.

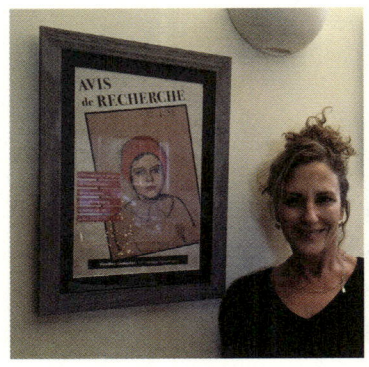

At Wendy Mines' home in El Cerrito, just north of Berkeley

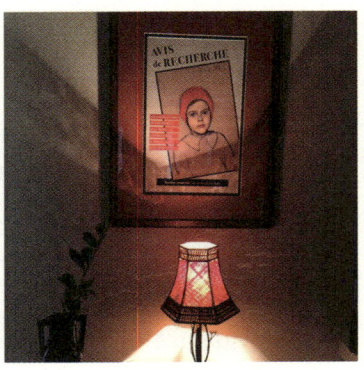

At Renee Ozburn's apartment in Chicago

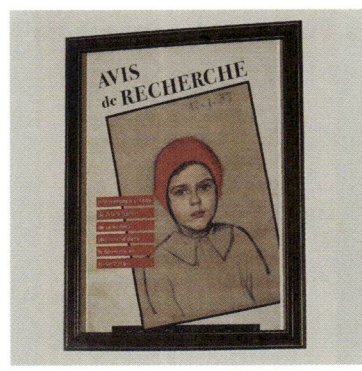

At David and Evy Jester's apartment in Paris

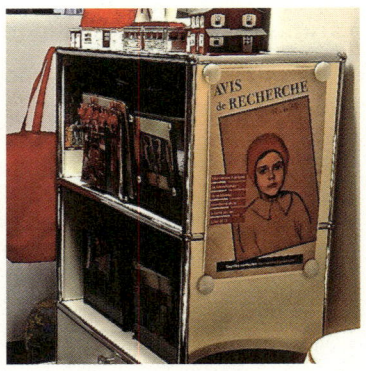

At a registrar's office at the Museum of Modern Art in NYC

Although the reproduced poster image packs a visual punch for most who see it, the auratic original offers far more: the opportunity to consider, to enter, the material surface itself, the "material memories" of the paint on the canvas, as the artist and critic James Elkins describes this pictorial alchemy in his fascinating book *What Painting Is*: "But a painting is a painting and not words describing the artist or the place it was made or the people who commissioned it. . . . The material memories are not usually part of what is said about a picture, and that is a fault in interpretation."

Once the painting is seen, the viewer interprets the memories planted in the material by the artist. In *The Success and Failure of Picasso*, John Berger describes the magic that takes place in the mind of the viewer in front of the painted surface: "Painting is the art that reminds us that time and the visible come into being together as a pair. The place of their coming into being is the human mind which can coordinate events into a time sequence and appearances into a world seen."

A whole world seen: the artist's two-dimensional representation (realistic or abstract), via the material memories and the viewer's interpretation of them. The viewer must allow the material on the canvas to penetrate past the eye, past the intellect, and past all the random, unimportant associations, to a deeper place. This is contemplation. Monet said, "Everyone discusses my art and pretends to understand, as if it were necessary to understand, when it is simply necessary to love."

Interpretation, however and wherever it happens in the brain, is a subjective experience. The Berkeley painter Jan Wurm told me after seeing *The Girl* for the first time that the artist had made a generalized portrait of a young girl, not a specific one. The artist either didn't want to see, or could not see, the specific features of a specific girl at a specific age. The lips, for example, are not real lips, Jan explained. They do not show the differentiation of color and texture that an upper and lower lip would reveal of this particular girl.

Jan's critique, based on a lifetime of figurative painting, may explain why some who view *The Girl* see themselves or someone they know in the portrait. One can more easily project onto *The Girl* because she is generalized.

Another Berkeley artist, Ann Arnold, doesn't agree with this interpretation. Her experience with painting children has taught her that the lips of a child have a softness, and the lower lip a bit of puffiness that is a kind of specificity. There's less detail than with adult mouths, she says, and they don't require as many lines to render them. "Grownups have been using certain expressions all their lives and their mouths have been slightly contorted based on those expressions. And that's not true of children."

Generalized or not, the girl in *The Girl in Red* is specific *to me*. As an exercise, putting myself once again in front of the portrait, I will try to pass through the retinal representation en route to Monet's "love" domain within the "material memories," the Holy Grail of the art experience.

What I see now is a half-figure, to use the technical term, a torso twisted very slightly to the left. The face of a girl is outlined in broad black and faint blue-black strokes that differentiate it from the background. This background is empty except for a date and a darkened (perhaps water-stained) area running along the bottom of the canvas. The bold outline of the face extends down through the neck to the torso in even broader strokes that form a support for this girl's head—a pictorial armature. Ann Arnold sees the unfinished collar—perhaps part of a schoolgirl's uniform—as a pedestal on which the face perches.

Above the face, the red of the head covering almost floats, its mass escaping in certain areas from its faint outline. It occurs to me that the head covering serves, symbolically, as a halo or a princess's crown, the mark of this child's innocence. It almost hides the brown hair, a few strands of which escape at the upper left side of the forehead. This would align with Elkins's view of art as alchemy. For alchemists and their search for the philosopher's stone (the transformation of base metal into gold), the color red or "redness" (the Latin *rubedo*) is associated, according to Elkins, with the heat of the golden-yellow sun, the final stage of the alchemical transformation. In Jungian terms this is the process of individuation, the making of a whole Self.

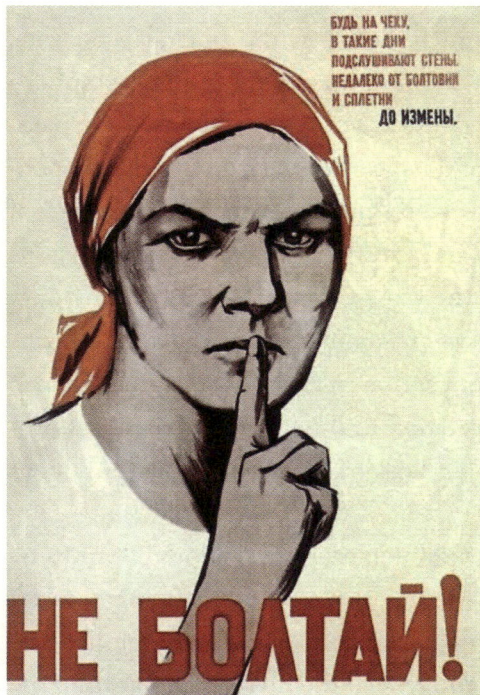

A Soviet-era propaganda poster of a young woman in a red scarf

Early in my journey, I thought the head covering might be a cloche, the close-fitting knit hat popular in France in the early 1930s. But a friend from Russia who believes that the girl in the portrait is Russian has argued convincingly that it's a scarf, stretched tight and tied behind the head as was common with "young pioneer" girls in Soviet Russia. Not a bonnet because, she points out, a bonnet is tied under the chin. The lack of detail supports multiple interpretations, but I'm leaning now toward scarf.

The Girl's non finito background serves as what Elkins describes as a "digestive area . . . where things almost are . . . they hold everything in suspension, letting the forms draw themselves almost into clarity." This "almost clarity" is mostly evident within the bold outlines of *The Girl's* upper torso where faint charcoal or pencil underdrawing hints at the folds and creases of a blouse or jacket.

The lack of anatomical detail in the portrait—no ears, arms or hands—brings to mind one of those photographer's props one puts one's head into at a carnival or amusement park, allowing only the oval of the face to appear through the opening. In any case, the face seems pushed forward by the lack of detail around it. The slightly stunted upper-body dimensions that I see in relation to the size of this girl's head (almost life-size) add to the impression of a painted prop, and also suggests caricature, as it is the convention in caricature (*portrait-charge*) to enlarge the head in relation to the torso. But there is absolutely no caricature in this face at all, a far cry from Dubuffet's portraits.

And what of color? Baudelaire said, "Color . . . thinks by itself, independently of the object it clothes." The many variations of red in the painting, seen in the scarf and the lips primarily, the hints of red and rose at the nostrils and around the eyes, indicate an artist of some talent and finesse. Standing close to the painting with a color chart in hand, I can make out cardinal, Venetian red, rose and vermilion. Most prominent in the scarf are the reds on the orange side of the blue–orange range of vermilion. This warm scarlet red is derived from the powdered mineral cinnabar, which combines mercury and sulfur. Vermilion or cinnabar is the red found throughout the history of art, from ancient Rome to the Renaissance, and ties classical painting closely to its earlier connection to alchemy. In the young girl's lips, the red matches the bluer end of the spectrum of cinnabar-based reds, as one might expect on a cold, snowy day in January.

Red is also associated with blood in alchemy, and brown with excrement. *The Girl in Red*'s rich palette of reds (lips and head cover) pop, and the browns (hair, eyes and eyebrows, and a shadow under the chin) blend with the neutral background. There is plenty of blood in this portrait, but the colorful trappings of everyday life—clothing and setting—are missing. The brown, almost black eyes tell a dark story that we feel but can only guess at.

Hovering above all is the power of the overscaled black date—12-1-1935—a material memory to be sure, not just a data point in a provenance report. John Berger says in his book *Ways of Seeing* that "the way we see things is affected by what we know or what we believe." The facts of *this* date are what I know and believe about *this* portrait, the history that's about to engulf Paris and the world—as if the painting's date were the missing "place" where the girl sits. This place, this history speaks to me through the eyes of a young life on hold in a dark, wintry freeze as a horrific shitstorm is about to be unleashed by evil alchemists draped in brown and gray, waving flags of red and black.

Monet's love domain can be found through careful contemplation of a painting's material memories, especially with *his* paintings—one can drown in the beauty of his *Water Lilies*. But with ghostly paintings like *The Girl in Red*, it's not always a pretty picture one finds.

A WHODUNIT
WITH TWO WHOS

o

A rtifact, a thing made. If, in an effort to transpose an artifact as text into an artifact as visual art, I was to fix my journey with *The Girl in Red* onto canvas, my palette would be limited to the following colors:

Red—For *The Girl in Red*, her headscarf and lips; and for the mineral cinnabar that gives lifeblood and power to art's vermillion

Black—For the brushstrokes that encircle *The Girl*'s face and sketch her non finito torso; and for the hideous Nazi swastika and the dark days in France and Europe after 1935

Blue—For the subtle blue tones in the outlines of *The Girl*; and for Django Reinhardt's bluesy 1939 ballad *Nuages* (*Clouds*), which became the alternate French anthem when the Nazis outlawed *La Marseillaise*

Gray—For the existential gloom that pervaded the prewar years in Paris; for Yuri Kuper, somber and elegant like his paintings; and for the château gris walls of the apartment where I have lived and worked in Paris over the years

Gold—For Gustav Klimt's *Woman in Gold* and the gilded frames of history's pictorial masterpieces; and for the golden-brown croque monsieur at La Palette that triggered the gleaning of *The Girl in Red*

Gold, also, for the art collector Foster Goldstrom, who has sparked a new attribution flame I thought had died out after my poster mission. A retired San Francisco art dealer and architectural history buff, Foster attended the open house when I put my home up for sale soon after my return from Paris. He was more taken by the eighty-year-old portrait mounted over the fireplace than the hundred-year-old Arts and Crafts house itself.

The agent holding the house open, a mutual friend, gave Foster my contact information. Although I had never met Foster, I was aware of his legendary Guy Hyde Chick House, a landmark in Berkeley designed by the École des Beaux-Arts–trained architect Bernard Maybeck, filled with Foster's impressive collection of modern and contemporary art and familiar to anyone involved in the Bay Area's *This Old House* subculture.

Unbeknownst to me, Foster took pictures of *The Girl* at the open house (technically a no-no, I believe) and began to explore some of his art sources for possible artists. Within days of seeing the painting, he notified me that he had come across the work of Xan Krohn (1882–1959), a Norwegian painter working between Norway, Russia and France. Krohn worked in Paris in the 1930s and Goldstrom believes this may be the artist of *The Girl in Red*.

Excited by the news from Foster, I did my own search and determined that most of Krohn's work has, I believe, very little in common with *The Girl in Red*. I agree with Foster that there are similar stylistic elements in some of his portraits, such as the one of Thomas Edison painted in Provence in 1920, with its thick black lines surrounding the face and upper body, and its non finito background. Though dubious, I await word from an Oslo art dealer Foster has contacted, Gidske Munthe, who sells Krohn's work in her gallery.

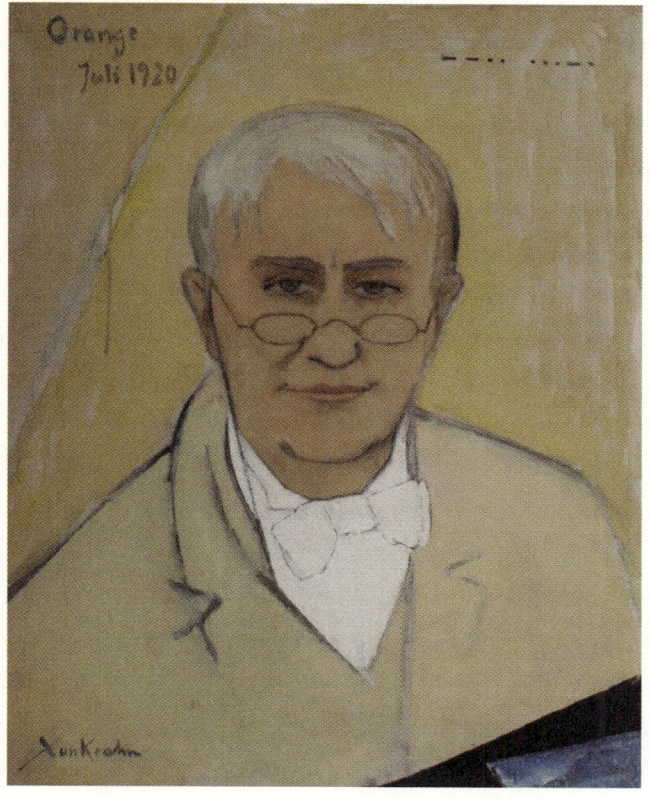

Portrait of Thomas Alva Edison *by Xan Krohn, 1920*

What is curious and ironic about Goldstrom's infatuation with *The Girl* and this possible attribution is that with all the effort I spent searching for clues in Paris with my Wanted posters, it's the authentic, auratic original now on display in Berkeley that has so moved someone to uncover the first credible lead. (Walter Benjamin, are you listening?) Even more curious is Goldstrom's connection to Yuri Kuper, as I soon discover at our first get-together. When he was a dealer in the 1970s, Foster met Yuri in Europe and bought one of his paintings. "Everyone in the art world knows everyone else," says Catherine Burns, the dealer I schmoozed with at Robert Johnson's Christmas party. She of course knows Foster and his collection.

The next time I meet with Foster to discuss *The Girl*, he offers me a catalog from a Yuri Kuper show he attended in Geneva, Switzerland, at Galerie Jan Krugier, one of the most important postwar galleries in Europe. I am just as astonished to find that the catalog's introduction is by John Berger as I was to find last year that Yuri's Pushkin Museum catalog had introductions by Peter Selz and Robert Johnson. Thanks to Foster's connection to Yuri, John Berger has now entered my narrative as a character, not merely as a brilliant, quotable critic. Six degrees of separation is a subset of heureux hasard.

I decide to contact Robert Johnson about Foster's possible Krohn connection. (Do I have to say that Foster and Robert knew each other back in the day?) Robert agrees with me that there are "a few superficial details" in common between Krohn's work and *The Girl*. "But," he continues with absolute certainty, "it's not Krohn. He is severe, yours is by someone softer and more emotionally sympathetic . . . like a painted 'snapshot' in the best sense, capturing the sensibility of childhood."

Then, an email from Gidske Munthe in Oslo, forwarded to me by Foster:

October 30, 2016

Dear Foster,

I am sorry this has taken so long. I have now been in contact with Kari Lien who is the author of the book "Xan og Julie Krohn-liv og kunst" that was published in 2015. She doubts this painting is by Xan—but cannot rule it out 100%. I am sorry that I am not able to give you further and better information. Xan Krohn has made some great paintings—one is exhibited in the exhibition "Modern Icons" in Paris right now. We do have a couple of great works for sale—in case you are interested.

Sincerely,
Gidske Munthe

Foster's hunch about Krohn was not off the wall, and his powerful attraction to *The Girl* has set off a chain reaction that keeps my journey alive, and Foster's. He is off to Paris to see some of the Krohns in the show Gidske Munthe mentioned in her email. That Krohn's biographer can't rule out Krohn 100 percent attests to Foster's instincts about art. Hidden behind his waggish, sometimes self-inflating, sometimes self-deprecating sense of humor, Foster has a deep knowledge of art that can seem surprising when revealed. He doesn't read books, he says, due to an ADHD disorder, but his years of gallery and collector experience are obvious when one is exposed to his private collection and public opinions.

After this unexpected close call with *The Girl*'s attribution, I consider my next steps. Some who read my online postings about *The Girl* in 2015 have advised me to follow a book about *The Girl* with a film that resolves its various mysteries fictionally. The idea has been percolating ever since I found the portrait.

If I were to transpose my journey from narrative text to a feature film, it would be, of course, in the form of a detective caper *à la* Tintin, a whodunit. In fact, a whodunit with two whos, the artist and the sitter. Well, three whos—add the idiot who threw out the painting.

The plot so far:

A girl is found sitting, dazed, on the sidewalk outside a café in Paris's Latin Quarter. It is January 1935. A regular at the café, a retired gallery owner, call him Gilbert, approaches the girl and determines she is suffering from amnesia following some unknown trauma. She does not know who she is, where she is, or where she lives. The only clue to her identity is a small painting she is carrying with her, her own portrait. It is dated several days before she is found but not signed. The café notifies the appropriate authorities who arrive to take the girl away, but not before Gilbert takes a photo of the girl and of the painting, resolving to try on his own to discover the identities of the two whos, the girl and the artist. Finding the artist will, Gilbert believes, uncover the girl's identity and the cause of her trauma. Gilbert, who has closed his art gallery, has been left idle and depressed, sitting all day in cafés playing cards with his former art-world cronies. The encounter with this "lost girl" offers him a road back to his former life and self.

The rest of the script remains to be written, but I imagine plot elements involving theft, extortion, abuse, even murder, all with the backdrop of a surreal art world in Paris in the 1930s. Tintin meets André Breton meets Georges Simenon.

Fiction has its dramatic advantages over nonfiction. The twists and turns of my journey, moored (mired?) in memoir, can't compete with the plot I am spinning for my whodunit, as Wikipedia defines the genre: "A complex, plot-driven detective story [where the] investigation is usually conducted by an eccentric, amateur, or semi-professional detective." Perfect! That's me. That's Gilbert. That's Tintin. But here's the stranger-than-fiction Wikipedia kicker: The term *whodunit* was coined by a literary critic writing for the American magazine *Variety* in . . . 1935.

THE END OF THE STORY?

○

I had naïve hopes that, one way or the other, Foster's efforts would mark the final finito of my non finito journey. Real feedback about real artists from real experts has satisfied my due diligence duty to explore *The Girl*'s provenance and authorship. But startling moments of heureux hasard continue to violate the boundaries I set. I understand better now why it took Patrick Modiano ten years to complete *Dora Bruder*. I am well into year two and counting.

Venturing out on a crisp January day into San Francisco's chic Hayes Valley, the neighborhood near the San Francisco Conservatory of Music I consider my Bay Area Left Bank, I enter the newly opened Jules Maeght (pronounced "mag") Gallery on Gough St. I'm curious about its connection to Galerie Maeght in Paris located on rue du Bac, just around the corner from my summer apartment.

I have walked past Galerie Maeght countless times in Paris, often stepping in to see its offerings. The gallery's specialty is twentieth-century art, and it's a showcase for many of the greats since the 1930s when the gallery first opened shop in Cannes—Matisse, Calder, Giacometti, Braque, Léger, Bonnard, Dubuffet and many others.

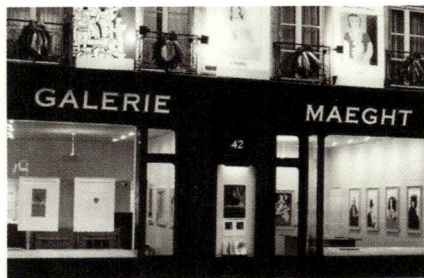

Galerie Maeght, rue du Bac, Paris

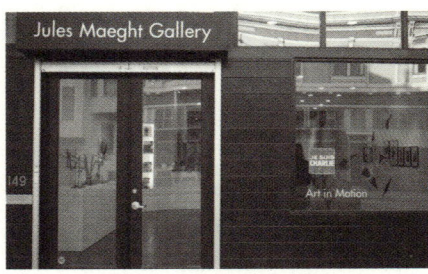

Jules Maeght Gallery, Gough St., San Francisco

The day I found *The Girl in Red*, I carried her back to my apartment along the Seine, up rue du Bac, past Galerie Maeght and on to blvd. Saint-Germain. I remember now wondering as I passed the gallery whether the mysterious painting was good enough to bring into a gallery of Maeght's stature. Now a Maeght gallery branch has opened just around the corner from a small studio apartment I stay in while working with my guitar collection at the conservatory, a second chance to show *The Girl* to this renowned dealer of modern art.

Engaging a friendly young man seated behind a large counter in the center of the ultrachic gallery space, I ask about the relationship between this Maeght and the Paris Maeght. Luc, the gallery manager, tells me that the owner, Jules Maeght, is the grandson of the legendary founders, Aimé and Marguerite Maeght. The new gallery will show contemporary art and some of the twentieth-century icons that made the family Maeght and its roster of artists famous.

I explain to Luc the coincidence of my apartment in Paris and now my studio in San Francisco both being so near a Maeght gallery. Giving him a brief rundown of my saga in Paris with *The Girl*, I show him the painting on my cell. It must have looked to him like a sad old Citroën in a showroom full of gleaming new Peugeots, but Luc expresses polite appreciation for the portrait. When I mention the book that I'm writing and ask him to send me a comment on *The Girl* from the point of view of a young gallerist in San Francisco, he agrees. I half-jokingly add that when my book is released, I would love to have a signing event at the gallery along with the painting on display. He smiles. I pause, then continue, "here in San Francisco *and* in Paris." He laughs and gently informs me that this Maeght gallery can be rented for private events.

Not hearing back from Luc, I return to the gallery and find him again behind the counter. This time he is sitting with a gentleman, mid-fifties I'm guessing, sporting a brightly colored Lacoste polo shirt and a well-trimmed beard. Jules Maeght.

Leaning against the reception counter after Luc introduces me to M. Maeght, I listen in while Luc describes my gleaning of *The Girl in Red* and the book that I'm writing about it. But when Luc explains my idea for an event at the gallery to celebrate the book with the painting on display, Maeght misunderstands. "*Non, non,*" he exclaims in his Frenchie English, "we only show our own artists and never give over the gallery to other artists." I flash on Gilbert telling me *non*, he would not give me Yuri Kuper's email address to send to Robert Johnson. The French have a way with their *non* that can be chilling. Ending hard on the consonant "n" gives the rebuff such finality and judgment.

Luc and I chime in, taking turns explaining that I am a writer with a book *about* a painting, not an artist *with* a painting, and that I want a reception for the published book, not a show. *The Girl in Red* would only be on display during the event. "Ah, *oui*, now I understand," Maeght replies.

With the ice broken, Luc pulls up on his computer the image I had sent him of *The Girl*. Maeght seems mildly interested but gives no opinion as to its artist and makes no judgment about its quality. He is more interested, it turns out, in the back of the canvas and asks about the stretcher bars. "You might be able to find the painter's name if you can identify the frame," he offers. When I tell him about the "15 F" written in pencil on one of the wooden bars and volunteer my conjecture that it represents the price in francs for the painting, perhaps at a flea market (*brocante* in French), Maeght responds dismissively, "*Non*, that's not the price; that's the frame's size."

I am startled and embarrassed, remembering how much time I had put into the inflation-adjusted estimate of what 15 francs in 1935 would mean in today's dollars. According to Maeght, frames in those days were sold in sizes—10 F, 15 F, 20 F, and so on—by just a few companies in Paris, and that one of them, he imagines, might still have records of the artists who bought 15 F stretcher bars in 1935.

I try joking with Maeght—"Seems like a stretch to me"—but the pun doesn't register, perhaps because it's in English. Maeght suggests that I send a photo of the painting, front and back, to an auction house in Paris to see whether they can identify the artist. Not Sotheby's, he cautions, because they are too big to care about my portrait and my story. But Piasa, a respected smaller auctioneer, would possibly respond.

I thank both gentlemen for their time and advice, and promise to report back on any response from Piasa. The idea of contacting an auction house had been suggested to me in Paris by one of the galleries near ground zero, but I never followed up. Now, with Jules Maeght on my team, or at least his name, I feel ready to try a Hail Mary pass. With the help of Lisa Taylor I craft a letter in French to Piasa that mentions Jules Maeght, and send it off with an attached image of the painting. The response is swift and surprising:

12 February, 2017

Dear Sir,

Thank you for your message. Unfortunately, in the absence of a signature, this picture could be attributed to quite a lot of artists. . . . The style [suggests], in my opinion, artists of the group "Forces Nouvelles," in particular Robert Humblot.

Sincerely,
Stéphane Corréard
Piasa

I learn online that Groupe Forces Nouvelles was officially launched in 1935 by the critic and artist Henri Heraut. That date, 1935 again! It's like an old dog on the street that won't leave you alone. My inner Tintin and his dog, Snowy, are back on the trail.

The Forces Nouvelles movement represented a pre–World War II effort to replace avant-garde trends associated with

Cubism and Surrealism with a more traditional approach, including elements of Impressionism and Fauvism. The movement's artists preached a return to figurative art, traditional drawing, and naturalism, but with modern subject matter. The only artist who escaped their censure was Picasso, an institution beyond reproach. To artists such as Robert Humblot and the young Pierre Tal-Coat, who took inspiration from Balthus and Manet, among others, earlier avant-garde styles were pretentious, overly political, and disconnected from art's traditional connection to classical beauty.

By the 1950s and '60s, however, it was clear who had won this *guerre d'art*. Tal-Coat had gone abstract (Tachism), Humblot faded into minor status and Groupe Forces Nouvelles was all but forgotten. Dubuffet's shocking Art Brut, along with Giacometti's ghostly bronze human extrusions, captured the Paris art scene. Abstract Expressionism conquered New York, and Francis Bacon's nightmare portrait bombs blitzed London. *La guerre est finie!*

In this context, I see Yuri Kuper as a survivor of that war, a contemporary synthesis. Whereas Dubuffet erases representation in his material fields and ghostly caricatures, Kuper retains representation, as did Giacometti and Bacon, but buries subjects in a muted material universe, coextensive with them.

On my next outing in San Francisco, I show Jules Maeght the response from Piasa. He is unimpressed. It sounds very vague to him and does not really offer a credible lead. The word he uses to describe Piasa's Forces Nouvelles suggestion is "conjecture." His *non* echoes in my brain. From my perspective, however, which I boldly share with Maeght, the response from Piasa confirms my own amateur critique of *The Girl*, especially the possible influence of Manet and Balthus, and now Robert Humblot and Pierre Tal-Coat. Although I have found nothing by them that is a match for *The Girl*, Tal-Coat's ghoulish portrait of Gertrude Stein from 1935 uses similar black outlining.

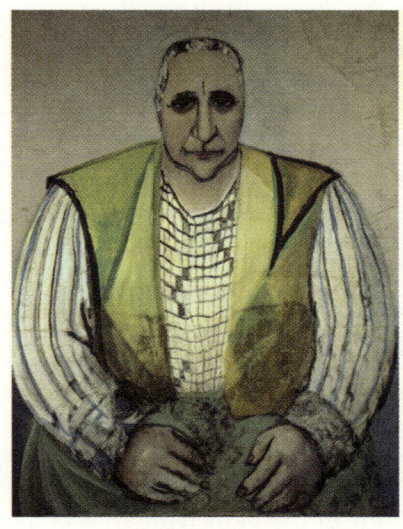

Portrait of Gertrude Stein
by Pierre Tal-Coat, 1935

Maeght is clearly unmoved by my analysis. He is right that the Piasa letter reveals nothing definitive. Going up against Maeght, I feel brave, but completely out of my depth. The Forces Nouvelles connection does play nicely into Dubuffet's 1940s rhetoric against nostalgia and the regressive return to tradition that this group of artists embraced, and one wonders if the Dubuffet of the mid-1930s was aware of the artists associated with this movement.

Leaving the gallery, another wild goose chase under my belt, I vow yet again to resist any further attempts—my own or others'—to establish *The Girl's* provenance and attribution. It's time to finish the book, not fish for clues—knowing, of course, that these vows are hopeless efforts at controlling a voyage that has an itinerary of its own, one that has not been shared with me.

Writing now at the kitchen table of a friend's comfortably ramshackle house in Stinson Beach, just north of San

Francisco, I am putting the finishing touches on my manuscript. I love being near the beach when I want to focus without interruption, especially when tidying up the loose ends of a project. The roar of the ocean, just a few hundred yards from the house, keeps me company, as do the primordial pelicans that lumber overhead as I gaze out the kitchen window.

After work this morning, I'll walk into town along the beach for lunch at the Parkside Café. There's a grilled ham-and-cheese sandwich on the menu, our dumbed-down version of the classic croque, which I've come to prefer. But I won't go near it. I have this idea that to end my book, I must cancel my subscription to ham and cheese. Luckily, the cheeseburger at the Parkside is very good. Beef and cheese.

Is this truly the end of the story? I feel like a juggler who stops, freeze-frame, with all the balls still up in the air. Maybe that's where they belong, up there, floating with Plato's forms, beyond my reach. And maybe one of the balls will fall and hit me on the head, like Newton's apple, launching me back into the journey.

Heureux hasard!

EPILOGUE

I

I've been living with and writing about *The Girl in Red* for at least seven years, since the summer of 2015 when I met her in Paris and started posting on social media. I have stood in front of *The Girl* countless times and have tried to express over and over again in words and images what I see and feel about her. I always see and feel something new. It's like any important relationship, or reality itself—it's always changing and, at the end of the day, always mysterious.

From a Paris sidewalk near the Latin Quarter to a Haussmann apartment in Saint-Germain-des Prés to an Italianate villa in Berkeley I moved into in 2017, and by some cosmic (and sometimes comic) process I characterize as heureux hasard, *The Girl* has become part of my life. I've added an exclamation point when I've used "heureux hasard" as a rallying cry, as in *Aux barricades!* (To the barricades!) But whatever you call the phenomenon—heureux hasard, serendipity, synchronicity, fate—I have submitted to it the way my alter ego Tintin submits to his escapades alongside Snowy, his canine companion—with dogged resolve.

And with gratitude too, because it would be foolish not to acknowledge a blessing. It's impossible for me not to think of *The Girl* as a blessing, though not from God via angels but metaphysically, or merely metaphorically or, on occasion, absurdly. Unless, of course, *The Girl* actually *is* an angel—from the ancient Greek word *angelos*, literally "messenger." I was born and raised in the City of Angels, after all, and must consider such possibilities.

The Girl has the uncanny power to grab and hold (obsess and hypnotize) whomever she meets, a *fétichisme d'art* in Benjaminian terms. In a sea of paintings and prints, sculpture, antique tapestries, vintage guitars and all the rest of the bric-a-brac displayed in my home's salon, she is always a surprise. When the Berkeley violinist Dan Flanagan came over recently to rehearse in front of a live audience the new compositions dedicated to him by his composer friends before an important New York concert—each piece inspired by a work from his impressive collection of nineteenth- and twentieth-century paintings—he made a beeline for *The Girl in Red*. He swept past my antic Picasso lithograph, a charming Bonnard sketch, a *trompe-l'oeil* sculpture by the contemporary ceramicist Richard Shaw, a stunning Elizabethan-era tapestry, my mother's dramatic portrait by Eckard Heidrich and many other intriguing works. All he saw in the room was the anonymous *Girl in Red*.

"What is *that*?" he exclaimed, facing *The Girl*.

Dan is a large man in his forties with boyish good looks. His imposing bulk belies the delicate finesse of his fiddling. I responded to his question with the short version of finding the painting and writing a book about it. He was fascinated by the portrait and amused by the story. Competitive collector types appreciate one another's embellished tales of acquisition. (I suppose one could describe my book as an "embellished tale of acquisition.") I truly believe that had I offered *The Girl* to Dan, he would have gone for it in a heartbeat, albeit at a price well short of the $1 million I teasingly posted on social media back in 2015. But after Christie's 2017 sale of Leonardo da Vinci's portrait of Christ, *Salvator Mundi*, to Mohammed Bin Salman for a record-setting sale price of almost $500 million (despite the portrait's dubious authorship and an excessive restoration I consider "distoration"), *The Girl* should by all rights go for double my earlier price. N'est-ce pas?

When my Paris Facebook posts about *The Girl in Red* expanded into a book-length manuscript in 2017, it failed to attract a publisher, despite the efforts of an agent who loved it. I shelved it and began another project, a collection of all my Paris food articles and illustrations published by *Zester Daily* (now defunct, *quel dommage!*). The croque monsieur survey that brought me to Paris in 2015 became a chapter in *Café French: A Flâneur's Guide to the Language, Lore & Food of the Paris Café*, published in 2019.

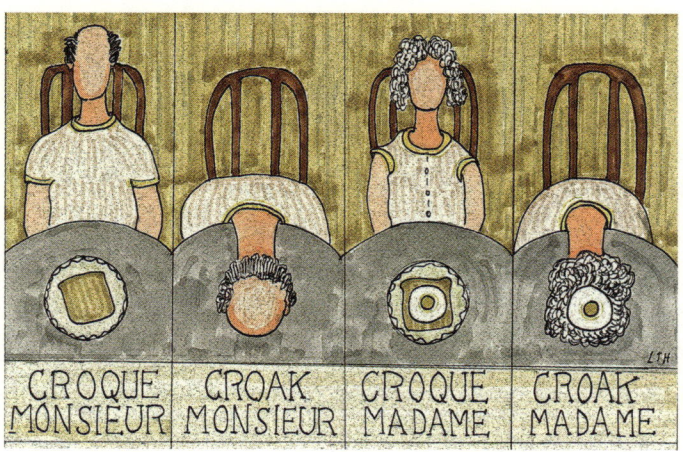

This illustration, "Croque/Croak,"
accompanied my Zester Daily *article in 2015.*

Since the publication of *Café French* and an illustrated COVID memoir in 2022—*My Little Plague Journal*—my connection to *The Girl in Red* has continued to unfold à la Tintin, but also à la Renoir and his corny but colorful cork theory of life. In a book about his father (*Renoir, My Father*), the filmmaker Jean Renoir relates the great impressionist's theory, which I paraphrase: we live our lives like corks following a river's current with no set destination and no real navigational control other than minor adjustments as we lean left and right.

So I document my travels with *The Girl in Red* down the river of life, in search of her factual and metafactual story, steering incrementally this way and that, hyperfocused on my pictorial *amour fou*. *The Girl* plays not only the love interest in my book's narrative but a central role in my life's narrative as well, joining me with family, friends, colleagues and, from time to time, an actual amour fou. Like all (or most) of these characters, *The Girl* will be with me, come what may, until the end.

II

Although my apparently never-ending quest for *The Girl's* provenance continues—more now out of casual curiosity than urgent necessity—my obsessive fascination with the painting has expanded to questions about art itself and its impact on my life as a part-time maker and full-time viewer. If I have learned anything during my adventures with *The Girl*, it's that the images viewers respond to most powerfully have a profound presence that live on in their eyes, minds and souls. These images are not merely artifacts; they are art-I-facts, existing not only as discrete objects with formal aesthetic qualities but in relationship to the intellectual, emotional and spiritual responses of their viewers. And of their artists too, for they are the first viewers of their work.

But I can't fully explain *why* this is so. Why do we respond so powerfully to art? My hunch—more than a hunch, a conviction—is that there is in our engagement with art something deeply psychological and, I believe, spiritual (or metaphysical if you prefer), but also connected to our very survival as a species. (See Denis Dutton's book *The Art Instinct.*) Our response to art's images can be so powerful, in fact (and this extends to all the arts), that some viewers experience what medical science has labeled Stendhal syndrome, a constellation of psychosomatic symptoms ranging from rapid heartbeat and fainting spells to confusion and even hallucinations.

This condition was first identified, or at least named, by a Florentine psychiatrist named Graziella Magherini in the 1970s after treating visitors to Florence's art treasures. She chose the name after reading Stendhal's description of being overwhelmed by the art and architecture he saw while in Florence in 1817 in his *Naples and Florence: A Journey from Milan to Reggio*: "I had palpitations of the heart, what in Berlin they call 'nerves.' Life was drained from me. I walked with the fear of falling." I had to laugh when I came across this comment because my response to Stendhal's art—*The Red and the Black*—was far from a "fear of falling." More like, as I've previously confessed, a fear of falling asleep.

If the *why* of a painting's power remains elusive and in philosophical flux after hundreds of years of Western aesthetic theory (what the contemporary philosopher Graham Harman describes as the ever-mysterious Je ne sais quoi of art) the *where* and *how* of art are becoming clearer. Neuroscientists such as V. S. Ramachandran at UC San Diego and Semir Zeki at University College London are giving us an increasingly vivid neurological map of aesthetic experience. They may not be able to tell us what a particular work of art means, or why it is so powerful, but they have identified the neural structures that "light up" when we see, read, hear, taste or touch objects we identify as beautiful, sublime or merely pleasurable. This is the medial orbitofrontal cortex (the OFC), according to Zeki, the reward center of our brain. Aesthetic pleasure connected neurologically to sensual pleasure, emotion and memory is, these researchers claim, innate in humans and part of our evolutionary inheritance. Beauty is in our DNA.

Clearly, *The Girl in Red* has lit up the reward center in my brain and one other area—the default mode network (the DMN) that has been identified with introspection and daydreaming. Flâneurs take note.

Having neurological mappings of where art appreciation is happening is hugely instructive and suggestive. It's as if when I found *The Girl* on rue Guénégaud, a map of my brain was overlaid onto a city map of Paris, weaving an infinite web of connections, imagined and real, where Saint-Germain-des-Prés and the Latin Quarter touch—ground zero. *The Girl in Red* has given me access to this composite psychic topography, a merger of romanticism and neuroscience, at its deepest point—my sweet spot in Paris. This is where I met my *Girl*. This is where Abelard met Héloïse.

The other big art lesson I've learned from my years with a lost and found painting relates to time and the duration of aesthetic contemplation. Julian Barnes laments what he finds when he goes to a museum and observes the crush of spectators, some of whom truly wish to linger with their favorite pieces. From *Keeping an Eye Open*: "How long do we spend with a good painting? Ten seconds, thirty? Two whole minutes? . . . Even such a spectator can come to the end of a big show with a truculent feeling of what might have been."

So much for the power of aura, adrift in a sea of cell phones and headphones.

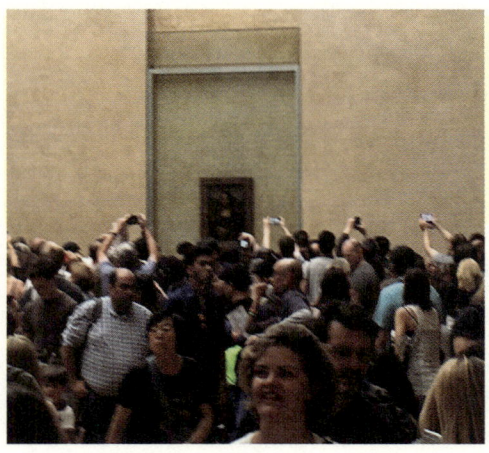

Navigating the crowds at the Louvre in front of the Mona Lisa *in 2016*

Likewise for the late, great philosopher of aesthetics and mind, Richard Wollheim, who taught philosophy and chaired the department at UC Berkeley in the 1980s and '90s. Serious contemplation of a painting requires time—time for the clutter of everyday consciousness to fade away, allowing for a deeply personal experience of the work to emerge via, according to Wollheim, psychodynamic processes that link the viewer's experience and the artist's intentions. Here is Wollheim poised in front of a painting, as quoted in Arthur Danto's poignant obituary of the philosopher in the *The Guardian* (November 5, 2003):

I evolved a way of looking at paintings which was massively time consuming and deeply rewarding. For I came to recognize that it often took the first hour or so in front of a painting for stray associations or motivated misperceptions to settle down, and it was only then, with the same amount of time or more to spend looking at it, that the picture could be relied upon to disclose itself as it was. I noticed that I became an object of suspicion to passersby, and so did the picture that I was looking at.

One has to admire a world-class philosopher who can express himself with such humility and humor, and in accessible prose, though his widely influential "seeing-in" theory (our ability to see images and meaning in a two-dimensional surface) is much less accessible. And though challenged by postmodernist critics, Wollheim's Freudian perspective on interpretation is something I share.

I don't have Barnes's or Wollheim's problem. I've had years with *The Girl in Red*, not minutes or hours. *The Girl* and her aura are on full display, day and night, in my home, and there are no limits on the duration of my contemplation. Days will go by, even weeks and months, when I don't look at her, but she comes vividly back to life when I see her again. Startling new associations reveal themselves.

III

In the back of my mind, ever since gleaning *The Girl*, I have had an inkling that the painting's impact on me has something to do with a painting from my childhood, a portrait of a young female, just the head and shoulders, hanging in the living room of the home my family moved into when I was five years old. Something about that face, though quite faint in memory, has always seemed linked to *The Girl In Red*. I've never explored the connection—until now.

There is no head covering in my memory of this young lady. Her hair is dark and straight and pulled back tight behind her head. The painting is an oil, perhaps late nineteenth century, perhaps British. There is possibly a young man next to her, but I can barely see him in my mind's eye. I see only her.

Heureux hasard! Going through a storage box in my garage soon after starting work on this epilogue, I found old magazines I'd saved from the 1970s and '80s that feature my food cartoons ("foodoodles") and foodie articles. Digging down into the pile, out popped a drawing in pencil and gouache of that girl in the portrait in my house, signed with my father's initials and dated January 1966, the year I left home to attend UC Berkeley. Glimpsing this drawing for the first time in decades (I had completely forgotten about it), I experienced a Stendhalian shudder that forced me to sit down. My art and memory neurons were tripping the light fantastic. I named the drawing right then and there: *My Father's Girl*.

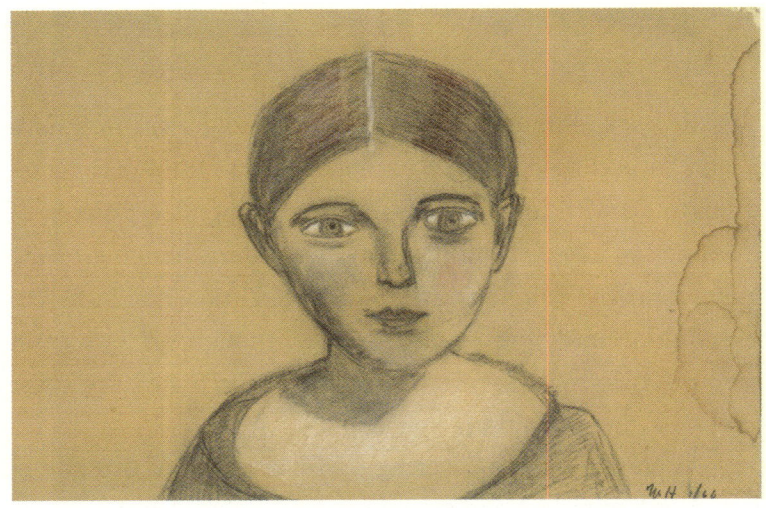

My Father's Girl *by Mervin Harris, January 1966*

What the drawing was doing buried under a bunch of old magazines, I have no idea. Perhaps I placed it in the box to protect it during one of my several house moves in the 1990s. It's as if I had buried my father—and my trauma regarding his premature death in 1969—under the food journalism I had begun in 1971, literally and psychologically.

My father's lost and found *Girl* has so filled in my memory of that faint image from my childhood that I really can't tell the difference now between the drawing and the memory of that painting, and the resemblances between *My Father's Girl* and my *Girl* are utterly uncanny: Both girls float in a non finito background; the hair of *My Father's Girl*, fastened behind her head, much like *The Girl's* scarf, has reddish highlights; both faces present bilateral facial dissonance; and the dark eyes— it's all about the eyes, the windows of the soul. Crazier still, both paintings have water stains, at the bottom of my *Girl*, and on the right edge of my father's drawing.

The effects of Stendahl syndrome (he called them "nerves") are indeed unnerving, and persist longer than I would have guessed. If heureux hasard strikes sharp as lightning, Stendhal syndrome rumbles on like thunder. I'm not as surprised at the appearance of my father in my narrative as I am mystified. Did my "inner lost girl" need her father? Did my unconscious call on my "old man," the archetype of the Wise Old Man who appears at the end of the individuation process described by Carl Jung? And is my father's *Girl* an image of *his* inner lost girl, as Susan Griffin commented when I showed her his drawing? In any case, my father is, like *The Girl in Red* (like Walter Pater's *Mona Lisa*), back from the dead.

If all of this seems more suitable for a therapy office than a book about art, I won't argue the point. Had Hergé's Tintin been a psychologist instead of a journalist, he could have gone on an adventure in my psyche and figured all this out. Bottom line, heureux hasard is not finished with me.

IV

Sorting through photographs from my 2016 Paris poster mission to select those that will appear in my book, I've come across the one I took of an affiche mounted next to mine (almost touching it) on rue Visconti that showed a girl in a blue head cover. The Russian artist, Ekaterina Aristova, was having a show that I had intended to go see but never did, one of many roads not taken in Paris that summer. I have now written to

Ekaterina about our "poster connection" and requested a copy of hers to frame and hang next to mine in my office (almost touching). I also invited her response to *The Girl in Red* and to the opinion I received from the Piasa auction house, that the artist of my painting might be among those in the art community known in the 1930s as Forces Nouvelles.

The email response from Ekaterina, which included a digital image of her poster, in her own very good English:

August 13, 2022

Dear Mr. Harris,

Thank you for your message. Such a surprise! It's a pleasure reading you.

I don't think the artist of your lovely painting was part of the Forces Nouvelles. I would suppose an artist involved at La Ruche or even the Russian artist Zinaida Serebriakova. Your *Girl in Red* is very similar to her unfinished style and love for red color accents. She used to paint her daughters Katia and Tanya, and in the 1930s she was very active here in France.

Please send me a copy of the book.

Greetings from Paris!

Ekaterina

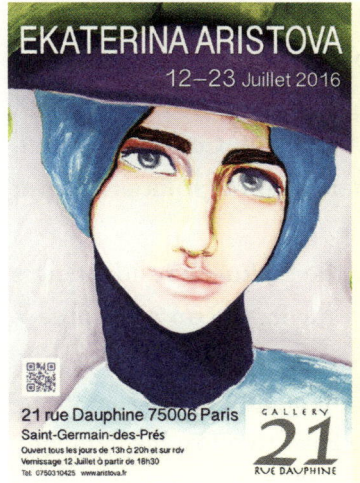

Ekaterina has sent me the poster from her 2016 Paris show. She informs me that her "girl in blue" is titled Belle Inconnue (Beautiful Unknown). *I inform her about Balzac's* Le Chef-d'Oeuvre Inconnu (The Unknown Masterpiece), *which she vows to read.*

Looking at Serebriakova's work on the web, I note a few of her portraits with unfinished backgrounds and upper bodies. One of a young fisherman from 1934 comes the closest to a match, but it's clear to me for a variety of reasons that Serebriakova is not the artist of *The Girl in Red*. Ekaterina agrees. From a second email: "Looking at the numbers in your painting's date, they don't look like those in her dated works."

Ekaterina's comment about La Ruche is an interesting lead that I pass on to future owners of *The Girl*. And to Foster Goldstrom, who hasn't given up on the possibility that Xan Krohn is the artist. He is intrigued by the possible La Ruche connection. Could Krohn have lived at La Ruche? I don't find his name among the artists described in a memoir I have located by the La Ruche artist Marvena, *Life with the Painters of La Ruche*.

The La Ruche building complex in Montparnasse dates to 1902, when it became a popular low-cost living and exhibition space for some of Paris's most famous artists-to-be, many of them Russian, many Jewish, all of them poor immigrants who came to Paris to be part of the École de Paris. La Ruche's roster is notable: Alexander Archipenko, Fernand Léger, Jacques Lipchitz, Chaim Soutine, Amedeo Modigliani, Constantin Brancusi, Diego Rivera, and many others. Although Picasso never lived there, he was part of the scene.

Perhaps most famous among the La Ruche residents was Marc Chagall. There are stories in my family on my mother's side (Dolkart) that they grew up near the Chagalls in Vitebsk, a Jewish shtetl in Belarus. One of them almost married Marc, it is claimed, before he went off to Paris to make his name. By 1935, Chagall, the Jew, was no longer being mentioned in Paris art publications, and by 1940 all École de Paris artists (Jewish or not, they were labeled degenerate) were forbidden by the Vichy government to exhibit their works in France.

La Ruche is still functioning today after a demolition threat was successfully resisted in 1968 by a group of artists, writers and filmmakers, including Jean-Paul Sartre, Jean Renoir and Alexander Calder. Perhaps the artist in a film version of *The Girl in Red*, along with the girl and her parents, will be Russian Jewish immigrants discovered to be living at La Ruche by the detective hero Gilbert, my repurposed Latin Quarter nemesis. La Ruche would be an exciting backdrop for a portrait of Paris's art scene in the 1930s and '40s.

V

Another potential breakthrough has emerged, or at least an opportunity to connect with experts in the field of provenance: the folks at DOMOS Art Advisers, headquartered in London. I gleaned DOMOS's Erin Martin and Ty Murphy after reading Martin's online article about a lost Picasso painting in Terrance Gelenter's *Paris Insider* newsletter. I immediately contacted Martin to pick her brain about a possible provenance search. She was so excited about the image of *The Girl* attached to my email that she insisted I talk to Ty Murphy, the head of her copany. She set up a three-way Zoom meeting from her home in Paris, and we were off and Zooming.

Murphy is an art advisor and authenticator—he calls himself an "art detective"—and a Picasso specialist who advises the Online Picasso Project, an important digital *catalogue raisonné* of the artist's work. He also publishes *Art & Museum*, a magazine for wealthy collectors.

At our Zoom meeting, while Ty, a jocular Brit, digs into a take-out order of fish and chips at his London residence (it was dinnertime there), he comments on Erin's first question about whether the painting is finished or not. His impression is that *The Girl* is unfinished. I chime in with my take on this debate that has raged on the issue since the Renaissance. Ty responds: "That debate could go on forever. Some artists, like Picasso, never finished works." When I quote Robert Johnson's position, that my portrait is indeed finished because of its having been dated, Ty challenges this with the example, again, of Picasso. "He never signed or dated his paintings, whether finished or unfinished, until they were sold."

Agreeing to disagree, we move on to *The Girl*'s possible Russian connection. "She really does look Russian," says Ty. "I mean, that's my first instinct." Erin may have prompted Ty on this because she works with a group of Russian collectors, consulting on their purchases, and has seen a lot of Russian portraits. The minute Erin saw *The Girl*, she thought the sitter was Russian.

"She doesn't look like a peasant," Ty continues. "She looks well fed, and her face is not skinny. It's not a poor person. Could be the artist's child or a family member. Or it could be a commission." And then, after more discussion, including Ty's conjecture that someone brought the painting to one of the dealers near La Palette to get a valuation and then "chucked it on the sidewalk" when they got the disappointing answer, he recommends that I contact a colleague in London, an expert on provenance, Angelina Giovani. He will be seeing her at the Paris Frieze show the following week and will discuss the painting with her. "Then," he adds, "we can have another Zoom to discuss her involvement in the search."

Our meeting comes to a close with an agreement to reconvene after Ty's conversation with Ms. Giovani. I was beginning to warm again to the idea, perhaps impressed by Ty's art-world status. "But it's not going to be cheap," Ty blurts out. "Her minimum is 3,000 euros, and I won't get a penny of it." And then his final seductive tease: "If you find out that the painting is by an important artist, you don't just have a book; you have a movie."

Word came back quickly through Erin that Giovani was overbooked and couldn't take on another client. And then another email from Erin: a friend of hers in Paris, a woman with "serious psychic gifts," had taken a look at *The Girl* and has the strong impression that she came to Paris from "somewhere around what is now Poland, but," she adds, "she is not Polish." Also, "the artist was unknown at the time of the painting and remains so." The psychic's email to Erin concludes with, "I agree with you that she has a very alluring and haunting look that pulls you in. A sadness and yet innocence."

I asked Erin if I could follow up with more questions for the psychic about the artist's gender and nationality, but, she responded, this is all her friend sees in the portrait. In other words, *non*. Finito.

After this latest flirtation with a professional provenance search, and combining the educated guesses and research suggestions of Ty Murphy, Ekaterina Aristova, Foster Goldstrom and Catherine Burns, I am ready to present an admittedly fanciful summary of my findings regarding *The Girl in Red*:

Summary Report on Provenance and Attribution*
September 12, 2022
The Girl in Red

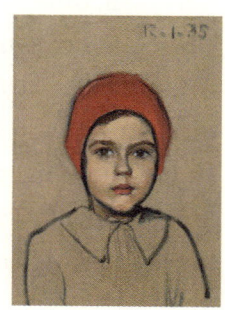

This oil portrait on linen of a young girl (probably Polish or Russian, according to the DOMOS Art Advisor Network**) was presumably painted in Paris, France, where it was found on a sidewalk in Saint-Germain-des-Prés on July 26, 2015, in front of 35, rue Guénégaud by its current owner, L. John Harris. It measures 17" × 22"and was completed (dated) on January 12, 1935, as written on the upper right corner of the canvas. The artist's signature or initials are not present. The pencil marking "15 F" on the back of the stretcher bars indicates the size of the frame.*** The numeral "1" in the painting's date is not in the French style (looks like our "7"), which suggests that the artist was not French. The "1" on the back of the frame is a French "1," suggesting that the canvas was put on the frame in Paris.

The subject's face and red head covering, presumably a scarf tied behind the head, are fully painted, and the torso and background are unfinished. Stylistic elements of the portrait suggest the work of the Norwegian artist Xan Krohn, but this attribution is doubtful, according to the artist's biographer, Kari Lien, though it "cannot be ruled out 100%."**** There are also similarities to the work of artists of the Groupe Forces Nouvelles in Paris during the 1930s, according to the Piasa auction house in Paris,***** and to the work of Russians living at the La Ruche artist colony in Paris from the same period, according to the Paris-based Russian artist, Ekaterina Aristova.******

No details of previous ownership have been uncovered despite an extensive Wanted poster posting campaign in Saint-Germain-des-Prés and the Latin Quarter carried out by Mr. Harris in July of 2016. Materials related to this project have been archived by Mr. Harris. The known details of the work have been submitted to the Art Loss Register in London for further investigation.*******

A Google Images reverse search turned up no close matches to *The Girl* in style, location, period and authorship.

*This report does not comply with the guidelines from the International Foundation of Art Research (IFAR).

**From a Zoom conference call between DOMOS representatives and the owner in October of 2022.

***According to Jules Maeght of the Jules Maeght Gallery in San Francisco from a conversation with the owner in January of 2017.

****Email to Foster Goldstrom in October of 2016, from Gidske Munthe, an art dealer in Oslo, Norway.

*****Email from Piasa to the owner in February of 2017.

******Email from Ekatrina Aristova to the owner in August of 2022.

*******The response from ALR will be attached to this report when received.

It may be presumptuous for me to prepare this summary report, but who else is going to do it? And it hasn't cost me the 3,000 euros Ty Murphy estimated for a professional report, though three thousand days in the grip of heureux hasard is payment enough. I will archive the report along with other material gathered on my journey: Yuri Kuper's Pushkin

Museum catalog; Jean Dubuffet's Acquavella catalog; the "mafia"-tagged avis de recherche poster; Ekaterina Aristova's poster of her *Girl in Blue*; my avis de recherche poster signed by all those present at the Terrance Gelenter salon in 2016; Yuri Kuper's Geneva gallery catalog with an introduction by the late John Berger; the student paper inserted into the Diderot book in London; and other items that may follow. (Heureux hasard!)

VI

At about the same time that I was corresponding with Ekaterina and Zooming with the DOMOS team, it was suggested that I have my own portrait painted. Curious that I've never thought to do this after years of investigating and writing about a portrait. (I suppose one could label my book a literary self-portrait.)

It was Marcia Masse of Masse's Pastries in North Berkeley's Gourmet Ghetto who made the suggestion. She saw *The Girl in Red* back in 2015 and knew I'd been writing a book about it. "It's definitely the time in your life for you to have your own portrait made," she argued, as I was purchasing one of her husband Paul's excellent almond croissants. (His are my favorite version of the butter-rich confection this side of Paris, though the butter content seems even higher in Paris. Marcia disagrees and takes pride in her husband's commitment to butter in Berkeley's olive oil–leaning food scene.)

The portrait artist that Marcia proposed to me, Max Thill, is a young painter and art restorer in Berkeley, the son of one of her customers. In his late twenties now, Max painted a portrait of poster artist David Lance Goines in whose Berkeley print shop he had apprenticed as a teenager. Marcia was impressed by it. Then followed portraits of the owners of Saul's Delicatessen, next door to Masse's, and, most recently, Paul Masse.

The idea of a formal portrait has, frankly, never appealed to me, especially if paid for by the subject—me. My friends in art school drew and painted me, as I did them, but it seems pretentious to pay for one's own portrait. Robert Johnson's potent pitch for painted portraits in a recent documentary film about another Berkeley portrait artist, Valentin Popov, by the filmmaker and artist Celik Kayalar makes the case: "A lot of photographs of ourselves end up in drawers after we die," Robert explains, "but paintings, especially if they are good paintings, are going to live a long time . . . a lot longer than we are." At this stage in my life, "living longer through portraiture" is starting to have a certain appeal. Curiosity eventually overcomes modesty, and I agree to meet with Max at my home to discuss the idea. If nothing else, I will get his professional impressions of *The Girl in Red*.

Standing with Max now in front of *The Girl*, he makes some interesting observations. The techniques used by *The Girl*'s artist suggest to him skill and talent, if not professional status. Max has studied Renaissance art and, prompted by David Goines, copied many classical paintings in true École des Beaux-Arts student style. In *The Girl* he sees the Renaissance practice of *sprezzatura*, an expression of nonchalance, as if the artist completed the painting with little effort. The seemingly dashed-off date reinforces this observation. The inclusion of the day and month in the date also suggests to Max a technique known as *alla prima*—"at the first attempt"—or, in one sitting.

There are some areas of paint that appear to Max to have been dry before color was added on top, suggesting that the portrait may have been worked on over the course of time, but to Max's eye much of the paint was applied "wet-on-wet," another property of alla prima.

Finally, Max doesn't see what I had assumed to be a water stain running along the bottom of the canvas. Instead, he speculates that the discolored area is where the applied primer (made of animal-skin glue, he surmises), darker in color than the raw linen, has pooled at the bottom of the canvas.

Hearing Max's analysis of *The Girl* reveals technical links to Leonardo's *Mona Lisa* I hadn't been aware of. I'm impressed. I promise Max that I will take a careful look at his work on his website and let him know if a commission is in the cards. But I still have my doubts. If an artist had approached me with an offer to paint my portrait because of, say, my interesting face, that would be another story. Or, as with Robert Johnson, had someone offered me a portrait of myself in exchange for writing something for their website or show catalog, I'd be inclined. But did Dr. Paul Gachet pay Vincent van Gogh for his two portraits in 1890? No. Van Gogh wanted to show off his ideas about portraiture and used his fellow artist and caretaker as his model. Of course Van Gogh had a means of support, his brother, Theo. Max has to earn his keep. Worth considering.

Then, soon after the meeting, an idea emerges from out of the blue (*all'improvviso*) that has resolved any lingering doubts. I can connect my portrait with *The Girl in Red*, literally and conceptually, a dual portrait, me and *The Girl*, side by side on the same canvas. I will play the role of the auratic original, *The Girl* a copy. And that was that—applied aesthetic philosophy meets conceptual art collaboration. My portrait becomes part of my journey, joining *The Girl* in her two-dimensional reality.

Fully on board now with this idea, I contact Max and pitch the concept: For the portrait, I will wear my usual fedora, its sage-green color altered to harmonize more closely with *The Girl's* red scarf. My three-quarter pose will turn in toward *The Girl's* position, which turns slightly toward me. My face and unfinished torso will be outlined with thick blue-black lines, matching *The Girl's*. Finally, and critically important, the canvas will be finished on January 12, with Max's signature at the bottom and dates in two places—12-1-35 above *The Girl* and 12-1-23 above me.

Max has agreed enthusiastically to the proposal, and I have agreed somewhat less enthusiastically to his price. Van Gogh and Dr. Gachet are still wandering around my brain, but Max's price is more than fair given that *The Girl* was free, a gift of the gods, and the two paintings average out to a more than reasonable price per portrait. (A strange-sounding collector's calculus, I admit.) We set a date for a photo shoot that will provide the basis for my portrait.

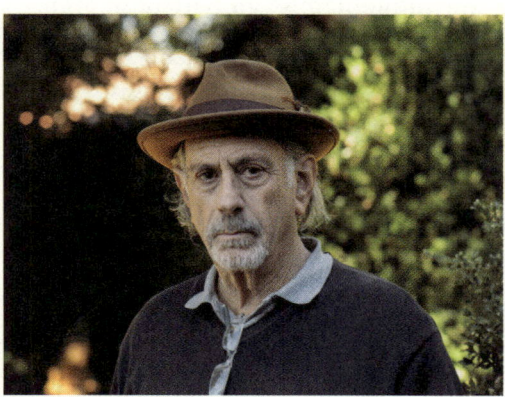

The photo by Max Thill to be used for the portrait

A truly gifted but shy young man with a certain Quattro-cento air about him, Max Thill is the perfect choice for the proj-ect. He is modest enough to sign on to my concept and talented enough to pull it off. Having been exposed to postmodern crit-ical theory in his undergraduate classes at the University of Chicago before turning to painting and drawing, Max is famil-iar with Walter Benjamin's concept of aura, and responsive to the theoretical and theatrical nature of the commission.

In terms of the traditions of portraiture, I'm not sure where to place this dual portrait (I'll call it *Dual Portrait with Aura*). It will have elements of conceptual art and pastiche, and there will be shades of Arthur Danto in it, an homage to his brilliant theories and narratives that have guided me to a basic understanding of the cultural shift from modernism to postmodernism and beyond. Some critics today are calling this "beyond" *metamodernism*, a synthesis of sorts, the best of both worlds, they seem to be saying. Although somewhat prema-ture in terms of naming a major new cultural "ism," and a bit New-Agey (though a welcome shift away from what the linguist and philosopher Noam Chomsky, a harsh critic of postmodern doctrine, describes as the unintelligible "gibberish" of France's radical intellectuals of the 1960s and beyond), proponents of metamodernism see a paradigm shift that makes sense: an "os-cillation" between overly optimistic modernist doctrine and overly pessimistic postmodern theory that allows for a synthe-sis of the naïve enthusiasms of the former and the cynical ni-hilism of the latter.

My attraction to Danto's perspectives on art, though *un peu passé peut-être*, is not so surprising given that my own sen-sibilities were shaped during that same period: the year Danto first saw Warhol's *Brillo Boxes*, 1964, is one year after my first trip to Paris to visit my older brother, who was attending the Sorbonne, and my first viewing of Picasso, Dali, Matisse and Manet outside of art books. But it may be that my attraction to Danto has more to do with his decades-long obsession with the *Brillo Boxes* than with his theories about them. Warhol must have triggered the same area of Danto's brain that *The Girl* triggered in mine.

A remarkable sentence from Danto's 1984 essay "The End of Art" describes far more eloquently than I can the aspirations of my art exercise with Max:

> All there is at the end is theory, art having finally become vaporized in a dazzle of pure thought about itself, and remaining, as it were, solely as the object of its own theoretical consciousness.

The essay was not predicting the literal end of art, according to the philosopher Noël Carroll, who teaches today at the City University of New York and considers Danto the greatest art critic of the second half of the twentieth century. Danto only meant that art would never be the same after Warhol, that the grand narrative of the Western art canon had come to an end.

Carroll thinks Danto was right about that. So do I.

Presumptuously, as with my provenance report, and prematurely—my portrait is not even finished—I will give the collaboration with Max a Danto-esque art-critical shot:

> *Dual Portrait with Aura* by Max Thill will be an experiment in collaborative portraiture by artist and sitter,

nostalgically embedded in mimesis, but realized perfor-
matively and ironically in the service of metamodernist
synthesis. Pairing my authentic, one-of-a-kind presence
on canvas with *The Girl*'s copied image will pass her aura
on to me—1935 to 2023—launching a hybrid presence
and provenance that oscillates between multiple time dimensions: past (hers), present (mine), and future (ours).

Assuming that *Dual Portrait with Aura* will remain beside
The Girl going forward in time, the preview here (along with
my book) can follow in their wake, to be noted in the provenance reports that accompany future transfers of ownership.
Although I am the first recorded owner of both the *Girl in Red*
and Max Thill's *Dual Portrait with Aura*, I will not be the last
(though perhaps the most verbose).

VII

I t's a late fall day in November, and I'm working at Stinson
Beach in the house where I often go to clean up manuscripts
and fish for endings. Endings are, obviously, harder for me
than beginnings and continuings. Louis Pons, the artist in Agnès Varda's gleaning documentary—he passed away just last
year—spoke in the film about art as "tidying up" one's inner
and outer world. He also described the found objects he put
into his reliefs and assemblages as his "sentences." My found
object, a painting, an obsession, has become many thousands
of sentences, and it's hard to stop—as if I've been "sentenced"
(by what court?) to continue. Hoping at the last minute to find

a way to extend my narrative, I've done some research into the formal structure of memoirs. There seems to be nothing after an epilogue except appendixes and, of course, sequels. (Note to self.)

Max Thill tells me he is making good progress on the portrait and will make the deadline. I can't wait to see it. But now it's time, after much fishing, to cut bait. I'll just get up from my desk, turn off my computer and walk out to the beach. I'll go up to that wavy line where the sand meets the sea and stop.

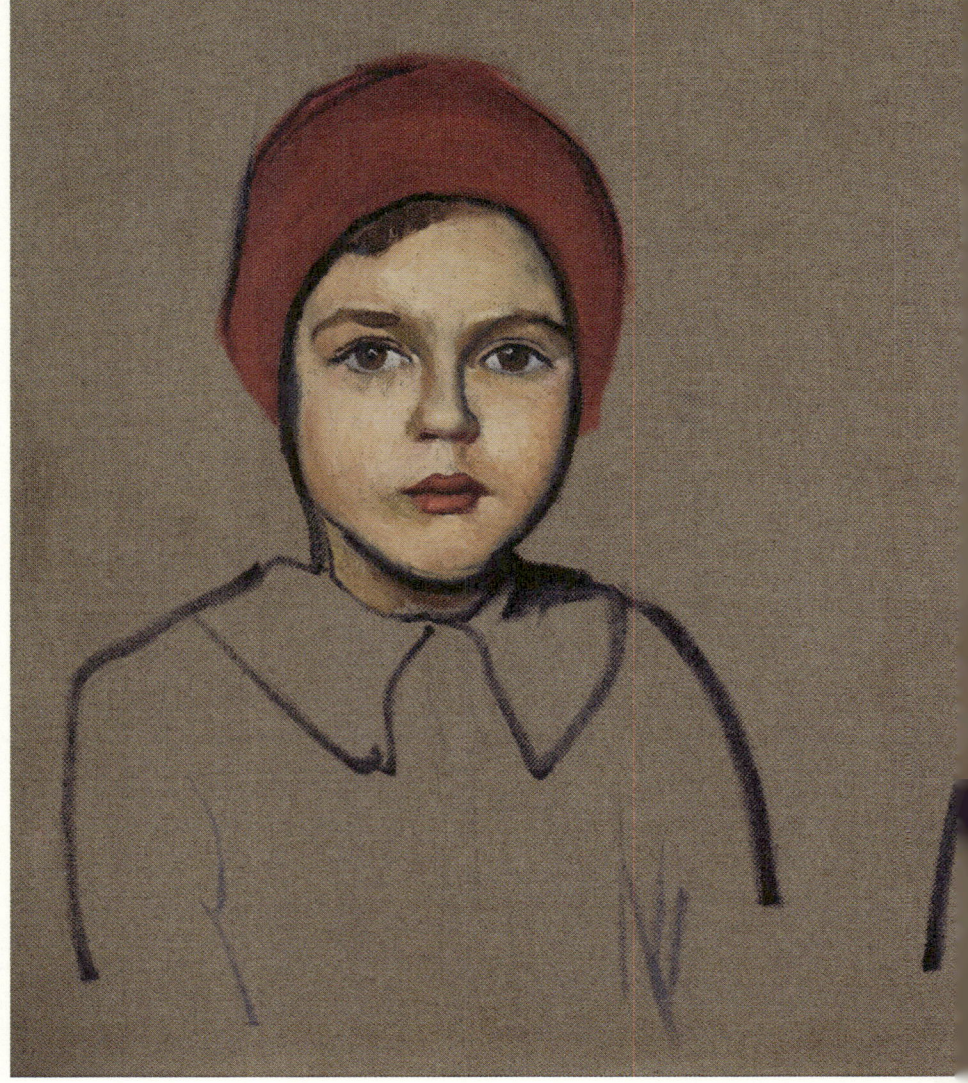

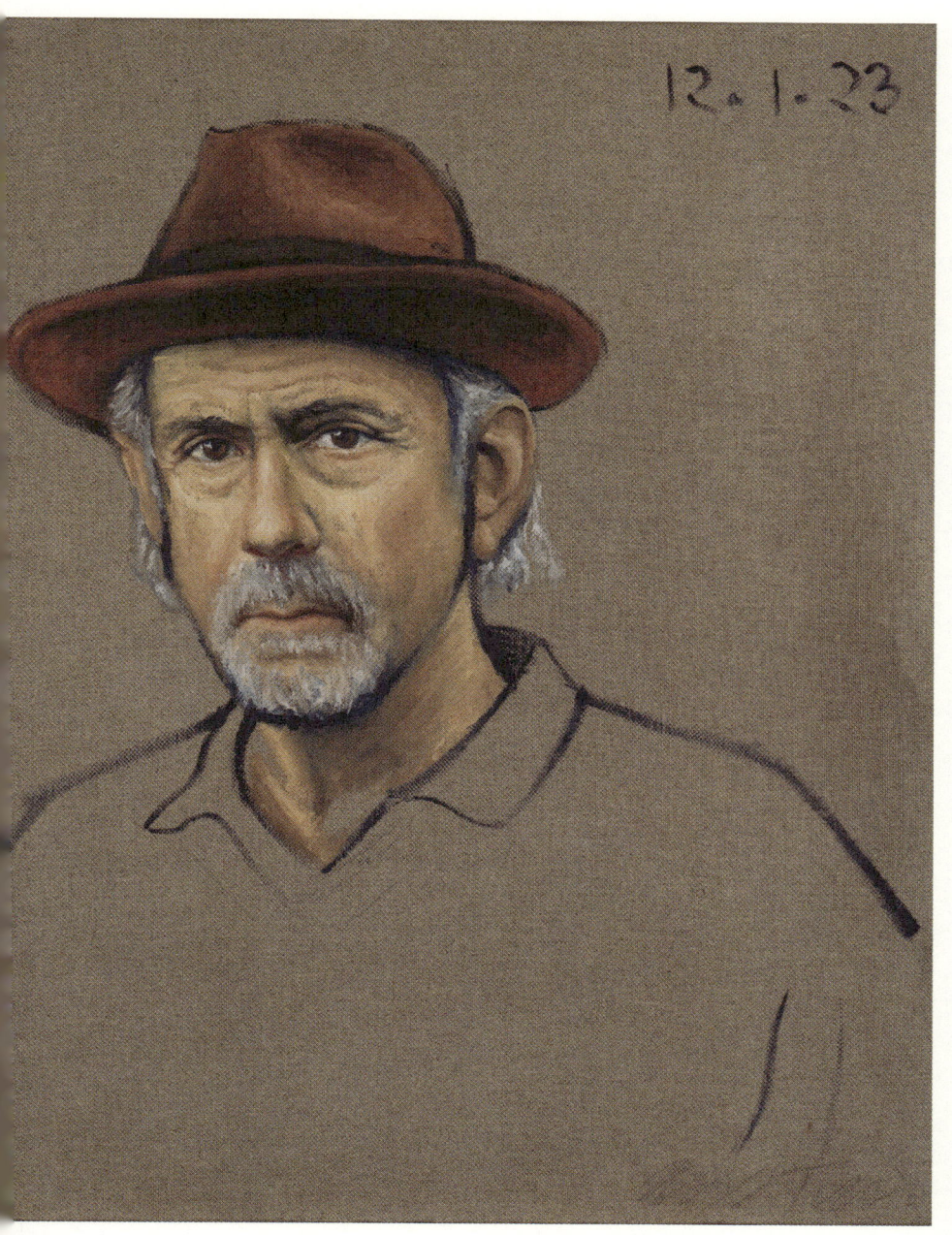

Dual Portrait with Aura *by Max Thill, 2023*

°

THE ART LOSS ■ REGISTER™

www.artloss.com

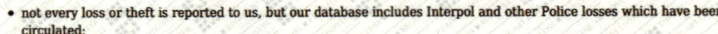

Mr John Harris
1569 Solano Ave #201
Berkeley 94707
United States

3rd January 2023   **ALR Ref: S00239079**

We have now carried out a search of the Art Loss Register database for the following item based upon the information that you have provided:

ITEM:	Portrait of a young girl wearing a red head cover
ARTIST:	Artist unknown
DATE / PERIOD:	January 12, 1935
MEDIUM:	Oil on linen
DIMENSIONS:	Height: 22 in Width: 17 in Depth: 3/4 in
CURRENT OWNERSHIP:	John Harris, Berkeley, CA, acquired on July 26, 2015.
HISTORIC PROVENANCE:	N/A

N.B. clause
Based on the limited information provided, the Art Loss Register recommends further research to be undertaken into the provenance of the object.

We certify that this item has not, to the best of our knowledge, been registered as stolen or missing on our database nor has a claimant reported this item to us as a loss between 1933 and 1945. It should, however, be noted that:

- not every loss or theft is reported to us, but our database includes Interpol and other Police losses which have been circulated;
- our database does not contain information on illegally exported or excavated artefacts unless they have been reported to us; and
- we do not have details of all items confiscated, looted or subjected to a forced seizure or forced sale between 1933 and 1945.

It is important for you to note that this Certificate is no indication of the authenticity of the item. Nor is this Certificate an export licence. The details above for Current Ownership and Historic Provenance are those provided to us at the time of this search and we do not guarantee the provenance of any item we have searched. Your search with the Art Loss Register demonstrates due diligence but may not excuse you from undertaking further research or providing further information if established at a later date. Should we become aware of any abuse of this Certificate we may find it necessary to take action.

Julian Radcliffe

Julian Radcliffe
Chairman, The Art Loss Register

The Art Loss Register, 16 Black Friars Lane, London EC4V 6EB
Tel: +44 (0)207 841 5780 Email: info@artloss.com Company number: 02455350

1/1

APPENDIX

o

J ust received from the Art Loss Register (ALR) in London, a certificate with the conclusion that there is "no match" for *The Girl in Red* in their vast database of stolen or missing art. Their recommendation: "further research to be undertaken into the provenance of the object."

ALR is one of the world's leading search vehicles for identifying and authenticating art for museums, galleries, auction houses, collectors, insurance companies and law enforcement. It was suggested that I contact ALR by Carla Shapreau, the founder of the Lost Music Project and one of my sources for technical and legal details regarding provenance and attribution searches. She is also, *par hasard*, the mother of Max Thill. Heureux hasard!

Along with the certificate came a note from a provenance expert at ALR in which she suggests that I look at the work of the artist Eugen Spiro. My brief online search reveals some interesting material on Spiro's life and work. A "degenerate artist" from Poland working in Paris, Spiro, a Jew, escaped to New York just as the Nazis arrived. One or two of his portraits share some characteristics with *The Girl in Red*. This also fits well with the comment from the psychic friend of DOMOS's Erin Martin who believes that the girl in the portrait came to Paris from Poland. But I think it doubtful that Spiro painted *The Girl in Red*.

The journey continues.

ACKNOWLEDGMENTS

o

I sincerely thank all those who have contributed to my journey with *The Girl in Red*—the painting and the book.

THE ARTISTS: Yuri Kuper gave me confidence that my attraction to *The Girl as art* was justified; Jan Wurm and Ann Arnold had revealing opinions about *The Girl*; Fanny Vanoye shared my avis de recherche poster with her friends in Paris; Ekaterina Aristova introduced me to artist history at La Ruche in Paris; Celik Kayalar kept me company at Saul's Deli while I finished my manuscript; Stuart Marcus cheered me on from Los Angeles; Leonard Pitt praised *The Girl in Red* from day one; Michael Haimovitz shared his memories of the Colby Street art commune; Bob Ward immediately identified the power of *The Girl* when he walked into my house; Alison Moeller designed my *avis de recherche* poster; Joe Slusky understood the metaphysical implications of *The Girl in Red*; Max Thill placed me into *The Girl's* two-dimensional reality with his remarkable *Dual Portrait with Aura*.

THE ART-WORLD PROFESSIONALS: Curator and collector Robert Flynn Johnson appreciated *The Girl* as an anonymous work and shared his curatorial and collector perspectives; the late art historian Peter Selz shared my shock that *The Girl* had been discarded; the collector and former art dealer Foster Goldstrom made a bold and educated guess about *The Girl's* artist; Gidske Munthe, an art dealer in Oslo, Norway, shared her information on the possible artist, Xan Krohn; the French gallerist working in San Francisco, Jules Maeght, gave me helpful advice about *The Girl*'s provenance search; Stéphane Corréard from the Piasa auction house in Paris had good ideas about *The Girl*'s possible artist; the violinist and art collector Dan Flanagan was riveted by *The Girl* when he performed at my home; Jazz guitarist and composer Steve Khan cheered me on from the very beginning; Ty Murphy and Erin Martin, art advisors at DOMOS in London and Paris, shared their speculations on *The Girl*'s history; art dealer Catherine Burns generously reviewed the manuscript and advised me on provenance issues; Carla Shapreau shared her legal and curatorial expertise on provenance issues and excerpts from the diary of Joseph Goebbels; gallerist Serge Sorokko in San Francisco shared his memories of Yuri Kuper; Dr. Lynne Ambrosini, the deputy director and chief curator emerita of the Taft Museum of Art in Cincinnati, Ohio, made helpful suggestions.

THE FOOD PROFESSIONALS: Many thanks to chef Peter Jackson for his croque monsieur collaboration in Paris; chef Jeremiah Tower for his description of blanquette de veau; restaurateurs Bob and Maggie Klein of Oliveto Restaurant and Community Grains for their introduction to the cookbook author Martha Rose Shulman, who introduced me to the editor at the late *Zester Daily* magazine; all the editors at *Zester Daily* for their work on my Paris articles and illustrations; the owners and staff at Saul's Delicatessen for their food and friendship while I worked on the book; Marcia Masse at Masse's Pastries for her introduction to the portrait artist Max Thill; Marilyn Rinzler of the late Poulet Delicatessen and Restaurant for listening to my endless Paris foodie stories.

Deep appreciation also for the readers of the manuscript at various stages of completion and their suggestions and encouragement: Nenelle Bunnin, Richard Collier, David Downie, Jane Ellis,

Tom Farber, Susan Griffin, W. Scott Haine, Lorri Holt, Michele Jordan, Kaaren Kitchell, Emily Moell, Gloria Polanski, Zack Rogow, John Weil, Andy Weiner and Lawrence Weschler.

Special thanks to my Paris friends for keeping me company on my journey: Anita Conrade, Varda Ducovny, Terrance Gelenter, the late Lucien Godin and Anne Godin, David and Evy Jester, Hank and Lou Resnik, Mary Schneider, Marc Selvaggio and Andrea (again) and Jacques Valerio; and my gratitude to all the café, shop and gallery owners in Paris who allowed me to post my avis de recherche poster in their windows and on their walls.

Much gratitude to those who helped in the research, editing and publishing process: Sharon Rudnick for helpful early comments; Ann Arnold for proofing and critiquing the manuscript along the way; Ellie Ziedman for her recommendation of Patrick Modiano's *Dora Bruder*; Marion Abbott for her finely tuned editorial eye and publishing advice; Lisa Taylor for her French-language consultation and editing; Lily LeaVesseur for her research assistance; Kimberley Cameron for her agenting efforts; Brad Bunnin for legal advice; and my publisher, Steve Wassermann, editor Emmerich Anklam, designer Archie Ferguson, copyeditor Michele Jones, publicist Kalie Caetano and all the fine folks at Heyday who brought my book finally, and beautifully, to fruition.

To my sons, Max and Alex; their partners, Alison and Allie; and their mother, Linda, my appreciation for your putting up with my endless talk about *The Girl in Red*.

BIBLIOGRAPHY

o

The books on this list have been my primary sources for material in art history and criticism, aesthetic philosophy and psychology, Paris cultural studies, world history, and literature. I have not included articles read online, YouTube videos, or the websites and blog posts I've consulted.

Atkins, Robert. *Art Speak*. New York: Abbeville Press, 1990.

Balzac, Honoré de. *Treatise on Elegant Living*. Cambridge, MA: Wakefield Press, 2010.

Balzac, Honoré de. *The Unknown Masterpiece*. New York: New York Review Books, 2001.

Barnes, Julian. *Keeping an Eye Open*. New York: Knopf, 2015.

Baum, Kelly, et al. *Unfinished: Thoughts Left Visible*. New York: Metropolitan Museum of Art, 2016.

Benjamin, Walter. *Charles Baudelaire: A Lyric Poet in the Era of High Capitalism*. London: Verso, 1997.

Benjamin, Walter. *Selected Writings, 1938–1940*. Cambridge, MA: Harvard University Press, 2003.

Berger, John. *The Shape of a Pocket*. New York: Vintage Books, 2001.

Berger, John. *The Success and Failure of Picasso*. New York: Vintage Books, 1965.

Berger, John. *Ways of Seeing*. New York: Penguin Books, 1977.

Breton, André. *Nadja*. New York: Grove Press, 1960.

Brunner, Kathleen. *Picasso Rewriting Picasso*. London: Black Dog, 2004.

Butler, Cornelia, et al. *Dubuffet Drawings, 1935–1962*. New York: Thames & Hudson, 2016.

Chomsky, Noam, and Andrea Moro. *The Secrets of Words*. Cambridge, MA: MIT Press, 2022.

Danto, Arthur C. *After the End of Art*. Princeton, NJ: Princeton University Press, 2015.

Davenport, Guy. *A Balthus Notebook*. New York: Echo Press, 1989.

De Waal, Edmund. *The Hare with Amber Eyes*. New York: Farrar, Straus and Giroux, 2010.

Diepersloot, Jan. *The Tao of the Species*. Berkeley, CA: Apprentices of Perception Press, 1982.

Downie, David. *A Taste of Paris*. New York: Saint Martin's Press, 2017.

Dutton, Denis. *The Art Instinct*. New York: Bloomsbury, 2009.

Elkins, James. *What Painting Is*. New York: Routledge, 2000.

Findlay, Michael. *The Value of Art*. Munich: Prestel, 2014.

Gluck, Mary. *Popular Bohemia*. Cambridge, MA: Harvard University Press, 2005.

Griffin, Susan. *The Book of the Courtesans*. New York: Crown, 2002.

Henri, Robert. *The Art Spirit*. New York: JP Lippincott, 1923.

Hergé. *The Adventures of Tintin: The Broken Ear*. New York: Little, Brown, 1978.

Johnson, Robert Flynn. *Anonymous: Enigmatic Images from Unknown Photographers*. London: Thames & Hudson, 2005.

Jung, Carl. *Two Essays on Analytical Psychology*. New York: Pantheon Books, 1953.

Lewis, Ben. *The Last Leonardo*. New York: Ballantine Books, 2019.

Marvena. *Life with the Painters of La Ruche*. New York: Macmillan, 1974.

McGilchrist, Iain. *The Master and His Emissary*. New Haven, CT: Yale University Press, 2009.

Modiano, Patrick. *Dora Bruder*. Berkeley: University of California Press, 1999.

Mourlot, Fernand. *Picasso Lithographs*. Boston:
Boston Book and Art Publisher, 1970.

Myers, Paul A. *Paris 1935*. Corona del Mar, CA:
Paul A. Myers Books, 2011.

Nin, Anaïs. *The Diary of Anaïs Nin*. Vol. 2, *1934–1939*.
New York: Swallow Press, 1967.

Oancea, Larisa. *Nancy Spanier: The Arc of a Dancing Life*.
Boulder, CO: Performance Inventions, 2021.

Renoir, Jean. *Renoir, My Father*. Boston: Little, Brown, 1958.

Robb, Graham. *Balzac*. New York: Norton, 1994.

Rosenthal, Mark, Kent Minturn, and Anny Aviram. *Jean Dubuffet: Anticultural Positions*. New York: Acquavella Galleries, 2016.

Sante, Lucy. *The Other Paris*. New York:
Farrar, Straus and Giroux, 2015.

Sebald, W. G. *The Emergence of Memory*. New York:
Seven Stories Press, 2007.

Sebald, W. G. *Vertigo*. New York: New Directions Books, 1999.

Shattuck, Roger. *The Banquet Years*. New York: Vintage Books, 1955.

Stendhal. *Scarlet and Black*. New York: Everyman's Library, 1938.

Tulka, Rick. *Paris Café: The Sélect Crowd*. Brooklyn, NY:
Soft Skull Press, 2007.

White, Edmund. *The Flâneur*. New York: Bloomsbury, 2001.

Winner, Ellen. *How Art Works*. New York:
Oxford University Press, 2019.

Wollheim, Richard. *Art and Its Objects*. Cambridge:
Cambridge University Press, 1980.

Wollheim, Richard. *Painting as an Art*. Princeton, NJ:
Princeton University Press, 1987.

IMAGE CREDITS

o

The following images are used with permission. All other images in the book (photographs, artwork, archival materials) are used courtesy of the author.

p. 18: Pablo Picasso, *The Italian Woman* (after the painting by Victor Orsel), 1953, printed 1955, Digital Image © The Museum of Modern Art/Licensed by SCALA/Art Resource, NY. © 2023 Estate of Pablo Picasso/Artists Rights Society (ARS), New York

p. 22: Gustav Klimt, *Adele Bloch-Bauer I*, 1907. © Neue Galerie New York/Art Resource, NY

p. 31: Paul Ordner, *Je vous en supplie, cessez mes enfants*, 1934/1939; © Paul Ordner LC_AFF_21864_1/Collection La contemporaine

p. 32: Paul Popper/Popperfoto via Getty Images

p. 33: Hilaire-Germain-Edgar Degas, *Combing the Hair ("La Coiffure")*, about 1896. © The National Gallery, London

p. 42: Gustav Klimt, *Adele Bloch-Bauer I*, detail, 1907. © Neue Galerie New York/Art Resource, NY

p. 51: Kees van Dongen, *The Corn Poppy*, c. 1919, oil on canvas, the Museum of Fine Arts, Houston, the John A. and Audrey Jones Beck

Collection, gift of Audrey Jones Beck. Photo © The Museum of Fine Arts, Houston; Jud Haggard, photographer. © 2023 Artists Rights Society (ARS), New York/ADAGP, Paris

p. 55: Yuri Kuper, *Garlics,* 1998, object number: 1166, Sainsbury Centre, UEA. Photo © James Dunne

p. 89: Hergé, *The Broken Ear,* cover artwork, 1937. © Hergé/ Tintinimaginatio 2024

p. 91: Perino del Vaga, *The Holy Family with Saint John the Baptist,* ca. 1524–26. The Courtauld, London (Samuel Courtauld Trust) Photo © The Courtauld/Bridgeman Images

p. 96: Jean-François Millet, *The Gleaners,* 1857. © RMN-Grand Palais/ Art Resource, NY

p. 116: Attributed to Daniele da Volterra, *Michelangelo Buonarroti* (1475–1564), probably ca. 1545. Metropolitan Museum of Art, Gift of Clarence Dillon, 1977

p. 120: Frida Kahlo, *Self Portrait with Curly Hair,* 1935. Private Collection Photo © Christie's Images/Bridgeman Images; © 2023 Banco de México Diego Rivera Frida Kahlo Museums Trust, Mexico, D.F./ Artists Rights Society (ARS), New York

p. 122: Keystone-France/Gamma-Keystone via Getty Images

p. 138: Leonardo da Vinci, *Head of a Woman (La Scapigliata),* 1500s. © Galleria Nazionale, Parma/HIP/Art Resource, NY

p. 202: Leonardo da Vinci, *Mona Lisa (La Gioconda)* detail.
© RMN-Grand Palais/Art Resource, NY

p. 246: Acquavella Galleries, catalog cover for the Jean Dubuffet
exhibit "Anticultural Positions," 2016. Featuring *Monsieur d'Hotel*, 1947
(oil and sand on canvas), Dubuffet, Jean (1901–85)/Private
Collection/Bridgeman Images; © 2024 Artists Rights Society (ARS),
New York/ADAGP, Paris

p. 247: Jean Dubuffet, *Lili Assise*, 1935. © Fondation Dubuffet;
© 2023 Artists Rights Society (ARS), New York/ADAGP, Paris

p. 261: Xan Krohn, *Portrait of Thomas Alva Edison*, Orange, 1920.
© Oslo Kunsthandel AS

p. 273: Pierre Tal-Coat, *Portrait of Gertrude Stein* (1874–1946), 1935.
Private Collection © Peter Willi/Bridgeman Images;
© 2024 Artists Rights Society (ARS), New York/ADAGP, Paris

ABOUT THE AUTHOR

L. John Harris is a writer and artist living in Berkeley, California. A contributor to California's food revolution of the 1970's and '80s, his *Book of Garlic* (Holt, Rinehart, Winston, 1974) launched a global "garlic revolution." Harris's Aris Books popularized single-subject cookbooks in the 1980s. Following the sale of Aris, Harris returned to food journalism and illustration and took up documentary filmmaking (*Los Romeros: The Royal Family of the Guitar* and *Divine Food: One Hundred Years in the Kosher Delicatessen Trade*). In the early 2000s Harris produced several illustrated memoirs under his own imprint, Villa Books. A lifelong classical guitar player and collector, Harris is the curator of the Harris Guitar Collection at the San Francisco Conservatory of Music and produces musical events at his Berkeley residence, Villa Maybeck. He is currently working on a history of Berkeley's Gourmet Ghetto food revolution of the 1970s and '80s.

A NOTE ON THE TYPE

This book is set in Athelas. Inspired by classic British bookmaking, Athelas features tasteful curves and serifs, eschewing hard edges in favor of a spacious, tranquil feel. Athelas was created in 2008 by the founders of TypeTogether, Veronika Burian and José Scaglione, who designed the font specifically for use in fine books printed on high-quality paper.